Social Media Marketing

FOR

DUMMIES®

by Shiv Singh

Includes contributions from:
Michael Becker, Jeannette Kocsis, and Ryan Williams

WILEY

Wiley Publishing, Inc.

Social Media Marketing For Dummies®

Published by
Wiley Publishing, Inc.
111 River Street
Hoboken, NJ 07030-5774

www.wiley.com

Copyright © 2010 by Wiley Publishing, Inc., Indianapolis, Indiana

Published by Wiley Publishing, Inc., Indianapolis, Indiana

Published simultaneously in Canada

For general information on our other products and services, please contact our Customer Care Department within the U.S. at 877-762-2974, outside the U.S. at 317-572-3993, or fax 317-572-4002.

For technical support, please visit www.wiley.com/techsupport.

Wiley also publishes its books in a variety of electronic formats. Some content that appears in print may not be available in electronic books.

Library of Congress Control Number: 2009936808

ISBN: 978-0-470-28934-1

Manufactured in the United States of America

10 9 8 7 6 5 4 3

WILEY

About the Author

A recognized digital marketer, **Shiv Singh** has been with Razorfish since 1999, and he has worked in the Boston, New York, San Francisco, and London offices. As the company's VP & Global Social Media Lead, Shiv helps the agency introduce its clients, such as Carnival Cruise Lines, Microsoft, Citibank, Ford Motor Company, Panasonic, Novartis, and Starwood, to social influence marketing. And he shows them how to incorporate social media and social technologies to support marketing and business objectives. His role also includes capability development, developing strategic partnerships, leading thought leadership efforts, and encouraging experimentation with social media across the agency.

Shiv has been published widely, and he has spoken at conferences such as South by Southwest Interactive, the Direct Marketing Association's Leader's Forum, OMMA Global, O'Reilly Graphing Social Patterns, the ARF Annual Summit, and the Social Ad Summit. He has also been quoted in the *Wall Street Journal* and by Reuters, Associated Press, *Adweek, Ad Age,* and several other noted publications discussing digital strategy and social influence marketing.

Author's Acknowledgments

I've always wanted to write, a desire that was constantly fueled by my parents, who encouraged me to write first by keeping a diary, and then exploring poetry and fiction, and finally, nonfiction as I grew older. And the same goes for my brother, who fueled the interest by patiently reading drafts of whatever I've written and providing valuable feedback. My teachers in school pushed me along in a similar fashion. Without all the continuous encouragement from my childhood days to put pen to paper, no book would ever have been written.

This specific book would never have been completed had it not been for my wife, who sacrificed what should have been many a family weekend to let me sit at my desk and churn out chapter after chapter. Her encouragement, which often took the form of incentivizing me with the lure of a nice wine if I finished a chapter before an agreed-upon deadline made all the difference, especially at a time when I was juggling a day job, a night job in the form of a wine magazine I copublish, and the birth of a son who thankfully started sleeping through the night rather quickly.

Professionally, I have had the good fortune to work with some incredibly inspiring, thoughtful, and talented people at Razorfish, one of the largest digital agencies in the world. They influence and challenge me every day, making me smarter, more informed, and more humble. The company global social media list has been a continuous source of inspiration, where employees share their opinions generously. No book can be written while holding down a day job without the cooperation of the company you work for, and for that, I thank Clark Kokich and Bob Lord, the company's Chairman and CEO, respectively, who wholeheartedly supported the book project and got the company behind it, too.

And finally, the editors at Wiley deserve acknowledgment. Especially Steve Hayes, who first saw the opportunity and reached out to me, and then coaxed each chapter out of me while providing incredibly valuable guidance to a first-time author. Their patience, especially, with the timeline as I struggled to deliver chapters on time, made the mammoth task all the easier.

Publisher's Acknowledgments

We're proud of this book; please send us your comments at http://dummies.custhelp.com. For other comments, please contact our Customer Care Department within the U.S. at 877-762-2974, outside the U.S. at 317-572-3993, or fax 317-572-4002.

Some of the people who helped bring this book to market include the following:

Acquisitions and Editorial

Project Editor: Rebecca Senninger

Executive Editor: Steven Hayes

Copy Editor: Heidi Unger

Technical Editor: Leah Jones

Editorial Manager: Leah Cameron

Editorial Assistant: Amanda Graham

Sr. Editorial Assistant: Cherie Case

Cartoons: Rich Tennant
(www.the5thwave.com)

Composition Services

Project Coordinator: Katherine Crocker

Layout and Graphics: Ashley Chamberlain, Christine Williams

Proofreader: Lisa Young Stiers

Indexer: Sharon Shock

Special Help
Linda Morris

Publishing and Editorial for Technology Dummies

Richard Swadley, Vice President and Executive Group Publisher

Andy Cummings, Vice President and Publisher

Mary Bednarek, Executive Acquisitions Director

Mary C. Corder, Editorial Director

Publishing for Consumer Dummies

Diane Graves Steele, Vice President and Publisher

Composition Services

Debbie Stailey, Director of Composition Services

Contents at a Glance

Table of Contents

Introduction

. . . .

On August 23, 1999, Blogger launched as one of the earliest dedicated blog-publishing tools. At that time, social media was considered a niche activity on the fringes of the Internet. But today, Blogger is the 16th most popular site on the Internet, hosting millions of blogs. In a span of three years, Facebook has grown to over 200 million users, and Wikipedia, for all practical purposes, has replaced Britannica as an encyclopedia. Social media is today the most important phenomena transforming the Internet.

There is more to it than the phenomena, though. It also presents unique marketing opportunities, which force marketers to revisit the core guiding principles of marketing while providing new ways to reach social influencers and allow for people to influence each other and do the marketing for the brand. Social influence marketing (SIM) forces companies to rethink how they market online, to whom they market, and how to structure their own organizations to support these new marketing opportunities. For anyone involved with social influence marketing — and Internet marketing, more broadly — this is indeed an exciting time.

Social Media Marketing For Dummies is written to help you make sense of the madness. Because it's such a hot topic, the press and the experts alike are quick to frighten marketers, like you, and introduce new terminology that confuses rather than enlightens. This book cuts through all that noise and simply explains what social influence marketing is and how you can harness it to achieve your objectives as a marketer. It also aims to help you prioritize what's important and what isn't.

About This Book

The social influence marketing space is changing rapidly, so by very definition, this book can't be completely comprehensive. It does, however, aim to distill the core concepts, trends, tips, and recommendations down to bite-sized, easy-to-digest nuggets. As social influence marketing touches all parts of marketing and all parts of the Internet, too, (from traditional Web sites to social platforms to the mobile Web), based on your own experiences, you'll find some sections more valuable than others.

As you read this book, keep in mind that the way people influence each other online and impact purchasing and brand affinity decisions is similar to the way they've done for thousands of years in the real world. The technology is finally catching up, and social influence marketing is fundamentally about allowing and encouraging that behavior to happen in a brand-positive manner online, too.

This book helps you understand why social media matters to marketers and how you can harness it to directly impact your own marketing efforts in meaningful ways. Targeted at both marketers in large organizations and those of you who work in small businesses or run small businesses, it includes advice for every business scenario.

Conventions Used in This Book

To make the book easier to read, I use the following conventions:

✔ Social influence marketing is sometimes abbreviated SIM. So whenever you see SIM, think social influence marketing!

✔ The terms *social media marketing* and *social influence marketing* are used interchangeably in the book, and that's largely because this is a book about both social media and the social influencers who are active within that media.

✔ When you see URLs (Web addresses) appearing within a paragraph, caption, or table, they look like this: www.dummies.com.

Foolish Assumptions

In writing this book, I imagined someone pulling a copy off a bookshelf in a Barnes and Noble or Borders and scanning it to see whether it's a valuable guide. And I wondered what that person would need to know to find this book interesting. Here are some of the assumptions I came up with about you:

✔ You have a computer with Internet access.

✔ You've visited a social media site like Facebook or Twitter.

✔ You're working in marketing or want to join the marketing field.

> ✔ You have customers or prospective customers who use the Web frequently.
>
> ✔ You sell a product or service that you can market online.
>
> ✔ You're curious about social media and whether it changes marketing.

How This Book Is Organized

This is book is divided into four distinct parts. As you progress through the chapters, you'll move from learning the fundamentals of social influence marketing to practical strategies for implementing SIM programs and campaigns for your brand.

Rather than have separate chapters for marketers at small businesses versus large corporations, each chapter addresses the circumstances of both using the differences between the two to explain the core concepts more strongly.

And unlike most books that deal with social influence marketing, this book looks at every dimension of the field holistically, with chapters dedicated to using SIM techniques on your Web site, in marketing campaigns, on mobile devices, and behind your company's firewall.

Part 1: Getting Social with Your Marketing

A common misconception about social influence marketing is that it's fundamentally about marketing on social platforms such as Facebook, Twitter, MySpace, and YouTube. But that's not the case, and Part I lays out the landscape of SIM, places it in the context of other forms of marketing, and then walks you through different stages of the marketing funnel.

With important statistics on the size of the social Web and consumer online media consumption, this section also explains why SIM matters.

Part II: Practicing SIM on the Social Web

Part II is very much the practitioner's part, explaining the nuts and bolts of SIM campaigns, including planning for them, managing participation, seeding viral video clips, and tips and tricks for turning a crisis to your advantage.

The chapters in this section also detail how, exactly, you can market on the mainstream and niche social platforms, what each platform allows you to do, and the best way to manage your influencers.

Part III: Old Marketing Is New Again with SIM

In Part III, you learn how to transform your own Web site to allow for social influence marketing. I also explain what it means to be an authentic and engaged advertiser — in other words, how to take your existing advertising efforts social and get more mileage out of them.

The chapters on mobile marketing and employee influence explain how you can encourage your employees to road test your SIM efforts. I also emphasize that you can't ignore the mobile Web today. And finally, the chapter on metrics explains how you can easily measure all your SIM efforts.

Part IV: The Part of Tens

And lastly, the Part of Tens, as with all *For Dummies* books, lists ten key SIM best practices that you must absolutely pay attention to. Also included are ten common mistakes — mistakes made by the best of us who have been practicing SIM time and again. The section ends with ten must-read blogs that will keep you updated with the world of SIM and digital marketing more broadly.

Icons Used in This Book

In the margins of the book, you'll find these icons helping you out:

Whenever I provide a hint that makes an aspect of social influence marketing easier, I mark it with a Tip icon.

The Remember icon marks paragraphs that contain a friendly reminder.

Heed the warnings marked with the Warning icons to avoid potential disaster.

Whenever I get technically inclined, I mark the paragraph with a Technical Stuff icon. If you're not technically inclined, you can skip these nuggets of info.

Where to Go from Here

The book is designed such that you can quickly jump to a specific chapter or section that most interests you in a particular moment. You don't have to start with the first chapter — although, if you're new to social influence marketing, I recommend that you do so. Understanding the foundation of social influence marketing (which I explain in the early chapters) will help you better apply the techniques that you learn in the later ones to the specifics of your business.

Part I
Getting Social with Your Marketing

The 5th Wave   By Rich Tennant

It was on the WhaleNet site one night that Capt. Ahab caught up with his obsession.

WHALE CHAT

White? Really? Where can we meet?

In this part . . .

Part I lays out the landscape of SIM, places it in the context of other forms of marketing, and then walks you through different stages of the marketing funnel.

Chapter 1 discusses the fundamentals of social influence marketing: what it is, how it works, and what it means in the context of your other marketing efforts. In Chapter 2, I highlight some of the key traffic statistics so that you have a sense of what to expect when you do your own social marketing research. In Chapter 3, I explain how you need to think about the big idea a little differently than you do with traditional marketing as you deploy social influence marketing to meet your marketing and business objectives.

Chapter 1

Understanding Social Influence Marketing

*W*hen designing Web sites, you display banners and push your Web site listings higher up in the search engine rankings to promote and sell products. It's easy to forget how people actually buy. It's easy to assume that the potential customers are lonely people crouched over their computers late at night choosing what products to add to a shopping cart — isolated from the real world and their family and friends.

But in reality, that's not how people purchase online today. It might have been the case in the early days of the Web, when the people spending time online were the early adopters and the mavericks, the ones willing to take the risk of putting their credit card numbers into a computer hoping for accurate charges and secure transactions. In those days, few people bought online, and the ones who did were on the fringes of mainstream society.

Those days are over now. With nearly 260 million people using the Web on a regular basis in the United States alone, using the Internet has become a mainstream social activity. Consumers approach purchasing online differently, too, and as a result, you need to approach your marketing online differently as well. Your approach must incorporate influence marketing.

This chapter discusses the fundamentals of social influence marketing: what it is, how it works, and what it means in the context of your other marketing efforts.

Defining Social Influence Marketing

A discussion of any subject needs to begin with a definition, and so here's the one for social influence marketing: *Social influence marketing* is a technique that employs *social media* (content created by everyday people using highly accessible and scalable technologies such as blogs, message boards, podcasts, microblogs, bookmarks, social networks, communities, wikis, and vlogs) and *social influencers* (everyday people who have an outsized influence on their peers by virtue of how much content they share online) to achieve an organization's marketing and business needs.

The definition warrants further explanation. Social media (which was probably one of the most hyped buzzwords in 2008) refers to content created and consumed by regular people for each other. It includes the comments a person adds at the end of an article on a Web site, the family photographs he uploads to a photo-sharing site, the conversations he has with friends in a social network, and the blog posts that he publishes or comments on. That's social media, and it's making everyone in the world a content publisher and arbitrator. It's democratizing the Web. WordPress.com, shown in Figure 1-1, is one popular blogging platform.

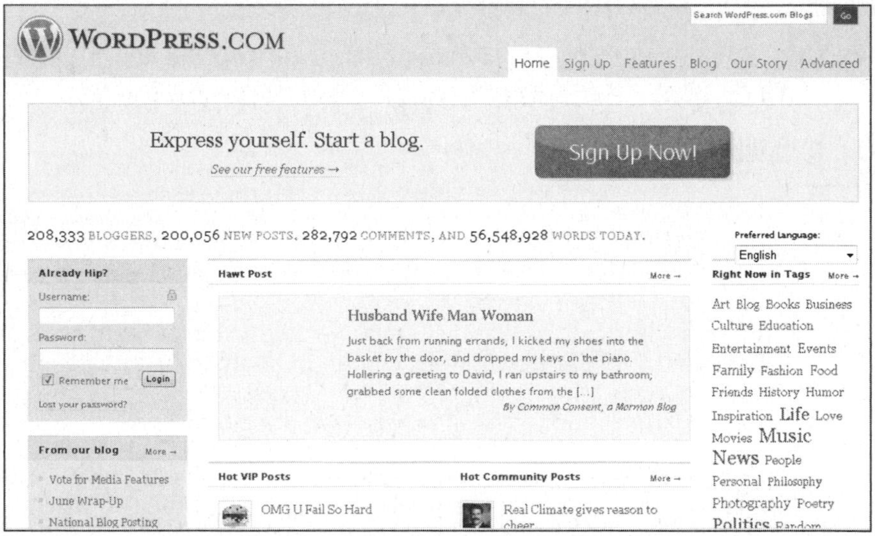

Figure 1-1: WordPress.com — just one example of many blog and social media platforms.

And then there are the social influencers. Are these people with special powers to influence a large majority of people? Not at all; rather, social influencers are the everyday people who influence the consumer as he makes a purchasing decision. Depending on the decision he's making, the social influencers may be a wife (or husband), friends, peers at work, or even someone the consumer has never even met in real life. Simply, the people who influence a brand affinity and purchasing decision are the social influencers. They may do this directly by rating products and commenting or by publishing opinions and participating in conversations across the Web. Anyone can be a social influencer, influencing someone else's brand affinity and purchasing decisions, and you, the reader, are probably one, too, without realizing it.

Social influence marketing is about recognizing, accounting, and tapping into the fact that as your potential customer makes a purchasing decision, he's influenced by various circles of people through the conversations that he has with them online, when he shares his own social media and consumes theirs. But wait a minute. How does social influence marketing tie into social media marketing? These terms are increasingly used interchangeably, but it's worth noting that when talking about social influence marketing, the emphasis is on the social influencers versus social media, which invariably implies just marketing on the social platforms like Facebook and Twitter. Since this book covers marketing with social influencers and social media on both the social platforms and company Web sites and also emphasizes the importance of social influencers, I use the relatively newer term *social influence marketing* throughout the book.

It isn't enough to market to the consumer anymore; as a marketer, you have to market to your potential customers' social influencers as well. And that's what social influence marketing is about.

Understanding the fundamentals of influence

To understand how social influence works, you need to look at how people are influenced in the real world, face to face. Social influence isn't something new. Long before the Web, people asked each other for advice as they made purchasing decisions. What one person bought often inspired another to buy the same product, especially if the original purchaser said great things about the product. That's how human beings function; we're influenced and motivated by each other to do things. We're social beings, and sharing information on our experiences is all a part of social interaction.

Is influence bad? Of course not. More often than not, people seek that influence. People ask each other for advice; they share decision-making processes with friends and colleagues; they discuss their own experiences.

How much a person is influenced depends on multiple factors. The product itself is the most important one. When buying *low-consideration purchases* (those with a small amount of risk), people rarely seek influence, nor are they easily influenced by others. Buying toothpaste, for example, is a low-consideration purchase because each product may not be that different from the next one, and they're all fairly inexpensive — so you won't lose much money if you choose one that doesn't fit your needs. On the other hand, buying a new car is typically a *high-consideration purchase* (a purchase that includes a large risk). The price of the car, the maintenance costs, and its reputation for its safety all contribute to making it a high-consideration purchase. Social influence plays a much bigger role in car purchases than in toothpaste decisions. Nissan recently used social influence marketing to sell its Nissan Cube, as shown in Figure 1-2.

Figure 1-2:
Selling the
Nissan Cube
with social
media.

Social influence matters with every purchase, but it matters more with high-consideration purchases than low-consideration ones. Most consumers realize that when they're making high-consideration purchases, they can make better and more confident purchasing decisions when they take into account the advice and experience of others who have made those decisions before them. That's how influence works.

Considering the types of influencers

When discussing social influence marketing, colleagues often ask me whether this means that they should add product review features to e-commerce Web sites or advertise on social networks. Yes, product reviews and advertising are important, but there's more to social influence than those two things. When you think about social influence in the context of your marketing objectives, you must separate social influencers online into three types: referent, expert, and positional. These categories come from thinking that social psychologists John French and Bertram Raven pioneered in 1959.

As a marketer seeking to deploy social influence marketing techniques, the first question to answer is this: Which social influencers sway your consumers as they make purchasing decisions about your product? After you identify those social influencers, you can determine the best ways to market to them.

Any major brand affinity or purchasing decision has referent, expert, and positional social influencers all playing distinct and important roles. Which one is most important may vary slightly based on the purchase, but the fact remains that you need to account for these three distinct types of social influencers in your marketing campaigns. If you're a marketer trying to positively affect a purchasing decision, you must market not just to the consumer but also to these influencers as well.

Referent influencers

A *referent influencer* is someone who participates on the social platforms. These users are typically in a consumer's social graph and influence brand affinity and purchasing decisions through consumer reviews, by updating their own status and Twitter feeds, and by commenting on blogs and forums. In some cases, the social influencers know the consumers personally.

Because the consumers know and trust their referent influencers, they feel confident that their advisers are also careful and punctilious. As they're people they trust, they value their advice and guidance over most other people. Referent influencers influence purchasing decision more than anyone else at the consideration phase of the marketing funnel, according to Fluent, the social influence marketing report from Razorfish.

For example, if I decide to make a high-consideration purchase, such as a car, I might start by going online and discussing different cars with a few friends in a discussion forum or on a social network. And then that weekend, I might meet those friends over coffee and carry on that discussion in person. They tell me about the cars they like, their own purchasing experiences, and which dealerships they've had experience with. This influence is considered *referent influence* because these friends sway me by the strength of their charisma and interpersonal skills, and they have this sway because I respect them.

Expert influencers

A consumer who's mulling over a high-consideration purchase might also consult an expert influencer. An *expert influencer* is an authority on the product that the consumer is considering purchasing. Also called *key influencers,* they typically have their own blogs, huge Twitter followings, and rarely know their audiences personally.

When I'm considering buying a car, suppose I don't turn just to friends for advice but also visit some car review Web sites like Edmunds.com (shown in Figure 1-3). On these review Web sites, experts rate, rank, and pass judgment on cars. As they put the cars through various tests and know the cars inside and out, their opinions matter. They're the expert social influencers — people who I may not know personally but are recognized as authorities in a certain field. Their influence is derived from the skills or expertise that they — or broadly speaking, their organization — possess based on training.

Positional influencers

A *positional influencer* is closest to both the purchasing decision and to the consumer. Called *peer influencers* sometimes, they are typically family members or part of the consumer's inner circle. They influence purchasing decisions most directly at the point of purchase and have to live with the results of their family member's or friend's decision as well.

Now I know that I can't make a high-consideration purchase like a car purchase without discussing it with my wife. Invariably, she'll drive the car, too, and sit in it as much as I will. It is as much her purchase as it is mine. Her opinion matters more than anyone else's in this case. After all, I need to discuss with her the relative pricing of the cars available and whether one is more suitable for our family versus another. This person derives her influence from her relative position and duties in relation to the actual consumer. She's closest to the purchasing decision and to the consumer and therefore has the most social influence.

Figure 1-3:
Edmunds.
com.

Influencing on digital platforms

As I discuss earlier in the chapter, social influence impacts every purchasing decision, and always has in some form or other. Each time people make purchasing decisions, they ask each other for advice. Sometimes, they depend upon an expert's guidance, and in other cases, that advice comes from people they know.

So why is influence such a big deal today? This is because Internet and social media consumption specifically have hit the mainstream. For example, as of February 2009, the social-networking phenomenon Facebook had 175 million users, giving it a population larger than most countries. That's a lot of people talking about a lot of things (including products) to a lot of people!

People are making more and more purchasing decisions online every day. It's as natural to buy a product online as it is to go into a physical store. They buy clothes and shoes online, not to mention high-consideration items such as computers, cars (yes, cars), and jewelry. But that's not all. Not only are consumers buying online, but thanks to social media, they're conversing, socializing, and influencing each other online in a scale never seen before.

Call it a shift in Web behavior, but the way people make decisions in the real world is finally moving to the Internet in a big way. The social media platforms such as Facebook (shown in Figure 1-4), MySpace, LinkedIn, Twitter, and YouTube are just a few of the places where people are asking each other for advice and guidance as they make purchasing decisions. Smart companies are realizing that they should no longer design their e-commerce Web sites to convince buyers to make purchasing decisions in isolation. Rather they need to design the Web sites to allow consumers to bring their social influencers into the decision-making process. As consumers, people expect and want that because that's how they're used to making their purchasing decisions. So that's why social influence marketing matters today. People are influencing and are being influenced by each other every day on the social network platforms, community Web sites, and destination sites.

You may need to put a lot of effort into convincing your managers how important the social media platforms are. Many of them may feel that it's a youth phenomenon, one that doesn't serve the interests of brands well. The best way to communicate these ideas and techniques to your staff is by organizing lunch-and-learn sessions and bringing in external speakers who can walk your managers through the major social platforms and how best to market on them. Sharing case studies from other brands always resonates well and goes a long way to establishing credibility.

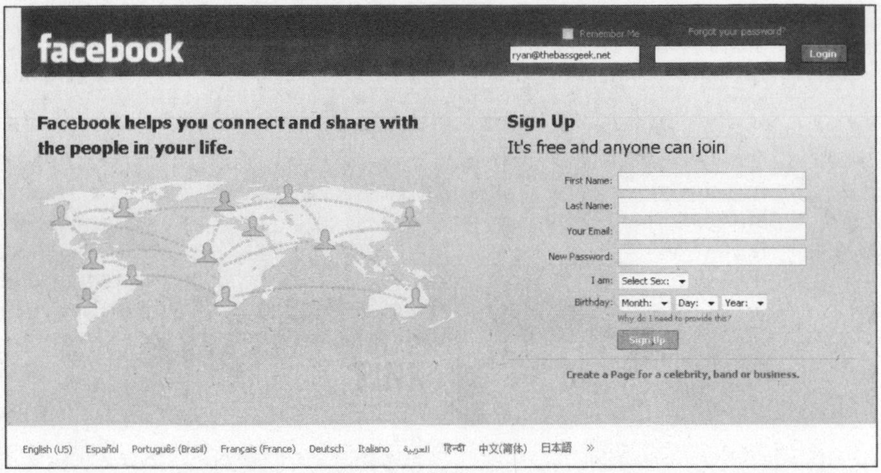

facebook

Remember Me   Forgot your password?
ryan@thebassgeek.net   [   ] Login

Facebook helps you connect and share with the people in your life.

Sign Up
It's free and anyone can join

First Name:
Last Name:
Your Email:
New Password:
I am: Select Sex: ▾
Birthday: Month: ▾   Day: ▾   Year: ▾
Why do I need to provide this?
Sign Up

Create a Page for a celebrity, band or business.

English (US)   Español   Português (Brasil)   Français (France)   Deutsch   Italiano   العربية   हिन्दी   中文(简体)   日本語   »

Figure 1-4:
Facebook.

Comparing Social Influence Marketing with Other Marketing Efforts

It isn't enough to deploy social influence marketing (SIM) in isolation of every other marketing effort. If you do, you're sure to fail. Your customers will notice that you have a disjointed, conflicted story — depending on where and how you're interacting with them. Therefore, it's important to understand how you can integrate your social influence marketing within your other more traditional marketing — direct mail, public relations, display advertising, and promotions.

Some of the social influence marketing philosophies are in conflict with traditional public relations, media buying, direct mail, and promotions tactics. It's no use damning those forms of marketing and alienating your peers who focus on those areas. Put extra effort in partnering with your fellow employees as you practice these marketing techniques. Explain what you're doing, why you're doing it, and how it complements their efforts. If you discredit the other forms of marketing and the people behind them, it only hurts you in the long run.

Direct mail

Direct mail is about managing an active customer database and marketing to members of that database via circulars, catalogs, credit card applications, and other merchandising materials delivered to homes and businesses. You've probably gotten a lot of direct mail over the years — perhaps mountains of it — and at some point, you've probably wished that these companies would stop mailing you. That's all direct mail, and whether you like it or not, direct mail has been a very successful form of marketing. The catalog industry logs billions of dollars in sales because of it.

That will change with social influence marketing. Of all the areas of marketing, direct mail is one that will be most affected in the long run. Before you start worrying that your mail carrier will stuff your mailbox (or your e-mail inbox through e-mail marketing) even more than usual, consider this: Direct mail is most successful when the mail is targeted and personalized. That means it's reaching the people who really care about the offers (or are most likely to take advantage of them), and it's personalized toward the recipients' needs in a voice and style that's appealing to them. Pretty straightforward, isn't it?

Direct mail is as successful as the marketer's customer database. The database should contain names and addresses of people who are open to receiving direct mail. But when people stop trusting the marketing efforts of large corporations and instead switch to each other for advice, that's when direct mail loses its power. Statistically, I know that consumers are now more likely to depend on each other for advice and information than they are on the corporations that are marketing to them. With consumers who are even more connected to each other through social media than before, it has gotten easier for them to reach out to one another for that advice. That means that when they see a piece of direct mail, they're less likely to depend on it. They'd rather go online and ask a friend for advice or search for a product online than look at that flyer in the mail. That's why direct mail dropped 3 percent in 2008. And as marketers harness social influence marketing tactics more, it will see further drops.

There's another side to the story, though. The more data that you can capture about your customers through social influence marketing tactics, the more opportunities you have to feed your direct mail database. That's just a factor of consumers doing more online, sharing more of themselves, and opting into direct mail efforts in exchange for information or acceptance into an online community. Your database may get richer with social influence marketing in the mix, but the value of it may decrease — although that doesn't mean that you can't use direct mail as a starting point to jump-start an online community, sustain interest in it, or reward participation through mailing coupons

Public relations

Among the earliest proponents of social media were digital-savvy public relations experts. Many of them entered this space by treating social media just as they have treated the mainstream media. These professionals equated *buzz* (how much people talk about a specific product or brand) in the social media realm with press mentions in the mainstream media. These PR experts identified the influential (*influence* defined as those having the most reach) bloggers and tweeters and started showering them with the same kind of attention that they had been bestowing on the mainstream media. They sent them press releases in advance, offered exclusive interviews, invited them to dinners, commented on their blogs, and carefully tracked how much their brands were mentioned and how positively.

For PR professionals, this approach made perfect sense. Arguably, they recognized early on how powerful social media could be and were among the first to track brand mentions and participate in conversations. In fact, many of the social media experts today are former public relations professionals who've taken the time to understand how social media works and how they can leverage it to support a company's or a brand's objectives. Many PR professionals also understand how bad press and traditional PR disasters can be amplified by social media if not addressed immediately.

But life isn't that simple, and the relationship between public relations and social media is a complex one — which is something that the savviest of PR professionals understand and have always understood. Public relations is fundamentally about managing the press (mainstream or alternative) and pushing a company's agenda out to the press as much as possible. Whether it's the mainstream or alternative media, it doesn't matter. From a public relations professional's perspective, the press is the press, and they're only as good as their ability to amplify a company's message. That's where the problem lies.

When I look at social influence marketing and how it harnesses social media, some of its core tenets are in conflict with public relations. For example, social influence marketing is about social influencers influencing each other through social media. The focus is on the social influencers influencing each other and not on the PR professionals influencing people in the social media realm. The difference is that as consumers, we're trusting and depending upon each other more for advice than on large corporations. The PR professionals, for all their sincerity and skill, will still push a company's message as forcefully as they can — and in that, it conflicts with social influence marketing.

Is there a remedy? Not necessarily, but as you deploy social influence marketing campaigns, be sensitive to the fact that your goals and aspirations may be in conflict with your PR organization if it hasn't embraced social media or social influence marketing. Have a conversation with them early on, find ways to collaborate and delineate boundaries, too — who does what, who reaches out to whom, and how much space is given to authentic social influencers to do the influencing versus the PR professionals. And as you do this, keep in mind that for many PR professionals, social influence marketing is an evolution of PR. That's a good thing providing for even more opportunities to collaborate.

Display advertising

When it comes to buying display advertising (also referred to as *media planning and buying*) on Web sites where your customers spend time, social influence marketing plays an important role. *Display advertising* is about identifying Web sites your target customers visit, buying ad space on those Web sites, and then measuring how much those ads are viewed and clicked upon. It's as much an art as it's a science because knowing which sites your customers visit, where they're most likely to engage with an advertisement (where on the site as well), whether the site charges the appropriate amount for the advertisement, and how much that advertising affects purchasing is not always easy. Trust me. I work with media buyers all the time, and their jobs are harder than you think.

But the display advertising space is important even in an economic downturn. The reason is simple: It's one of the most measurable forms of advertising, especially in relation to print and television, along with search engine advertising. You can track who views the advertisement, what they do with it, and in some cases, whether they eventually buy the product based on that advertisement. It's no surprise that the relationship to social influence marketing is an important one as a result.

This relationship with social influence marketing takes various forms. Here are some of those connection points:

- ✓ **Market to the social influencers who surround the customer, as well as the customer.**

  One of the ways in which you market to those influencers is using display advertising. So rather than just placing advertisements on Web sites that your customers visit, you place some advertisements (doesn't have to be a large percentage of your budget) on Web sites that their social influencers frequent, too. Is this as measurable as those advertisements targeting your customers directly? Maybe not, because these influencers are less likely to click the ads and make a purchase. But nevertheless, they remember the brand and they influence your customers.

- ✓ **Place display advertising on the social platforms — like Facebook, MySpace, and YouTube — that your customers frequent.**

  Most social platforms accept display advertising in some form, and this serves as an important part of their revenue model. Figure 1-5 shows display advertisements on YouTube. See Chapters 6 and 10 for more on this.

Figure 1-5:
Placement
ads on
YouTube.

Granted, display advertising on social platforms generally produces
bad results (users don't notice the advertisements, and they don't click
them) but the ad formats for social platforms are still evolving. One
example is *appvertising,* where advertisements are placed within applications that reside on social networks. These produce better results.
Another innovation is where consumers are asked to rate the ads that
they're viewing. This helps the platform target ads more appropriately
to them in the future.

✔ **Use interactive, social advertising.**

Think about this scenario for moment: You visit a major Web site like
CNN.com and see a large advertisement on the right side. The advertisement asks you a question, and you're invited to respond to that question
from within the ad unit. What's more, you can see other responses to the
question within the ad unit. That's an example of the ad unit becoming
a platform for a social conversation. There aren't too many examples
of social ads online, but I'm seeing more companies experiment in this
space. Figure 1-6 shows how one ad appears on CNN.com. See Chapter
10 for more on this.

Promotions

Promotions is another important type of marketing activity that's affected by
social influence marketing, due to the fact that as people communicate with
each other more, they have less time to participate in product promotions.
But it also presents unique opportunities for marketers to put the potential of
social influence marketing to good use.

Consider this: Promotions are primarily about incentives that are designed to stimulate the purchase or sale of a product in a given period. Promotions usually take the form of coupons, sweepstakes, contests, product samples, rebates, and tie-ins. Most of these promotions are designed as one-off activities linking the marketer to specific customers. However, by deploying social influence marketing concepts, you can design promotions that require customers to draw in their social influencers, whether it's to participate in the contest or sweepstakes with them or to play an advisory role. By designing the promotion to require social influencer participation (it needs to be positioned as friends participating), the specific promotion may get a lot more attention than it normally would have. I discuss this in Chapters 4 and 6.

For example, the promotions that Victoria's Secret has run around virtual gifting on Facebook all require the participants to identify people to whom to give the gifts. By virtue of the promotion definition, twice the number of people are exposed to Victoria's Secret in that promotion than normal.

Taking Social Influence Beyond Marketing

As I hint in the earlier sections, the benefits of social influence marketing extend beyond the core domain of marketing. If you harness the power of social influence marketing to change other parts of your business, you stand to gain the most. You can use SIM to mobilize groups of people to take specific actions, make marketers better corporate citizens, and further social change — and through those efforts, enhance a brand, too.

Using social influencers to mobilize

Social influencers, obviously, play an important role in getting people to do things. And this extends beyond the world of marketing. What makes it different on the Web is that it's a lot easier to do now. Author Howard Rheingold was one of the first thinkers to identify this phenomenon in a book titled, *Smart Mobs: The Next Social Revolution* (Perseus Books). He discussed how the street protestors of the 1999 Seattle World Trade Organization (WTO) conference used Web sites, cellphones, and other "swarming" tactics to organize, motivate each other, and plan protests. The smart mobs (an intentionally contradictory term) could behave intelligently because of their exponentially increasing links to each other. Through those links, they influenced and motivated each other to perform tasks, form shared opinions, and act together. They used social influence marketing tactics on themselves to accomplish specific objectives.

More recently, in *Here Comes Everybody: The Power of Organizing without Organizations* (Penguin Press), Clay Shirky also focuses on the power of organizing and influencing using social technologies. As he explains, every Web page can be considered a latent community waiting for people to interact, influence, and mobilize one another. People with shared interests visit the Web page at various times and often seek out their peers' opinions — not just opinions from the Web page's author. Shirky also discusses how Wikipedia, a user-contributed encyclopedia, can grow exponentially, publish efficiently, and self-correct using nontraditional corporate hierarchies.

I use the Seattle WTO protests and Wikipedia as examples to demonstrate how much social influence extends beyond the traditional realms of marketing into dramatically different domains. Driving the success of the Seattle WTO protests and the Wikipedia publishing model were two factors: social technologies that allowed people to contribute, participate, and converse easily, and technologies that allowed people to see what others were doing. The social influencers were at the heart of these efforts and many of the other smart mob initiatives over the years. Most recently, Twitter directly enabled protesters in Iran to organize in the wake of their recent elections, to such an extent that the U.S. State Department asked Twitter to delay a scheduled maintenance so that it wouldn't disrupt communications among the Iranian citizens as they protested the reelection of President Mahmoud Ahmadinejad.

But bringing this back to your company, it also demonstrates that you can harness those very same social influence marketing philosophies to achieve other corporate objectives as well. I discuss them further in Chapters 3 and 12.

Social influence marketing isn't just about how people influence each other by what they say on the social media platforms and on Web sites across the Web. It also happens when people observe what others are doing online. As a result, if you'd love others to mimic a certain type of customer behavior, make that behavior visible to everyone visiting the Web site. I don't just listen to people I admire; I also copy what they're doing.

Marketers as better corporate citizens

As has been the case in the last few years, marketers are increasingly supporting and furthering specific social causes that are in alignment with their brands. This win-win situation results in the marketers getting more favorable press for their brands and the specific causes getting much needed sponsorship, too. One area where marketers are increasingly harnessing social influence marketing tactics is in amplifying their efforts in the cause realm.

Why causes? The causes have all the ingredients to make a successful social influence marketing effort. They are usually time bound, have broad appeal, and are subjects that people like to discuss with each other. Marketers who tap into causes see their brands benefiting from halo effects by being associated with important social concerns and by gaining visibility with much larger audiences than they normally would have. If you're a marketer, it bodes well to directly support a cause, encourage its supporters to harness social influence marketing tactics, or sponsor it indirectly. And then even more so, it makes sense to market your own cause efforts using social influence marketing tactics in a measurable fashion

Early in 2009, Procter & Gamble (one of the largest consumer-goods companies in the world) organized a social media education session for all its marketers. But instead of having a series of presentations by employees, P&G invited social media experts to visit their headquarters. The company divided the social media experts into teams and paired them with their own marketers. The teams were tasked with raising money for Tide's Loads of Hope disaster relief campaign using social media platforms to sell T-shirts. (The Loads of Hope Web site is shown in Figure 1-7.) The winning team raised $50,000, and Tide matched their contribution. Through this effort, P&G positioned itself as a better corporate citizen, raised money for a good cause, and was able to educate its marketers about the potential of social media by actually practicing social media marketing. Some detractors argued that this was just a one-day effort that got more attention than it deserved, but the fact that so much money was raised in so little time is admirable.

As you consider tapping into social influence marketing to amplify your brand's efforts in the cause realm, keep in mind that consumers are increasingly skeptical of these efforts. Make sure that you're donating enough to make the effort genuine and meaningful for everyone involved.

Figure 1-7:
Tide's Loads
of Hope.

Social graphs for social change

There's more to social causes than your ability to amplify your efforts around causes using social influence marketing tactics. A larger change is afoot that demands attention, even if doesn't directly relate to your objectives. The Web allows individuals to financially support a cause at the very moment that they're inspired and then encourage their friends who reside in their social graphs to do the same.

When an individual provides monetary support for a cause, he can — in that very moment, using the social platforms and his own social media — broadcast his effort to his network of friends and associates. By doing so, he becomes a social influence marketer, spreading the word about the cause and socially influencing his friends to contribute as well. This instant, *viral affect* (the phrase comes from diseases and how they can spread rapidly from person to person) is collectively (and strongly) influencing how causes are promoted and funded — more so than the traditional big corporation backing strategies. This means that you, as a marketer, benefit from the halo affect of supporting a cause, but you can't just support it — you must be willing to participate in this viral affect the same way. Here are a few examples in this realm:

✔ **Causes:** This Facebook and MySpace application (which is available at www.causes.com) is a perfect example of nonprofit organizations using social media as marketing and fundraising tools. (You can see the Causes application's home page in Figure 1-8.) It allows you to choose a nonprofit, contribute funds to it, and track how many of your friends go on to support that cause after seeing your contributions or receiving your invitation to contribute. Within a year of its launch, the application had 12 million users supporting approximately 80,000 nonprofit causes worldwide. Users raised $2.5 million for 19,445 different charitable organizations. Facebook reported 60,000 daily uses of the application, while MySpace tracked 25,000 daily uses.

✔ **Oxfam Unwrapped:** The English charity Oxfam uses technology to help donors understand a problem more deeply and help them appreciate the difference that they're making. If you'd like to give the gift of giving, you can go to www.oxfamunwrapped.com (shown in Figure 1-9) and buy books, bags of seeds, clean water, and even goats in your friend's name. Oxfam delivers the gift to someone in need, and also sends your friend a gift card. The site is a core component of Oxfam's fund-raising efforts.

When Oxfam launched this program, the fact that you could buy a goat for someone in Darfur was more buzz worthy than any other marketing effort. Needless to say, it got people talking about Darfur, Oxfam, and goats, with people forming online communities based on these topics and the other charities that they support. In this case, the donors become social influencers.

✔ **charity: water:** This U.S.-based nonprofit provides clean water to developing communities using a Twitter festival (www.twestival.com) to promote the charity and encourage others to donate money as well. (See Figure 1-10.) The Twitter festival was held in 202 cities around the world, bringing together people from Twitter to support a cause. On February 12, 2009, the participating cities raised $250,000, with counting still going on. This was done with micropayments by participants related to the cause. Participants spread the word about it and socially influenced each other to contribute as well. The event was organized 100 percent by volunteers and 100 percent of the money raised went directly to the charity. You can find out how much your city raised on this Web site: www.charitywater.org/twestival/index.html.

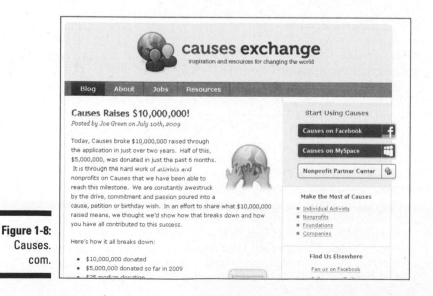

Figure 1-8:
Causes.
com.

Figure 1-9:
Oxfam
Unwrapped.

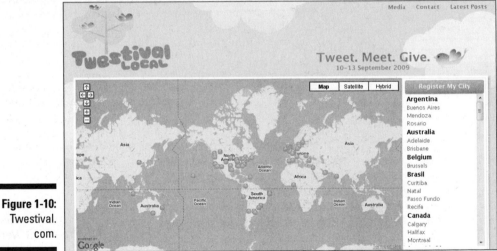

Figure 1-10:
Twestival.
com.

Chapter 2

The Lay of the SIM Land

Knowing which consumers are using the social Web is a subject of much debate. For some skeptics, the social Web is equated with Facebook. They consider the social Web to be a youth phenomena and of no consequence to adults. But they are just as wrong as the evangelists who believe that everyone is using the social Web all the time.

The truth is that who is using the social Web is a difficult question to answer. This is because the term *social Web* is most commonly used to describe how people socialize and interact with each other across the Web. With every passing day, many Web sites are becoming social platforms where visitors can interact and learn from one another. So then how can you find out which consumers use the social Web? The best way is by understanding the different kinds of usage behavior and looking at traffic on specific social media platforms.

In this chapter, I explain how to do that while also highlighting some of the key traffic statistics so that you have a sense of what to expect when you do your own research. Having a firm grip on the lay of the land in the social Web makes it easier to craft a marketing plan that works with it.

Measuring the Size of the Social Web

When you're convincing yourself or someone else that launching a social influence marketing campaign is an important project, a good first step is to measure the size of the social activity on the Web. When you see the numbers of possible customers (who fit your demographics, psychographics, and techno-graphics) you can reach using social tools, it's usually a no-brainer that a social influence campaign is a good thing. Fortunately, several strong online tools show how to measure social activity on the Web.

Many of these tools are free and serve as a good starting point for your research efforts. Each of these is important for a different purpose. Later in the chapter, I discuss these tools in more depth and explain how you can use them and what they tell you. Some of the tools include the following:

- **Technorati** (www.technorati.com): An engine for searching blogs.

- **BlogPulse** (www.blogpulse.com): Another engine for searching blogs. Some consider this tool to be more powerful than Technorati.

- **Google Blog Search** (blogsearch.google.com): This search engine is a strong alternative to Technorati and Blog Pulse for searching blogs.

- **Quantcast** (www.quantcast.com): A Web service to view and analyze Web sites' statistics. When the site is quantified, the results are most accurate.

- **Compete** (www.compete.com): Also a Web service to view and analyze Web sites' statistics.

- **Nielsen BuzzMetrics** (www.nielsen-online.com): A buzz-monitoring service for the social Web; see Figure 2-1.

- **comScore** (www.comscore.com): A high-end Web service for analyzing Web sites' statistics.

- **Lexicon** (www.facebook.com/lexicon): A Facebook service that you can use to understand buzz within Facebook.

- **BoardReader** (www.boardreader.com): A tool to view and analyze activity on discussion boards.

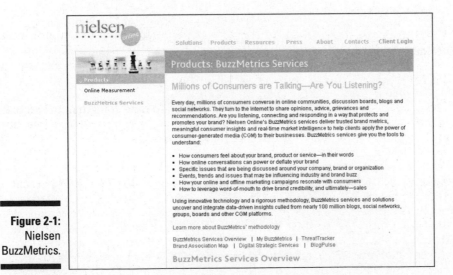

Figure 2-1:
Nielsen
BuzzMetrics.

Of course, all the tools in the world won't help you if you don't know what to measure. You should look at a few big social media categories to gather information on your key demographics. I delve into those first to give you a more tangible feel for the social Web.

No single tool is perfect for capturing Web usage. Therefore, it's always useful to use multiple sites together to get the best data. Also, looking at the relative changes in the statistics over a period of time (versus the raw numbers, which may not always be totally accurate) may be a safe approach to take.

Measuring blogosphere activity

A good place to start measuring social activity on the Web is the blogosphere. The *blogosphere* is a collective term encompassing all blogs and their interconnections. It's the perception that blogs exist together as a connected community.

Technorati is a leading blog search engine, and it indexes 112.8 million blogs and 250 million pieces of tagged social media. Every year, it publishes a State of the Blogosphere report that identifies who is blogging. In the report for 2008, 36 percent of bloggers are 25–34 year olds, 27 percent are 35–44 year olds, 15 percent are 45–54 year olds, 13 percent are 18–24 year olds, and 8 percent of them are 55+. It also says that more than 75 percent of bloggers have college degrees, 42 percent have graduate degrees, and more than half have household incomes of more than $75,000. So, these are the people publishing the blogs.

It also helps to know how many people read blogs so that you can understand what percentage of your total customer base you'll reach via marketing on blogs. According to market research firm eMarketer, in 2007, 94 million Americans read a blog. And they estimate that in 2008 the number grew to 104 million Americans, or 54 percent of the Internet population.

Check out www.emarketer.com to find more up-to-date stats than the stats I had available at the time I wrote this book. Most of the summaries are free, but for the detailed report, you need to become a paid subscriber.

Forrester, another market research firm, estimates that one in three Americans who are online read a blog at least once a month. And 18 percent of those people comment on the blogs. Similarly to eMarketer, Forrester publishes a lot of summary information for free (often in the form of analyst blogs that they post on their Web site, at www.forrester.com, or through their socio-technographics Profile Tool), but you'd need a paid account for the detailed reports. Figure 2-2 shows the Profile Tool at www.forrester.com/Groundswell/profile_tool.html, where you can start doing your own research.

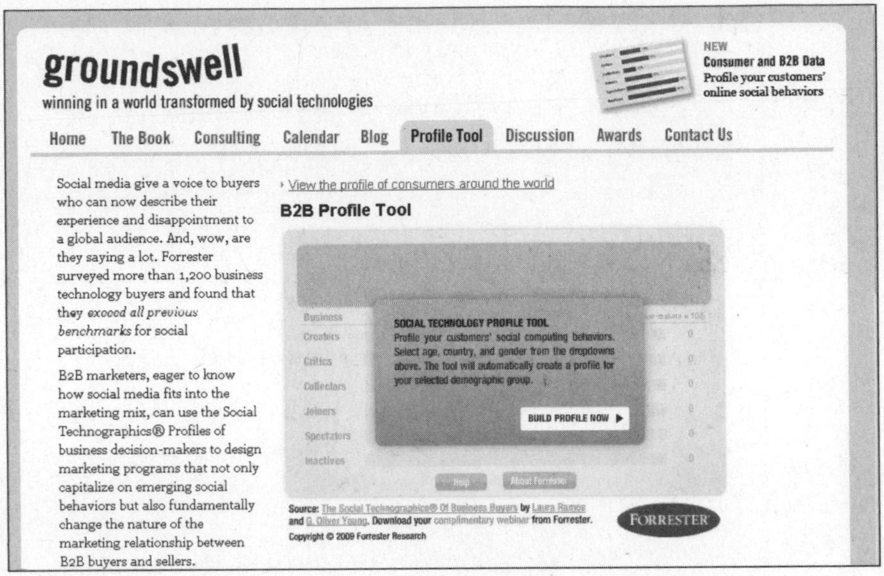

Figure 2-2:
Forrester's
Groundswell
Profile Tool.

In terms of age demographics, generally speaking, the younger the user, the more likely he reads a blog. But there's no question that reading and writing blogs isn't just a youth phenomena. Just by these numbers alone, you can assume that participating in the blogosphere by writing, reading, and commenting is very much a mainstream activity.

Social network usage

The mainstream social networks — MySpace, Facebook, and LinkedIn — are on every marketer's radar. But you need to also consider niche networks as marketing platforms as well. These smaller social networks are targeted towards a specific audience. Examples of these include CafeMom (for mothers; www.cafemom.com), BlackPlanet (www.blackplanet.com), VegetarianPassion (www.vegetarianpassion.com), and a SmallWorld (www.asmallworld.net; targeted towards the social elite and mostly European based). Figure 2-3 shows CafeMom. The adoption of niche social networks often causes the most debate as marketers are never sure how many users use them and how consistently.

Quantcast (www.quantcast.com), an independent media measurement service, finds basic traffic patterns for mainstream and niche social networks. Quantcast determined that in December 2008, MySpace averaged 68 million visitors per month, while Facebook averaged 45.2 million visitors per month. The results indicate that if you have a product targeting a very young crowd, these might be the sites you should focus most of your efforts on.

Figure 2-3: CafeMom.

These results show that although MySpace and Facebook lead the social networking pack, they might not be the best places to market to an older, professional audience. (Or at the very least, they may not be the best place to put all your marketing dollars if you're trying to reach an older audience.) LinkedIn (www.linkedin.com), however, is a social networking site that targets business professionals, who use it, primarily, as a networking tool. The site averages 5.5 million visitors per month, and the LinkedIn user's average age is 36. That's a significantly older average compared to MySpace and Facebook.

If you look a little further to Ning (www.ning.com), which is a platform allowing anyone to set up a private social network, you notice that it averages around the same number of monthly visitors as LinkedIn, with the largest demographic being the 35–49 year olds at 38 percent of its population. Figure 2-4 shows Ning.

And Eons.com, which averages around 4.1 million visitors per month globally, has 53 percent of its United States traffic coming from the 50 demographic, followed by the 35-49+ year olds at 29 percent. 58 percent of its visitors are female.

You can use Quantcast to find statistics on almost any site on the Web. Just type the site's Web address (for example, **Ning.com**) in the Advanced Search box at the top of the home page and click the Find button.

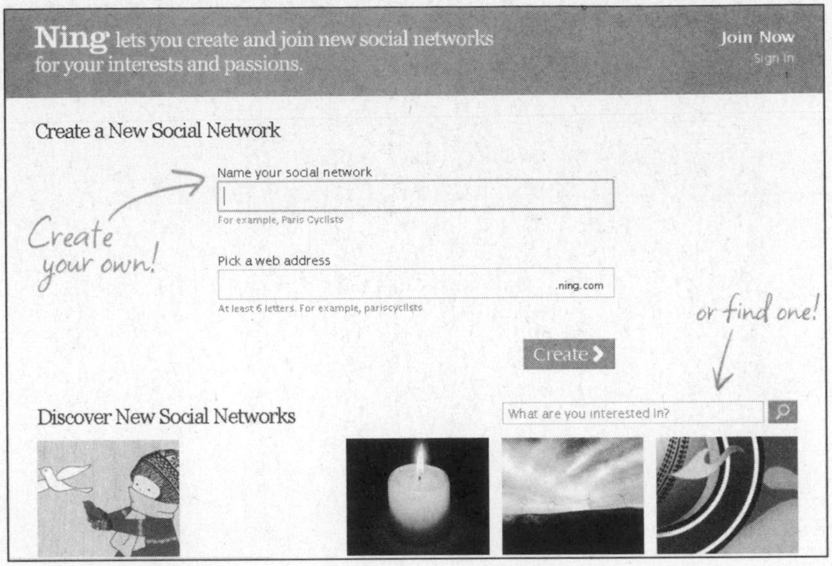

Ning lets you create and join new social networks for your interests and passions.

Join Now
Sign In

Create a New Social Network

Name your social network

For example, Paris Cyclists

Pick a web address

.ning.com

At least 6 letters. For example, pariscyclists

Create ▸

Create your own!

or find one!

Discover New Social Networks

What are you interested in?

Figure 2-4:
Ning.

Measuring YouTube, Flickr, and Wikipedia popularity

Measuring the top user-generated video, photo, and wiki Web sites can also offer a good indication of the size of the social Web.

YouTube averages an astounding 69 million visitors per month, according to Quantcast, with its breakdown going like this.

- ✔ Its largest demographic is 18–34 year olds (36 percent).

- ✔ The 35–49 age group (23 percent) is the next largest.

- ✔ Both the 12–17 and the 55+ age groups come in at 19 percent.

Flickr, a photo-sharing Web site owned by Yahoo! and shown in Figure 2-5, averages 22 million visitors per month. Here's who you find:

- ✔ The largest demographic is the 18–34 year olds (39 percent).

- ✔ It's followed by 35–49 year olds at 31 percent.

Wikipedia has similar statistics, too. It averages 76 million visitors per month:

- ✔ 37 percent are 18–34 year olds.

- ✔ 35–49 year olds comprise 27 percent of its traffic.

I discuss all three of these sites more in Chapter 6.

Figure 2-5:
Flickr.

You're probably wondering what all of this data means. That question is best answered by comparing these numbers to Google's traffic. Why Google? Because Google is the most visited Web site in America, with 142 million visitors per month. Guess who the largest demographic on Google is? The 18–34 year olds, at 37 percent of its total traffic, followed again by the 35–49 year olds, with 29 percent of the traffic. The traffic is also evenly split between male and female visitors.

You can conclude from this comparison to Google that activity on the social Web mirrors activity on the broader Web in terms of traffic patterns and age demographics. Sure, the social networks skew slightly younger, but it also quickly becomes a question of which social network you're talking about. With regard to gender, the social platforms skew slightly toward females. Another interesting statistic: research by Forrester emphasizes that 75 percent of all Internet users participate in the social Web in some form or other. In other words, it couldn't be clearer that the social Web is blurring with the mainstream Web.

Identifying High-Traffic Sites

Each time you run a social influence marketing campaign, you need to determine what the most popular sites are and on which sites you should run the campaign. The tools for identifying the sites with the most traffic are readily available online. I discuss several of them in this section.

Measuring traffic across the mainstream Web

The leading services that can help you understand the high-traffic sites are Nielsen Online (www.nielsen-online.com) comScore (www.comscore.com), Compete (www.compete.com), and Quantcast (www.quantcast.com). Each one uses slightly different methods for measuring traffic. Nielsen Online, comScore, and Compete (shown in Figure 2-6) are mostly fee based, while Quantcast offers the most features for free. Table 2-1 lists the top ten trafficked Web sites in July 2009, according to Quantcast.

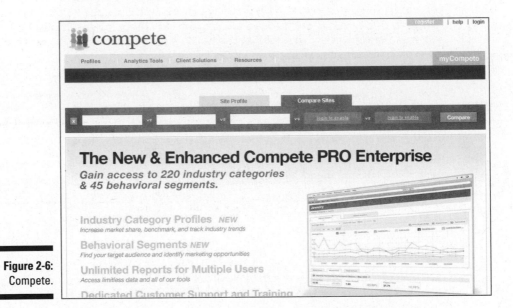

Figure 2-6:
Compete.

Table 2-1	Top Ten Trafficked Web Sites
Site	*Visitors (Approximately)*
Google.com	142 million
Yahoo.com	124 million
Facebook.com	94 million
YouTube.com	83 million
Microsoft.com	83 million

Site	Visitors (Approximately)
MSN.com	79 million
Wikipedia.org	69 million
MySpace.com	61 million
eBay.com	61 million
AOL.com	58 million

A slightly different way to look at the list is to use comScore's top ten properties. This list combines all the Web sites belonging to a specific company. For example, Google sites combine Google Search (ranked as the number one Web site, in terms of traffic) with Google News, Videos, Images, Blogs, and so on. In other words, Table 2-2 shows companies with the largest audiences versus just Web sites with the most traffic for July 2009.

Table 2-2	Top Ten Properties
Site	**Visitors (Approximately)**
Google sites	159 million
Yahoo! sites	157 million
Microsoft sites	129 million
AOL LLC	105 million
Fox Interactive Media	81 million
Ask Network	79 million
eBay	73 million
Amazon sites	67 million
Wikimedia Foundation sites	62 million
Apple Inc.	58 million

Measuring traffic on the social Web

Measuring traffic on the social Web ranges from very simple to a bit more challenging. The simplest task is discovering the most influential blogs. Technorati can help you, using its authority rankings. A Technorati authority ranking indicates how many other blogs linked to a blog within the last six months. The idea is that when blogs link to other blogs, the content is more valuable than the content on blogs that don't link to other blogs. (And, logically, blogs that link to more blogs are more influential.) These scores place extra importance on blogs that have the maximum number of other blogs linking to them. Table 2-3 lists the most popular blogs by authority ranking as of August 2009.

Table 2-3	Top Ten Blogs
Blog	*Ranking*
Huffington Post (Social & political commentary)	17,521
TechCrunch (Silicon valley startups)	11,073
Mashable (Social Web news)	9,413
Engadget (Consumer gadgets)	7,749
Boing Boing (Culture and lifestyle)	6,675
Gizmodo (Consumer gadgets)	6,498
The Official Google Blog (On Google)	5,996
Lifehacker (Tips and downloads for hacking)	5,756
Ars Technica	5,679
TMZ.com (Celebrity gossip)	5,073

As you scan Table 2-3, notice that many of the top ten blogs are technology focused. That could be pure coincidence, or it could be because technology bloggers are more apt to exchange links with other blogs in order to pump up their authority rankings.

Visit Technorati (http://technorati.com/pop/blogs) to find out the top blogs by authority ranking at any given moment.

In terms of measuring the social platforms, things get a little harder. There isn't a running top ten list of social platforms made available on a consistent basis. If you want to know the largest social platforms, you have to use a service like Quantcast or comScore to get traffic estimates. However, occasionally, Nielsen Online and Compete publish top ten lists. Table 2-4 shows the U.S. top ten social networks and blog sites for April 2009, according to Neilsen based on the number of minutes spent on each site. The year-over-year percent growth is important to analyze which sites have the most momentum behind them.

Table 2-4	Top Ten Social Networks	
Social Network	**Total Minutes (000)**	**Year-Over-Year Percent Growth**
Facebook	13,872,640	699
MySpace	4,973,919	-31
Blogger	582,683	30
Tagged	327,871	998
Twitter	299,836	3712
MyYearbook	268,565	105
LiveJournal	204,121	273
LinkedIn	202,407	69
SlashKey	187,687	N/A
Gaia Online	143,909	-17

You can check this information at comScore (www.comscore.com), which is shown in Figure 2-7. While most of its data is for paid subscribers only, they do make this information publicly available.

Figure 2-7: comScore.

It isn't enough to know which social networks are the largest; you also need to know how well the social networks do compared to other categories of Web sites. After all, social networks are not the only Web sites that people visit online. Table 2-5 includes the U.S. top ten growing site categories between the months of March 2009 and April 2009 according to comScore.

Table 2-5	Top Ten Gaining Site Categories by Percentage Change	
Site Category	*Total Unique Visitors 000*	*% Change*
Social networking	139,781	21
Entertainment/music	95,511	12
Real estate	48,357	12
Gaming information	44,370	10
Retail/computer software	37,685	10
Retail/flowers, gifts, greeting cards	31,019	10
Community/home	29,857	10
Community/teens	24,142	9
Business/finance/taxes	20,585	9
Online gambling	12,754	9

While certain site categorizes (such as Business/finance/taxes) spike in the April timeframe, few other categories are seeing the explosive growth rate that the social networking category does. It's worth noting that outside of the social networking category, other categories that emphasize community are experiencing a lot of growth as well.

Measuring Internet usage on mobile devices

Internet use on mobile devices has jumped dramatically since the iPhone launch in 2007. iPhone users surf the Web from their phones in such large numbers that other device manufacturers, such as Research in Motion (the company who brings us the BlackBerry), are pressured to introduce phones into the marketplace that make surfing the Web as simple as the iPhone does. It's no surprise that the list of top Web sites visited via mobile devices looks similar to the list of top ten most trafficked Web sites. Table 2-6 shows data from the November 2008 International Data Corporation (IDC) and Openwave report, "Monitor, Manage and Monetize the Mobile Internet."

Table 2-6	Top Ten Web Sites Visited from Mobile Devices
Web Site	*Percent of Mobile Internet Visitors*
Google	27.9
Yahoo!	21.1
MySpace	15.4
Facebook	13.7
YouTube	11.8
The Weather Channel	11.2
MapQuest	10.4
Wikipedia	8.5
ESPN	7.7
eBay	7.5

Classifying Consumer Activities

Before you launch a social influence marketing campaign, you need a feel for what activities consumers undertake on the social Web. After all, your marketing campaign is far more likely to succeed if it is in harmony with what consumers are trying to accomplish on the social Web. Consumer activity on the social Web is classified into these eight categories:

✔ **Information:** The Internet, with its academic roots, was conceived as a virtual library and an information-sharing tool. And to this day, consumers use the Internet for finding information more than anything else. In fact, it's no surprise that Google, Yahoo!, and MSN are the top three Web destinations. It's because they're primary search engines, helping consumers find the information that they're looking for. That hasn't changed, and even with the Internet going increasingly social, searching and finding information remains the number one consumer activity online. If you're running a marketing campaign for a product or service that consumers seek, you're most likely to get strong results. When people are in the "information seeker" modes, they're most apt to participate in campaigns.

✔ **News:** One primary use for the Internet is news. More people read the news online than watch it on cable television. The instant, real-time nature of news makes it particularly suited for the Internet. Many cable television channels promote their Web sites to their TV audiences. But what's even more interesting is that practically all the major news Web sites integrate social media functionality into their user experience. When you go to www.cnn.com, www.nytimes.com, or www.washington post.com, you notice that journalists have blogs and the articles allow for commenting and ratings. Figure 2-8 shows the blogs offered by *The New York Times*. News sites often integrate video clips as well.

With news, your marketing opportunity differs slightly. Consumers are more receptive to the campaigns if your product or service is either contextualized in some form to what they're reading or is directly targeted toward them.

✔ **Communication:** The Internet continues to be a core communication medium for most people. With the advent of social media, this communication takes place within social networks versus personal Web sites or via e-mail and instant messenger programs. *Microcommunication* technologies such as Twitter, which let you communicate in short bursts of information, are also gaining traction. The medium allows consumers to communicate with one another in new, dynamic ways, whether it be microblogging, leaving notes on friends' Facebook Walls, commenting on personal blogs, or instant messaging from within Web sites. When consumers are communicating with each other, they're less receptive to marketing campaigns, unless the campaigns incorporate their communications with their peers in a permissible fashion. This is why social influence marketing campaigns that incorporate groups of people are so important.

Figure 2-8: Blogs on the New York Times Web site.

✔ **Community:** Online communities and social networks have seen explosive growth in the last few years. The amount of time that people spend on community Web sites is significantly higher than anywhere else on the Web. Online communities include social platforms, such as Facebook, Twitter, and MySpace, and the more private online communities and forums that are often tied to company Web sites.

For example, The Well (shown in Figure 2-9) is one of the most famous online communities, just as Facebook is the most popular social network in the U.S. as I write this. The reasons people participate in online communities are myriad. (See Chapter 7 for more information on online communities.) Suffice to say, community participation is a key type of activity online. However, when people are engaging with each other, they participate less in marketing campaigns because engaging with one another captures all their attention. They have no time for advertising, as they're just hearing each other's opinions. Rather, when searching for information or looking to buy a product is when consumers are more open to advertising. This is exactly why social influence marketing, with its unique approach, is important.

Figure 2-9:
The Well.

✔ **E-Commerce:** Consumers across the country continue to choose to buy more goods online. The fact that the products have to be shipped has done little to hinder many consumers from using the Internet to make retail purchases. The largest online retailer continues to be Amazon.com, with approximately $20 billion in sales each year. However, e-commerce represents just a fraction of total retail sales and, as a result, only a small percentage of total consumer activity online. According to the Census Bureau of The Department of Commerce, retail e-commerce sales were just 3.6 percent of total retail sales in the second quarter of 2009. There are some very obvious marketing opportunities in this, especially when peers are asked to recommend products. Great social influence marketing opportunities here.

✔ **Entertainment:** There's no doubt that consumers look to the Internet for entertainment. The explosive growth of YouTube and the most recent adoption of high-end video sites like Hulu (shown in Figure 2-10) are testament of this trend. Social games like Scramble and Pet Society on social networking platforms and the major portals are just another example of this trend. Arguably, entertainment is becoming a driving reason for people to spend more time online, and this is in part thanks to the proliferation of high-bandwidth access across the country. As long as the marketing campaign is entertaining, consumers will respond to it. They don't care as much whether it's an advertisement in these instances.

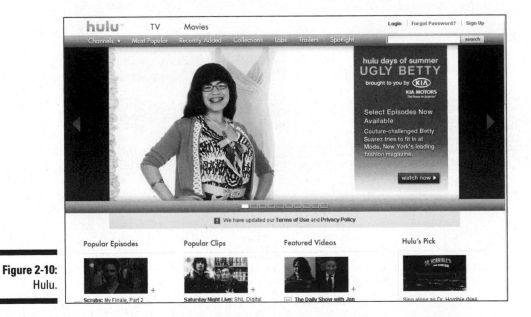

Figure 2-10:
Hulu.

✔ **Services:** Another popular consumer activity online is the use of services to allow a person to lead a more efficient and productive life. Whether they're paying bills, checking bank balances, looking up phone numbers, finding jobs, or searching for apartments, consumers use the

Internet as a tool to lead more productive lives. Many of today's businesses, such as banks and airlines, provide services on the Internet. Consumers are typically very task oriented when they're interacting with online services; as a result, they don't expect to participate in advertising campaigns and, especially not social influence marketing campaigns, when they're in this mode.

✔ **Business:** And of course, the Internet is used to conduct business. This may take the form of companies talking to each other and exchanging information, establishing online marketplaces, and initiating brand launches. Businesses engage with their customers online by marketing and selling products and services and providing customer service via the Internet. Consumers expect these online conveniences from brands that they interact with, and they increasingly engage with businesses on the Internet. They also use the Internet to start their own businesses. Depending on the business, social influence marketing campaigns can certainly help here.

Researching Your Customers' Online Activities

When developing a social influence marketing campaign, it's important to determine what your target customers are doing on the Internet. You can use several tools to find out where your target customers are going online. Without this information, you can't formulate a smart social influence marketing strategy. You'd be simply shooting in the dark.

Tools that help you research online activity fall into two basic categories: free and not free. The free tools you can simply register for and use. Tools and services for which you must pay can get expensive very quickly. In this section, I discuss some of the free tools. In Chapter 4, I discuss the pay tools and services, which are more appropriate when you're planning a specific SIM campaign.

✔ **Blog search engines:** These search engines *crawl* (sort through) just the blogosphere for the terms that you input. They search for those terms in the blog posts and the comments, and the searches generally include all publicly viewable blogs on the Internet. If you just want to get a sense of the conversations in the blogosphere about a specific topic or brand, these search engines can help you do that. The most popular ones include Technorati's blog search engine (http://s.technorati.com), Google's Blog Search (http://blogsearch.google.com), BlogPulse from Nielsen BuzzMetrics (www.blogpulse.com), and the more recently launched BlogScope (www.blogscope.net), which is shown in Figure 2-11.

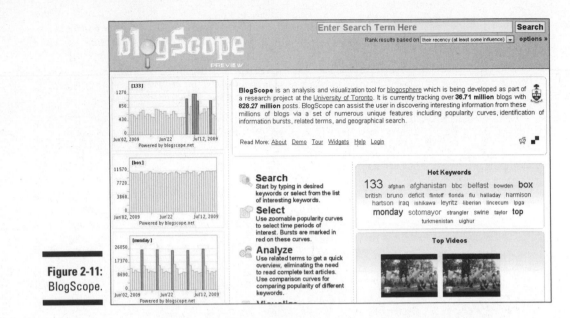

Figure 2-11:
BlogScope.

A discussion on blog search engines wouldn't be complete without mentioning the official Twitter search tool (http://search.twitter.com). Twitter is the most popular microblogging platform. *Microblogging* is similar to blogging except that you're restricted to a certain number of characters per post. Another microblogging search engine to consider is Tweet Scan (http://tweetscan.com). Tweet Scan is shown in Figure 2-12, where you can searches Twitter and its closest competitor Identi.ca.

Figure 2-12:
Tweet Scan.

✔ **Buzz charting:** Similar to the blog search engines, there are a few buzz charting tools. These tools focus on giving you a comparative perspective on how much different keywords, phrases, or links are discussed in the blogosphere. They search for the terms and then organize the responses into a chart with the x-axis being time and the y-axis the number of posts. Typically, you can choose the duration of time for the x-axis. Nielsen BuzzMetrics has probably the most popular blog buzz charting tool, at `http://blogpulse.com/trend`. Omgili does similar buzz charting for discussion forums (`http://buzz.omgili.com/graphs.html`), as shown in Figure 2-13.

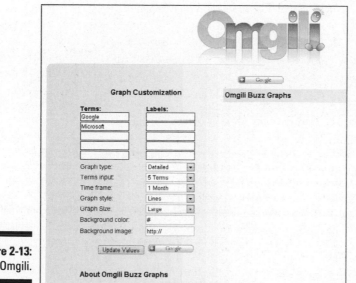

Figure 2-13:
Omgili.

✔ **Forums and message boards:** To understand online behavior in the social Web, you must be able to scan the conversations happening in forums and message boards as well. BoardReader (`http://boardreader.com`) allows you to search multiple boards at once. You can use it to find answers to questions that you may not find on a single board. Also, back to a marketer's point of view, you can find research peoples' opinions of brands or products. BoardReader is so popular that it powers a lot of the forum searches that the fee-based brand-monitoring tools conduct. Another player worth mentioning in this space is Omgili (`www.omgili.com`), which similarly focuses on forums and message boards. BoardTracker, which is shown in Figure 2-14, is another popular way to search forums and message boards.

Figure 2-14:
Board-
Tracker.

✔ **Video and image search:** Earlier in this chapter, I mention entertainment and the increasing number of people going online to watch videos — professionally created videos and personal ones, too. But how can you find the videos that are of interest to you or your brand? For video search, you have to depend on a couple of tools, as no single one truly captures all the videos created. All video searches must begin with YouTube (www.youtube.com), as it's the largest, but then you should also look at Metacafe (www.metacafe.com), Viral Video Chart (www.viralvideochart.com), which also tells you how much the clip is being discussed, and Truveo (www.truveo.com), another notable player, shown in Figure 2-15.

On the image side, you'd want to use the Flickr search (www.flickr.com), and to a lesser extent Google Images (www.google.com/images).

Google Images also searches professionally produced and published images, not just user-generated ones, so you might not get an accurate picture of what people are talking about.

Figure 2-15:
Truveo.

Analyzing Competitor Efforts

Just as it's important to understand where your consumers participate in the social Web, it's necessary to understand how your competitors engage in the social Web. After all, if your competitors are already running marketing campaigns similar to what you plan to do, yours won't attract much attention. A combination of sleuthing and third-party tools can help you.

Setting up Google Alerts

You can set up these free alerts for keywords related to your competitors. These keywords can include company names, brands, senior manager names, and partner names. Every day, you receive a Google Alert in your e-mail inbox with summaries of news stories and blog posts that include those keywords. It's a good starting point and completely free.

To set up a Google Alert, follow these simple steps:

1. **Go to www.google.com/alerts.**

    The Google Alerts page opens, as shown in Figure 2-16.

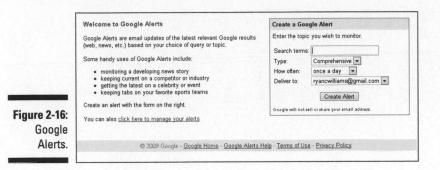

Figure 2-16:
Google
Alerts.

2. **Enter the search terms for which you want alerts.**

   Try to keep these to one word or a commonly used phrase.

3. **From the Type drop-down list, choose what type of content you want Google to search.**

   I generally choose Comprehensive so that I don't miss news items.

4. **From the How Often drop-down list, choose the frequency you want the alerts delivered to you.**

   I find Once a Day to be the best frequency.

5. **Enter the e-mail address where you want the alerts to be sent.**

   Remember that you can edit these alert settings at any time.

6. **Click the Create Alert button.**

Setting up Twitter alerts

Similarly, create Twitter alerts that track those same keywords in the Twitter world. Services like Twilert let you follow keywords and observe all the microblogging posts in which those words appear.

A few services like OneRiot (www.oneriot.com), Tweetmeme (tweetmeme. com), and Scoopler (www.scoopler.com) allow you to scan not just Twitter but all the other microblogging platforms at once and in real time.

To set up a Twitter alert, follow these simple steps:

1. **Go to www.twilert.com.**

   The Twilert home page opens, as shown in Figure 2-17.

   In order to set a Twitter alert, you have to be signed in to your Twitter account. If you don't have one, you can sign up at www.twitter.com.

Figure 2-17:
Twilert.

2. **Type the keyword that you want the alert set up for.**

3. **Click the Create a Twilert button.**

Monitoring blogosphere conversations

While Google Alerts can include blogs, they don't encompass the conversations that surround a blog post. For that you need to depend on Technorati. Visit Technorati (www.technorati.com) and type a blog address. You can see all the posts for that blog and all the links to it (and their related conversations) elsewhere on the Internet. The buzz charting tools discussed in the earlier section are helpful, too. Another tool to also consider using is BlogPulse (www.blogpulse.com), which is a blog search engine similar to Technorati.

Monitoring social networks

You probably want to observe what your competitors are doing on the various social networks. That's a little harder to do, as most social networks are closed gardens. Meaning, except for the public profile pages (a very small percentage of all the pages on the network), you can't search them with external tools, and typically, once you log in, you can't search the universe of activity on them. However, what you can do is search and follow the pages, profiles, groups, and applications created by your competitors. Keep in mind that some users hide their profiles, so you won't be able to track them. Search engines, such as Facebook's Lexicon, within the social networks can be helpful, too. Figure 2-18 shows Lexicon.

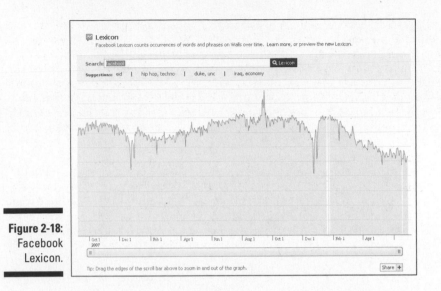

Tracking competitor Web sites

Look at the social media efforts that may reside on your competitors' Web sites. Often, those efforts are promoted or anchored in the company Web site or company-sponsored microsite through links. In fact, many of your competitors probably have (as they should) corporate blogs and Twitter accounts. (Start tracking those directly, too.)

Researching Your Competitor's Campaign Support

Practically every marketing campaign today has a social media component to it. As you see a competitor launch a major marketing campaign, scan the Web and the competitor's Web site for that campaign's digital and social components. The social activity surrounding the campaign (elsewhere on the Web) gives you a sense of how successful it is and how much it helps the brand. Also, watch prominent bloggers in that product category, as they may be part of an outreach program and could be promoting the campaign.

Conducting qualitative research

Using the free tools and observing competitor activity is all well and good. But more often than not, you need to conduct qualitative research that doesn't just tell you what your consumers are doing, rather the goals, needs, and aspirations that drive their behavior. Here, there's good news and bad news.

First the good news. Qualitative research, as you probably know it in the traditional marketing world, hasn't changed. You can still use interviews, focus groups, shadowing, and other ethnographic research techniques to understand your consumers. There are dozens of authoritative books on the subject — including a few excellent ones from the *For Dummies* series, such as *Marketing For Dummies,* by Alexander Hiam (Wiley Publishing) — on qualitative research, so I won't go into those research formats. All the same best practices of recruiting effectively, knowing your objectives, and having good interview guides and moderators apply.

And now for the bad news: the questions have changed, and you won't get all your answers from the qualitative research. Unlike qualitative research in the past, which focused on understanding a specific consumer's goals and needs, you must pay attention to the consumer's surrounding community and influencers within that community. For example, you need to ask who influences your consumers when they make specific purchasing decisions.

Running surveys and quantitative research

Similarly, quantitative research in the form of statistically significant surveys can be most helpful. Keep in mind that you must run surveys at regular intervals to get valuable, statistically significant results. The reason is that influence changes more rapidly in an online environment, and the social media platforms on which people participate change, too. Don't run extensive surveys irregularly. Run short, quick surveys about your audiences on a frequent basis to glean important insights.

Pay attention to where you run the surveys, too, as that can affect the results. A good strategy is to run the survey on your corporate Web site but simultaneously use a third-party survey vendor to run the same survey on the social media platforms. This way, you're gauging how people participate and socialize in their own contexts. Very often, the quantitative research can give statistically significant results about influence, with the qualitative research being used to explain the hows and whys of the responses. The two kinds of research go hand in hand.

Some of the survey vendors that you can use include these:

- **SurveyMonkey** (www.surveymonkey.com); see Figure 2-19
- **Zoomerang** (www.zoomerang.com)
- **SurveyGizmo** (www.surveygizmo.com)
- **Key Survey** (www.keysurvey.com)

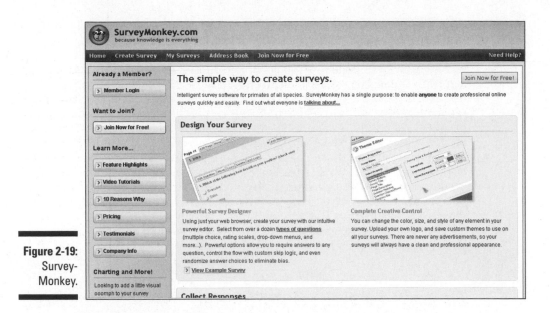

Figure 2-19:
Survey-
Monkey.

As you may know, there are other important forms of research, such as content, discourse, and network analysis, which take on additional importance in the sphere of social influence, but those can be relatively laborious. Generally, they're appropriate only when much deeper behavioral insights are required.

The psychology behind social influence

Consumers have always been heavily influenced by each other when they make purchasing decisions. They ask each other for advice, they observe and mimic each other's decision making, and, frankly, they let peer pressure inform their decisions, whether they like to admit it or not. What's changed is that digital behavior has caught up with offline behavior, and that's why social influence marketing matters to anyone who has a future in marketing.

Communication technologies such as social networks, prediction markets, microblogging solutions, location-based, networked mobile phone applications, and even virtual worlds make it possible for consumers to influence each other more directly and dramatically than

ever before. According to Harvard psychologist Herbert Kelman, this influence occurs in three ways:

- ✔ **Compliance:** Public conformity while keeping one's own private beliefs

- ✔ **Identification:** Conforming to someone who is liked and respected, such as a celebrity or a favorite uncle

- ✔ **Internalization:** Acceptance of the belief or behavior and conforming both publically and privately

Aside from making for good copy in behavioral psychology textbooks, these concepts do translate into tactics for social influence marketing.

All Consumers Are Not Created Equal

A chapter on the SIM landscape wouldn't be complete without addressing the fact that, in discussions about social influence and social influence marketing, all consumers aren't created equal. Social influence doesn't simply mean recognizing that every consumer may influence every other consumer, rather in specific marketing contexts, specific consumers have an outsized influence on their peers around them. For example, on my social network, one of my friends posts more comments than anyone else. Just by virtue of his volume of postings, his opinion is taken into account more than that of my other friends who aren't commenting as much. Like some of my other friends, I've grown used to his commentary, and I follow his opinions quite actively.

In this regard, three steps help you gain a marketing advantage from influential consumers.

1. **Discover the influential consumers.**

   As you launch a social influence marketing campaign and identify your consumers, pay extra attention to who is influencing your potential customers. Who are the consumers that are influencing your customers, and where is this influence taking place? (You can find out more about influencers in Chapter 8.)

2. **Activate the influential consumers.**

   After you identify the influential consumers, whether they're bloggers, forum leaders, or just conversationalists with lots of friends on the social networks, develop relationships with them and find ways to activate them to do the marketing on your behalf. In later chapters, I discuss how exactly you can do this.

3. **Turn customers into brand advocates.**

   And finally, once a consumer becomes a customer, deepen your relationship with her so that the customer becomes a brand advocate. That's not a new strategy except that now you can ask her to take specific actions within her social networks as a brand advocate. Rather than just asking her to talk about your product, you can have her actually reach out to her peers and then reward her for her participation.

Chapter 3

Getting in the Social Influence Marketing Frame of Mind

In This Chapter

▶ Applying social influence marketing to the marketing funnel

▶ Deploying specific tactics at each stage of the funnel

▶ Complementing brand marketing

▶ Making direct-response and social influence marketing work together

*T*he true power of social influence marketing comes from applying its principles to all parts of your business in a rigorous fashion. This begins with examining social influence marketing in relation to your marketing funnel and then understanding how it relates to brand marketing and direct response — the two traditional pillars of marketing that support the marketing funnel. Understanding the differences helps you better know when to deploy social influence marketing tactics versus when to depend upon brand or direct-response ones.

In this chapter, I also discuss how big and little ideas relate to social influence marketing. The marketing world has historically been driven by the big ideas. Whether it's been the glamorous advertising campaigns (Apple's iconic 1984 commercial comes to mind) or the clever in-store promotions that you see when you walk down the aisle at your local Whole Foods, ideas drive marketing. That changes with social influence marketing. I explain how you need to think about the big idea a little differently as you deploy social influence marketing to meet your marketing and business objectives.

Putting SIM in the Context of the Marketing Funnel

The marketing funnel is one of the most important metaphors in marketing today. It differentiates between prospects and customers and maps out the journey from the point where a prospect learns about a product to when he becomes a loyal and repeat customer. As practically every marketer uses some form of the marketing funnel, it serves an important framework through which to understand social influence marketing.

The traditional marketing funnel typically has five stages, as defined by Forrester. These five stages are awareness, consideration, preference, action, and loyalty (as shown in Figure 3-1). The last stage (loyalty) has the fewest people. Those customers are the most loyal and, therefore, among the most valuable. For many marketers, marketing is fundamentally the act of moving people from having an awareness of a product, considering it along with other products, establishing a preference for the product over the others, to eventually taking action such as purchasing it and developing loyalty towards it.

You employ different marketing strategies and tactics at every stage of the marketing funnel to move the prospects along. The movement of prospects and customers is measured precisely (especially when you do this online), and if there isn't enough movement, you need to devote more marketing dollars to pushing people through the funnel. How you spend these dollars and which investments do the most for moving people through the marketing funnel is always a subject of much debate and varies by product category. Regardless, social influence marketing and tapping into the social influencers with differing tactics can help with this journey.

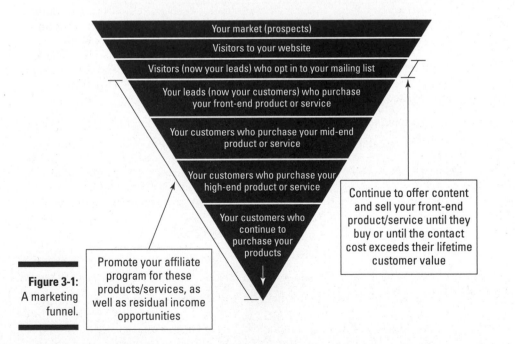

Figure 3-1:
A marketing funnel.

Your market (prospects)

Visitors to your website

Visitors (now your leads) who opt in to your mailing list

Your leads (now your customers) who purchase your front-end product or service

Your customers who purchase your mid-end product or service

Your customers who purchase your high-end product or service

Your customers who continue to purchase your products

Promote your affiliate program for these products/services, as well as residual income opportunities

Continue to offer content and sell your front-end product/service until they buy or until the contact cost exceeds their lifetime customer value

The stages of the marketing funnel may vary from company to company. Some link online funnel tracking with offline efforts, while others don't. You don't have to use the stages as I defined them rigorously. It's more important that you look at SIM in the context of how your company tracks leads and sales. In some cases, you need to consider how you can apply SIM at the different points in an advertising campaign. Regardless, the same principles apply whether you're looking at SIM in the context of the funnel for your entire marketing efforts or for just an online advertising campaign.

SIM at the awareness stage

The awareness stage of the marketing funnel is where you introduce potential customers to your brand. You build awareness and encourage prospective customers to remember your brand name so that when they do make a purchase in the future, they include your brand in their consideration mix.

Typically, marketers use television, radio, print, and direct mail to build awareness. They also sponsor events, conduct promotions, and invest in product placements to get further exposure. Marketers also use public relations professionals to influence editorial content in magazines and newspapers.

In the digital realm, you typically create awareness using display advertising on major Web sites, paid searches for category-related keywords, and sponsorships across the Web. E-mail marketing historically has been extremely successful at building awareness. Arguably, creating awareness online is a lot cheaper but without the same mass scale affect of a 30-second television spot.

You can use social influence marketing to build awareness of your brand, too. The reason is simple. As a marketer with a loyal customer base, you can encourage your customers to build your brand by talking about your product with their friends. Many a marketer has incentivized existing customers to tell their friends and families about their purchasing decisions. You aren't the first. In fact, you can also reach out to expert influencers to help you here.

Expert influencers are the people who are experts in a field and have large audiences.

Here are some SIM tactics to consider for building awareness:

✓ **Publish advertisements to YouTube and tag them with category terms.**

For example, if you're publishing advertisements for orange juice on YouTube, use the tags *orange*, *orangejuice*, *beverage*, *vitamin*, and *drink* in addition to the brand name. Highlight these YouTube video clips on the corporate Web site, too. Figure 3-2 shows your orange juice video would be in good company on YouTube.

Figure 3-2:
Does your
orange
juice video
belong
here?

✔ **Nurture relationships with expert influencers, such as bloggers who publish content related to the specific product category you're marketing.**

Take the time to share product samples with this group, answer their questions, and invite them to special events. If required, sponsor a post on an influential blog. These expert influencers build awareness for your brand.

✔ **Set up a Facebook fan page, a Twitter account, and a MySpace profile.**

Run polls, offer special discounts, publish games, promote coupons, and give members of these pages or accounts product sneak peeks. Share entertaining and educational information through them.

✔ **Provide RSS feeds for content on the corporate Web site.**

An RSS feed is a content format that easily allows anyone to pluck the content from your site and place it on their blog or in an RSS reader. Google Reader is probably the most popular RSS reader today. Just visit www.google.com/reader for instructions on how to set it up. Then each time you see the RSS icon on a Web site, you can click it and have that content fed into your RSS reader on an ongoing basis. Figure 3-3 shows how Apple has set up its RSS feeds.

✔ **Allow for the easy sharing of information from your corporate Web site onto the social networks.**

Services from companies like Popular Media (www.popularmedia.com) and ShareThis (www.sharethis.com) allow you to make your content sharable. See Chapter 9 for more information on this.

✔ **Allow new customers to broadcast their purchases to their social networks.**

Figure 3-3:
One of
Apple's
corporate
RSS feeds.

Each time a customer makes a purchase, you can ask them whether they would like to announce the purchase on their favorite social network. Services like Popular Media and ShareThis, along with Facebook Connect, allow you to set this up on your Web site for your customers.

If you're planning to broadcast their purchases, be sure to ask the customer for permission to do this before broadcasting the purchase.

✔ **Leverage social ads.**

Because social ads are highly engaging — by virtue of the fact that they tell the customer what his friends are doing — they're useful for building awareness and establishing consideration. For example, if a customer sees an endorsement from his friend in an ad unit for a movie, he is more likely to go for the movie. See Chapter 10 for more on social ads.

✔ **Support a cause via a social network.**

Promise to match the contributions of participants who encourage friends to participate in the cause as well. The Causes application on Facebook and MySpace allows you to do this very nicely. Go to www. causes.com for more information.

SIM at the consideration stage

The consideration stage of the marketing funnel is where you make sure that, as the prospective customer goes about making a purchasing decision, she considers your product.

To be included in the consideration stage, use tactics like product comparisons, special promotions, sales discounts, decision tools, and calculators to convince prospects.

The consideration stage is arguably the most important one because it's at this point that you can snag a loyal customer or forever lose one to a competitor.

Social influence marketing plays an integral role at this stage. This is because the referent, expert, and positional influencers (which I define in Chapter 1) help a prospect determine whether he should make the purchasing decision. Increasingly, while making choices between different products, prospective customers look to each other for advice and guidance. They ask their friends for advice, search the Web for customer reviews, and read expert opinions from credible third-party sources. In fact, according to a global Nielsen survey of 26,468 Internet users in 47 markets conducted in 2007, consumer recommendations are the most credible form of advertising among 78 percent of the study's respondents. That percentage could only have increased in the last year and a half.

Your role at this stage is, primarily, connecting that prospective customer with these credible third-party sources of information. Now, you may feel that connecting a prospective customer to a bad review or to another customer who may not have liked the product is a bad idea, but it isn't necessarily so. Prospective customers are looking for the best information about a product, and they respect companies that help them research the product more thoroughly. You can't hide bad reviews on the Web, and by pointing to all the reviews and not just the good ones, you establish credibility with your prospective customer. (Besides, I would hope that the positive reviews far outweigh the negative ones.) This is important as 63 percent of consumers indicate that they're more likely to purchase from a site if it has product ratings and reviews, according to an iPerceptions study in January 2008.

Here are some SIM tactics that you can use at the consideration stage:

- **Publish customer ratings and reviews on the corporate Web site.**

  Make sure ratings and reviews appear for all product and that you do not censor them. Even if a product gets negative reviews, publish them. Invariably, customers will choose other products from your company. You won't lose the customer completely.

- **Point to authoritative third-party reviews.**

  It's important to point to credible third-party reviews from recognized experts so that you build trust. Doing so can make the consideration stage a shorter one.

- **Encourage prospects to discuss the products.**

  When you're designing your online catalog, encourage prospects to discuss the product with their friends and family. Make it easy for them to take the product into Facebook to solicit opinions from others using the services like ShareThis (`www.sharethis.com`), pointing users to the brand's fan or profile page on the social networks and including e-mail links, too.

✓ **Connect prospective customers to each other.**

By setting up discussion forums, you can create spaces where prospective customers can exchange notes on the potential purchases that they're considering. Also point them to existing satisfied customers or real-world testimonials that visitors can rate and comment upon.

✓ **Set up a Twitter account and respond to customer queries.**

It's important to watch the chatter about your products and brands across the social Web. Where appropriate, respond in a thoughtful, helpful manner to the questions raised. Correct misrepresentations of your products in a similar way.

Twitter is useful for customer service. Companies like Comcast have had great success in using it for responding to customer queries and concerns. But the tone you respond in is critical, as you always run the risk of sounding defensive. You'll probably be doing more damage to your brand than good if you allow yourself to get defensive on Twitter.

✓ **Track a list of Web sites, blogs, and discussion forums where the product's target customers spend their time.**

Track activity on these sites and participate in conversations about the category, competitors, and customer needs in an authentic, productive, and useful manner.

SIM at the preference stage

At the preference stage, the prospective customer leans toward making a purchase. He's considered several products and established his favorites. He likes the product that you're pushing him toward. By this time, the prospective customer is more concerned with confirming that he's getting good value for his money and that his purchase will be suitable for his needs. At this stage, you may offer free trials and 30-day money-back guarantees. Generally speaking, you hope your prospective customers have developed an emotional attachment to your brand that will push them to purchase your products.

By the time a prospective customer is at the preference stage in the marketing funnel, he's probably evaluated all the competitive alternatives to the product. He's found information about them through product brochures, the product Web sites, and customer reviews across the Web. As he enters the preference stage, he's likely to talk to his friends some more and get their opinions. This may have less to do with whether one product is better than another from a feature standpoint, but the customer can also get a feel for your brand as well. The prospective customer also views user-generated content about your brand at this stage.

You must be very careful at this stage. It's important that you establish a trusted relationship with the prospective customer. The prospective customer needs to feel that he will get good customer service after he makes the purchase. He wants to believe that his decision will be a good one over the long term, too. You can build that trust and allay those concerns by talking to the prospective customer in an authentic, personal, and genuine fashion.

This is when your product blogs play an important role, as they make the prospective customers realize that actual people are behind your product or brand. Make sure to spend time answering questions, resolving product issues, and discussing how the product is evolving.

Consider these SIM tactics at this stage:

- **A blog — or several — that discusses the product:** Granted, blogs are valuable at the awareness and consideration phase as well, but they matter the most at the point of preference. Customers want to hear from you at this stage more than ever.

- **Podcasts with interviews and product explanations:** As a supplement to blogs, podcasts are an appealing way to explain the product to prospective customers in an appealing fashion when you're not in the room with them. To learn all about *podcasts,* which are audio blogs that are easily distributed online, take a look at *Podcasting For Dummies,* by Tee Morris, Chuck Tomasi, and Evo Terra (Wiley Publishing). Figure 3-4 shows the podcasts available on CNET.com.

Figure 3-4: CNET's podcast page.

> ✔ **YouTube clips of product demonstrations:** With prospective customers establishing their preference for the brand, video clips demonstrating the product and explaining its benefits are helpful. Publish your videos on a site such as YouTube so that customers can easily find them and also give others the opportunity to comment and rate them.

SIM at the action stage

The action stage is when the prospective customer makes the purchase and becomes an actual customer. He goes through the process of buying the product, whether he does this online, via the phone, or in a store. During the action stage, focus on making the process as smooth, efficient, and hassle-free as possible. You should put a lot of effort into making the purchasing experience a positive one, as it is one of the first direct interactions that the customer has with your company.

Most marketers will argue that at this point in the funnel, you should not play a role. Either the customer was positively influenced to make the purchasing decision or he wasn't. If he's at the point where he's taking action, he should be allowed to take that action without any distractions whatsoever, as even a positive distraction is still a distraction. However, if the purchase is a high-consideration one, you can make the purchasing process social in a way that doesn't distract from the purchasing but enhances it instead.

At the point of purchase, the customer wants to know whether he is making a suitable purchasing decision and if his social influencers approve of his decision. Providing him with data points that he can share with those influencers and a means to broadcast the purchasing decision helps him. He can broadcast his purchasing decision and influence his friends to make similar purchasing decisions. And by providing valuable tidbits of information, he'll have valuable information to share.

The point of purchase also serves as an opportunity to upsell other products and services. This is a traditional marketing tactic that's been used in both the digital world and in physical stores as well. By highlighting other products that customers just like him purchased, social influence can play a role in encouraging that customer to make additional impulse purchases at the point of sale. For example, I'm buying a pair of Gap jeans from Gap.com (shown in Figure 3-5) and as I'm about to check out, I'm told about a nice shirt to buy and that most people who bought the pair of jeans bought the shirt, too. I'm more likely to add the shirt to my shopping cart. That's using social data to influence a purchasing decision.

Figure 3-5:
Gap.com.

Consider these SIM tactics at this stage:

- ✔ **Highlight related popular products:** As depicted with the Gap.com example, showcasing popular products relating to the ones already in the shopping carts often leads to impulse purchases.

- ✔ **Provide tools to broadcast the purchase:** This is necessary to allow for the customer to do remarketing for you. The customer should have the tools to easily broadcast his purchase to his various social networks.

SIM at the loyalty stage

The last stage of the marketing funnel has the fewest people. These are the customers who have purchased your product and are consuming it now. At this stage, it's most important to encourage customers to spread the word about the product and encourage others to buy it. Loyal customers are often the best marketers for your company. With social influence marketing, this plays an even larger role.

You must first focus on making your customers loyal and repeat customers. It's no use encouraging a customer to talk about your product if she isn't loyal or an advocate of the product. You can incentivize your loyal customers to encourage their peers to test the product and make a purchase as well. You can do this using social influence marketing tactics.

The best way to encourage loyal customers to influence their peers is to start by encouraging them to talk about the product. Having them rate and review the products is the first step. You'll be surprised how many customers are happy to rate and review products. What's more is that as they rate and review the products, they're also happy to broadcast the reviews to their social network. Allow them to do that. Provide the technological means for them to share their own reviews of the product with their friends and family. See Chapter 9 for more information on ratings and reviews.

Another way that social influence marketing can help at the loyalty stage is by connecting prospective customers with loyal customers. In some cases, you can link prospective customers with loyal customers who they know in the real world. For example, if you're looking to buy a Ford Taurus and you have a network of 350 people in LinkedIn, there may be someone else in your network that drives a Ford Taurus. Now wouldn't it be valuable if Ford told you which friend drives the Ford Taurus so that you could ask him his opinion? That's increasingly possible to do in the social networks.

Regardless of whether you have any friends who own Fords, you might be interested in learning about Ford from other Ford customers. Social influence marketing is about connecting customers to one another so that they can socially influence each other to make better decisions. In this instance, Ford should definitely try to connect all the prospective Ford Taurus owners with the current ones. One simple way to do this is to set up a Facebook fan page or a LinkedIn group for Ford Taurus owners in specific locations and then point prospective customers to that page, where they can ask existing owners questions. It can only help them make more purchases.

The loyalty stage of the marketing funnel is important because that's where the most remarketing happens by your own customers. Just because the customer has already bought the product, it doesn't mean you should care about him less. In fact, with his ability to spread the word (positively or negatively) about your product across his social network and the social Web in an exponential fashion, you had better take good care of him. Otherwise, you may have a PR disaster on your hands.

Probably the most classic example of a PR disaster at the loyalty stage has to do with JetBlue Airlines back in 1997 when a snowstorm forced cancellations and travelers were stranded in airports and even on runways. Passengers of one JetBlue flight were stranded on the runway for more than 11 hours! Clips of the horrible ordeal were published on YouTube and the airline was slow to respond. Irreparable damage was done to the JetBlue brand because they had not done enough to take care of their existing customers. On the bright side, the JetBlue CEO decided to issue an apology via YouTube — using the very same social platform that was responsible for the propagation of the JetBlue runway fiasco. That made a difference, and it helped even more when he announced a Passenger Bill of Rights. These actions showed that he was engaging with his current and prospective customers on their own terms and on their platforms of choice.

There are hundreds of examples of brands facing online firestorms, often due to something stupid that they did. Table 3-1 highlights some of the more notable firestorms, according to Ad Age (April, 2009). Also listed is whether these online firestorms had offline ripples in the mainstream media.

Table 3-1	Notable Online Firestorms	
Company	*Online Noise Levels*	*Offline*
Taco Bell's rats	High	High
Domino's boogergate	High	High
Facebook changes terms of service	High	Moderate
Dunkin' Donuts/Rachael Ray wears kefiya	High	Moderate
Burger King employee bathes in sink	Moderate	Low
Motrin moms	High	Low
#amazonfail	High	None
SpongeBob SquareButt	Moderate	Low
Starbucks nipples on a mermaid	Negligible	Imaginary

Treating SIM Differently from Brand Marketing

Because of the power of peer influence, social influence marketing is increasingly approached differently than brand and direct-response marketing. The differences stem from the fact that the philosophical approach, strategies, and execution tactics of SIM are more community and socially oriented.

Social influence marketing is fundamentally about engaging with expert, referent, and positional influencers and strategically leveraging social media in all its forms to meet marketing and business objectives. As a result, you need to understand how social influence marketing fits into the context of brand and direct-response marketing.

SIM in the context of brand marketing

Brand marketing focuses on building equity around a brand, its personality, and attributes. Customers purchase products based on the brand promise. Through various forms of advertising and communications, the brand promise is brought alive to generate awareness, build excitement, and get specific products included in a consideration set. Mass media channels are typically used to build awareness for the brand, reposition it with more powerful attributes, or ultimately, sell product. This will always be central to marketing efforts. All brands require significant effort to penetrate a market and generate desire.

SIM complements brand marketing in some key ways:

- ✔ **SIM places extra emphasis on peer-to-peer marketing and allows for peer-to-peer decision-making in a digital context.**

  The focus is on understanding how consumers are interacting with each other on social platforms versus how they're interacting with the brand. Consumers are asked to do the marketing for the brand by layering their own voices and perspectives on top. The result is the socialization of a message or story in a way that's meaningful and relevant to their world.

- ✔ **SIM rarely uses mass media, whether television, print, or radio.**

  Interactive channels that allow for the socialization and redistribution of a message are more important. But the brand cannot be simply pushed through the channels. Instead, invite consumers in the channels to experience the brand and make it their own.

- ✔ **SIM is about becoming a part of all media streams, across all channels, where consumers are responding to and discussing the brand messages.**

  In many cases, they're self-organizing these conversations on the fly. In other instances, they gravitate toward existing community hubs where the conversations are already taking place. These conversations can also take on your own corporate Web site.

Because of this, messaging, advertising campaigns, and even the products themselves don't define successful brands as much as the communities that surround them do. A brand supported by a large and influential community becomes more successful than one with a weak, disparate, and disjointed community. You have a huge opportunity to learn from their consumers as they listen in on these conversations. This is an opportunity you shouldn't miss.

SIM in the context of direct response

Direct-response marketing is designed to solicit a specific, measurable response from specific individuals. Unlike brand marketing, with direct response, for every dollar invested, there is a traceable return. The measurable relationship is established between you and the consumer.

Some of the core attributes around direct response include a call to action, an offer and delivery of enough information to elicit a response, and guidance on how to respond. Television infomercials, which encourage consumers to call a number or visit a Web site, and direct-mail offers, which invite consumers to purchase a product or send a reply, are the most common forms of direct response. Online advertising campaigns that are designed to drive clicks and purchases on brand Web sites are the most common online equivalent.

SIM complements direct response but lacks some of the measurability found in direct response. Social influence marketing isn't typically geared toward a specific individual with the goal of soliciting a specific, measurable response. With SIM, communities of consumers are targeted with the goal of enticing them to positively influence one another and other people within their networks of online relationships. The goals are to convert consumers into potential marketers for the brand and provide them with the tools and mechanisms to further influence others. It's very different from asking an isolated consumer to perform a specific task.

SIM isn't as measurable as direct response marketing is. Tracking how social influencers work is still difficult; when a consumer shows brand affinity or makes a purchasing decision, it's hard to tell which factors or influencers impacted those choices most directly. In that sense, SIM is more akin to brand marketing, where the measurability is weak and needs to be based on feedback similar to that collected in attitudinal surveys. It's easy to track expert influencers online using social media measurement tools, but that's just part of the equation. Often, the social influencers who sway purchasing decisions aren't the most public and noticeable brand advocates.

Another factor to consider with SIM is that the call to action can't be too heavy-handed. As a result, some would argue that SIM is much more about social influence and much less about marketing. Social campaigns that blatantly push the call to action generally fail because they lack credibility and appear calculated. For this reason, you can't always easily recognize or measure your successful SIM campaigns.

Tying SIM with brand marketing and direct response

Social influence marketing, which is about harnessing and categorizing the local spheres of influence, complements brand marketing and direct response with its focus on reaching social influencers across a variety of channels and platforms at every stage of the marketing funnel. This is done so that influencers socialize the message in their own communities and conduct the marketing for the brand. Not all social influencers have platforms to project strong opinions; some are more anonymous, localized, and less recognizable — that's the bad news. The good news is that influencers obviously like to influence and have a meaningful and integral role to play in marketing online or offline.

Social influence marketing resembles relationship marketing, in that both focus on the relationship, not just the point of sale, and are more personal in nature. The difference is that relationship marketing focuses on establishing deeper, longer-term relationships with customers over a lifetime, while social influence marketing relies on customers marketing the brand.

Part II
Practicing SIM in the Social Web

The 5th Wave   By Rich Tennant

"Woo!"

In this part . . .

Part II is very much the practitioner's part, explaining the nuts and bolts of SIM campaigns, including planning for them, how to manage participation, seeding viral video clips, and tips and tricks for turning a crisis to your advantage.

In Chapter 4, I discuss the components of a successful SIM campaign and how you can make it work in harmony with other digital marketing efforts. Chapter 5 discusses why you need a SIM voice, how it differs from a brand voice or personality, where it gets manifested, and who can play that role. When you're ready to start your campaign, Chapter 6 helps you choose which of the four major social platforms — Facebook, MySpace, Twitter, and YouTube — on which to launch, sustain, and promote your brand. Chapter 7 moves away from the big four to discuss the niche social platforms. In Chapter 8, I discuss why social influencers matter, how you can reach them, and what best practices to deploy in the process of doing so.

Chapter 4

Launching SIM Campaigns

*L*aunching a social influence marketing campaign is, in some ways, similar to launching any other digital campaign. But at the same time, you need to approach certain aspects of it very differently to maximize the results.

In this chapter, I discuss the components of a successful SIM campaign and how you can make it work in harmony with other digital marketing efforts. I also discuss how best to respond to criticism, how to turn a crisis to your advantage, and finally, some tactics for turning the campaign into a long-term marketing asset.

Discovering the Types of SIM Campaigns

At this point, it's important to talk about the different types of campaigns. After that, I discuss the rules and guidelines that make SIM campaigns successful. In the realm of social influence marketing, how you implement a campaign is nearly as important as what you implement.

Before you launch your SIM campaign, make sure you've done an inventory of all the other major SIM campaigns going on at the same time that target your customers or are within your industry. The last thing you want is to launch a campaign in which you're asking your customers to do basically the same thing that they may have just done for a competitor.

The FTC (Federal Trade Commission) plans to impose regulations on how pharmaceutical companies can market using the social Web. Those regulations will cover blogger liability in the realm of sponsored conversations. If you're a pharmaceutical company or are operating in another regulated industry, be sure to check with your lawyers about what you're allowed and not allowed to do before launching the SIM campaign.

Blogger outreach

Probably the most common form of a SIM campaign is the blogger outreach program. This campaign typically takes the form of identifying influencer bloggers who reach your customers. They're the expert influencers who cover a topic and have a fan following. The best way to think of them is as media properties. Many accept advertising but typically have day jobs that they're balancing as well. Blogger outreach programs incentivize these bloggers to write about your brand or product. You can give them incentives by inviting them to the R&D labs of your company and treating them with the same deference that the mainstream press gets, to sending them sample products and providing them with prizes with which to run contests on their blogs. Campaigns are sometimes built around these influencers.

It's important to note that there's a debate raging in the blogosphere about blogger compensation. Some bloggers absolutely refuse to accept compensation, while others are comfortable with it. You must know where your targeted blogger stands on this debate before reaching out to him or her. For more information on the blogger compensation debate, read GeekMommy's post at http://geekmommy.net/2009/06/09/hostedcontests.

Knowing how to reach these bloggers without coming across as heavy handed, commercial, and ignorant is critical. Before you reach out to them, be sure to read their blogs so that you know how they cover your brand or category, scan the comments on their blog posts so that you get a feel for the readers and how they participate, understand their policies with regards to brands engaging with them (some prefer to go through representatives, for example), and ideally try to develop a personal relationship based on the content that they publish and the topics they cover before approaching them with an idea. These are all common-sense ideas that apply if you were attempting to do something similar in the real world. But as the saying goes, common sense is often uncommon, and many a company has done exactly the opposite.

UGC contests

Contests in all their various forms have always been a big hit in the marketing campaign arena. But now contests structured around user-generated content (UGC) are all the rage. And with good reason: They are invariably extremely popular, engaging, and fun. You structure a contest built on participants contributing something in return for rewards. This can be something as simple as crowdsourcing a TV advertisement, as General Motors did with its Tahoe campaign in 2006, to asking users to contribute video clips of their funniest moment with a product. The best clip (by the predetermined criteria) gets a prize, with all the other participants getting some sort of recognition. As *Wired* magazine reported, in the case of the Tahoe campaign, the microsite attracted 629,000 visitors with each user spending more than nine minutes on the site and a third of them going on to visit the main Chevy.com Web site. Sales took off from that point, even though environmentalists tried to sabotage the UGC campaign. Not too long ago, HP ran a successful contest in which it asked designers around the world to help design the exterior of one its new laptops. HP got tons of press, rallied a lot of support for the contest among budding designers, and also got some great ideas in turn.

Sponsored virtual gifts

Sponsored gifts are getting more popular every day on the social networks. The reason is simple. They make money for the social network platform (Facebook sees huge revenue potential in this area), the brands discover that they get more user engagement per dollar than through any other campaign, and the participants invariably encourage others to engage, resulting in a multiplier effect. For example, Honda provided 750,000 free virtual gifts for Facebook users to gift to their friends early in 2009. The gifts were fuel gauges shaped like hearts. The gifts were gone within four days and touched 1.5 million people (the senders and the receivers of the gifts). But what's more, according to the COO of Facebook, 130 million page views brought up one of the Honda heart gifts. I don't know how much the virtual gift program cost Honda, but it certainly got a lot of engagement. Other social networks, such as Cyworld and Second Life, have virtual gifting programs too but none are considered as successful as Facebook's.

Brand utilities

The basic idea behind brand utilities is that instead of providing the consumer with some advertising, you build their trust (and get their dollars) by giving them a utility application that provides actual value. If the utility serves a purpose, users adopt the application and think more favorably of your brand. Dollars that would have normally gone towards buying media go towards building the application instead.

For example, Nike has launched several brand utilities, with one of the most recent examples being the Ballers Network on Facebook, as shown in Figure 4-1. It lets basketball players find games, organize their leagues, and connect with other players. Nike's philosophy is to build applications like this one that provide a useful service and enhance an athlete's enjoyment of the sport. This social application does exactly that and strengthens Nike's position in the social realm. This application doesn't always have to take the form of an application or a widget on a social network. The famous Nike + solution, which is considered the world's largest running club, is a virtual community that helps users of it track the amount they've run and compare themselves to their peers. The advertising industry moves between trends very quickly, and it seems that brand utilities are already out of the limelight.

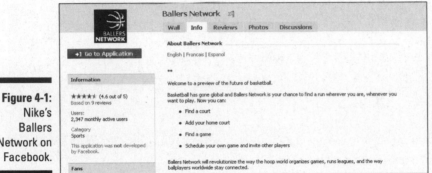

Figure 4-1: Nike's Ballers Network on Facebook.

Podcasting

A *podcast* is a digital audio file that is made available via Web syndication technologies such as RSS. Although strictly speaking, it's not social media, it's often classified as such because it allows anybody to easily syndicate their own audio content. You can use podcasts as a way to share information with your audiences. Often, podcasts take the shape of celebrity interviews or discussions about your product or brand. A successful example of a podcast is the Butterball *Turkey Talk* podcast. It's a seasonal podcast including stories from Turkey Talk hotline workers. You can subscribe to it via iTunes and other online podcast directories.

Podcasts typically don't form a whole SIM campaign in and of themselves, but work well with other SIM ones.

Sponsored conversations

Sometimes the most effective SIM campaigns are the simplest ones. These campaigns engage with consumers in a straightforward, authentic fashion on a social platform while also aggregating other conversations, pointing to new ones, and stoking the community. Recently, Disney partnered with SavvyAuntie, an online community focused on aunts without kids for one such effort, which is shown in Figure 4-2. Melanie Notkin, who runs SavvyAuntie, tweeted about Disney's *Pinocchio* movie in March 2008 to coincide with its Disney anniversary release. She tweeted about themes in the movie, often in question form, encouraging others to respond. Her 8,000 followers on Twitter knew that she was doing this for Disney (every tweet about Pinocchio had a special tag), but because the tweets were appropriate for the audience, entertaining, and authentic, the campaign was a success.

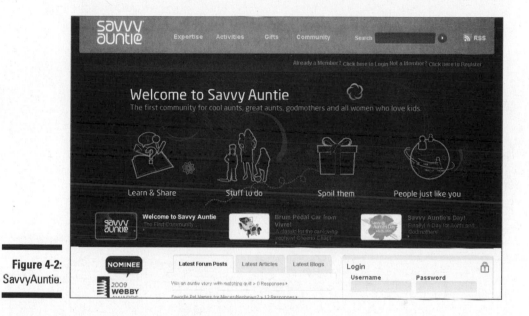

Figure 4-2:
SavvyAuntie.

Recognizing What Makes a Good SIM Campaign

A *social influence marketing campaign* is one that specifically allows for social influence to take place digitally. Social influence marketing campaigns are a relatively new phenomenon. A few years ago, marketing through social media was a niche activity and the notion of targeting influencers was an obscure one. The closest comparison was word-of-mouth campaigns conducted in the offline world to build brand awareness for a product by incentivizing people to talk about it among themselves. Digital campaigns, for the most part, were about display advertising across large publisher Web sites, complemented with paid search campaigns and maybe e-mail campaigns. These campaigns were used to drive prospects to a *microsite* (a site devoted to that particular campaign) or a Web site, where they were encouraged to make purchases or engage with the brand.

With a SIM campaign, you mustn't drag people away from the social platform on which they're communicating and interacting with each other. They don't want to be distracted and you'll probably only waste precious marketing dollars trying to lure them to your Web site. Instead, it's more important to execute the campaign on those very platforms where your potential customers are in conversation. You have to engage your customers where *they* want to participate, not where you want them to be. And unlike a digital marketing campaign of yesteryear, the customers of a SIM campaign ignore you unless your SIM campaign is aligned with their objectives and behavior patterns on those social platforms. In the following four sections, I outline specific guidelines you should follow when launching a SIM campaign.

A good example of a failed "build it and they will come" attempt was Bud.TV by Budweiser. They tried to create an entertainment destination bypassing YouTube. The effort failed miserably as they had to spend valuable advertising dollars to encourage consumers to do something that they had no interest in doing — moving away from YouTube, where they had the most entertaining content (and all their friends) to a corporate-sponsored Web site. What's more, the fact that users couldn't embed the video clips elsewhere (including YouTube) hurt the effort. Bud.TV launched in January 2007 and was shut down early in 2009.

Define your objectives

This may seem obvious, but it is amazing how many of us forget about articulating the objectives when it comes to a SIM campaign. Your objectives need to be tightly defined, and they must be practical and actionable too. The objectives must be specific to the stage of the marketing funnel that you're playing in as well. See Chapter 3 for more on the marketing funnel. Saying that the objective of the campaign is simply to take a TV advertisement and make it *go viral* is definitely not enough.

The objectives must also specify *where* you're planning to run the campaign, *whom* you're targeting (which customers and which influencers), the *duration* of the campaign, and *how it synchronizes* with other digital and offline marketing efforts. It is easy to forget that no SIM campaign happens in isolation. How you participate on the various social platforms is always a mirror of what you do and think in the physical world. If you ignore that fact, you'll lose your customers even before you've had a chance to meaningfully engage with them.

Execute for influence

Traditionally, most campaigns have focused on getting a potential customer to take a specific action or to view a specific brand message. The focus has always been on that individual engaging with the brand in some form.

However, with a SIM campaign, it is necessary to design for sharing, influencing, reciprocity, and social currency.

Unlike most other campaigns, a SIM campaign needs to accomplish two objectives concurrently:

- **It needs to engage the individual who's being targeted via the campaign.**

  This is similar to any other type of digital marketing campaign. You want to engage with your target audience in a specific fashion and solicit a specific response.

- **You also need to design the campaign so that the target person shares or discusses it with someone else.**

  This is the social currency element. The person should feel that by sharing the campaign with someone else, he derives greater value from it. This could be something as tangible as further discounts or intangible as status among his peers. The point being is that the more people the person shares the campaign with (or discusses it with), the more value he generates from it. In this sense, the campaign takes on a network effect, with its value growing each time someone participates.

Create partnerships

Few SIM campaigns are successful in isolation. Just as regular digital campaigns come together through a serious of partnership between the agency, the advertiser, and the publisher, so too is the case with a SIM campaign. However, in this case, the participants vary slightly. Rather than having a regular publisher, you have the social platform with whom to contend with. Your campaign must be in compliance with their policies; otherwise, they won't let it run on their platform. For example, Facebook (www.facebook.com) and YouTube (www.youtube.com) have strict terms of service regarding the type of advertising that can appear on their platforms.

But the platform players aren't the only ones you have to worry about. Invariably with most large brands, ad hoc user groups spring up that have a sense of ownership over the brand or product category on the social platform where you're planning to run the campaign.

For example, on Facebook, if you were to search "Ford," you'd find not just the Ford Motor Company page (shown in Figure 4-3), but literally hundreds of groups created by and for people interested in Ford Motor Company. If you're a marketer at Ford, when you're planning a SIM campaign on Facebook, it's not enough to talk to Facebook and your own agency about the campaign. For it to be a truly successful SIM campaign, you must engage with these ad hoc groups when the campaign is starting. They can be your biggest marketers, helping the campaign succeed. On the other hand, if you upset them, they can turn into saboteurs.

Figure 4-3:
Ford's
Facebook
page.

Irrespective of the social platform you're running a SIM campaign on, the ad hoc user groups are already there. Be sure to engage with them. A SIM campaign means new players and new partnerships that need to be forged early on for it to be a success. Finding and engaging with those communities of people becomes critical.

Track the results

There's a saying in the world of social media that only successful SIM campaigns can be measured; failures can't be. The point is that marketers often say that SIM could not be measured if in their heart of hearts they know that their campaign has failed. If the campaign is a success, you bet they'll be telling you about it and explaining why exactly it was a success.

You can measure a SIM campaign a lot of different ways: The best method depends on the objectives, the targeted audience, and the social platform on which the campaign is running. But you must determine what you're going to measure and how *before* you run the campaign. Otherwise, you're never going to know whether it's a success. Sure, SIM campaigns often spiral out of control and the law of unintended consequences starts applying. That's not a bad thing, but it doesn't take away from the fact that the campaign you're running is being run for a purpose and you'll only know whether you've achieved that purpose if you're measuring the results. It's also important to measure a baseline of online activity before you begin the SIM engagement and decide what to measure. This will help you determine how successful your campaign is, relative to the level of conversations and online activity before running it.

I get into measurement later in the book (see Chapter 13), but it's sufficient to say that you must not just measure how many people you reach or who is aware of your campaign, but also the influence generated, the *brand lifts* (increased awareness of the brand), and most importantly, whether any of this effort led to purchases. With the measurement tools in the marketplace (many of which are free or close to free), you can easily track your SIM campaign to the point of sale on the Web site or potentially even in a physical store. Don't hesitate in trying to measure this.

Participating — Four Rules of the Game

Many different factors can make or break a SIM campaign, and sometimes it's even just a matter of luck. But four rules matter above all else when it comes to SIM campaigns.

These rules don't always apply to other forms of marketing. So pay attention to them and make sure that your SIM campaign abides by these.

Be authentic

Authenticity is a tricky word. It's tricky because it's overused in the context of social media. Everybody talks about being authentic when marketing in the social media realm, but what that means is rarely explained. Authenticity is being honest and transparent: It's as simple as that.

Here are some examples.

> ✔ **When you set up a blog as part of your campaign, make sure that you're using your own voice.**
>
> Don't outsource the publishing of content to a third party or to your PR team. If you have to, make sure that the writer accurately identifies himself as contributing on your behalf. Jonathan Schwartz's Sun Microsystems blog is a great example, as shown in Figure 4-4. The blog is written in the first person by Schwartz himself. Anyone who knows him can tell that it really is Jonathan Schwartz writing.
>
> ✔ **When you're publishing your thoughts, opinions, or simply sharing information, don't do so anonymously.**
>
> In the world of social media, your consumers don't relate and care about brands as much as they care about the people behind them. People build relationships with each other and not with anonymous brands. So let your customers know who is behind the voice blogging, tweeting, or the contest on Facebook. You're not authentic if your customers don't know who you are.

Years back, Sun was under pressure in the market. Although many users loved our core Solaris operating system, others thought it was built for high end computers, not grid systems. Our computer business had failed to keep pace with the rest of the industry - which meant our volume systems looked expensive. In combination, and with a poor track record of supporting Solaris off of Sun hardware, we gave customers one choice - leave Sun. Many did. Those were the dark days.

Where did they go? They went to GNU/Linux, a free and open source operating

system built by a growing community, running on x86 systems. Why? Because the pair ("Linux on a whitebox") delivered, then, better grid performance, with more flexibility. We didn't erect barriers to exit, we promoted customer choice. Even when it cut the wrong way, as it did here. And yes, it hurt.

With business down and customers leaving, we had more than a few choices at our disposal. We were invited by one company to sue the beneficiaries of open source. We declined. We could join

Figure 4-4: Jonathan Schwartz's Sun Micro-systems blog.

✔ **Learn from the community and respond to their feedback.**

A key part of being authentic is telling your customers the way it really is, hearing their feedback (both positive and negative), and being willing to respond to it. It's no use participating in the social realm if you don't respond to commentary or feedback. If you're worried about not having the time to respond, consider not participating at all.

✔ **Be humane in your approach.**

It is easy to forget that for every comment and every unique visitor, there's an actual person somewhere in the world. Make sure that you participate with consideration and with the same respect that you'd reserve for someone you're talking to face to face.

For more information on authenticity as it applies to word of mouth marketing and social influence marketing, visit the Word of Mouth Marketing Association Web site (`http://womma.org/ethics/code`) and review its ethics code.

Operate on quid pro quo basis

For all the altruism associated with the social Web, it's easy to forget that it operates on the premise of quid pro quo. We're all good human beings, but most people expect something in return if they're giving you their time. As you develop a SIM campaign in which you'll be demanding your customers attention (and often a lot more than that), think about the possible quid pro quo. Are you giving enough back in exchange? If you're not giving something back, your customers won't participate. They'll simply ignore you. The social Web is littered with marketing campaign failures. These campaigns assumed that just by putting a banner advertisement in front of customers, they would achieve their objectives.

Here's an example of a SIM campaign that provided a strong quid pro quo for its audiences and was highlighted by Adweek. The all brand of laundry detergent created a promotion that aired April 5th, 2009 on the TV show *Celebrity Apprentice*. Instead of focusing on the attributes of their detergent (how much can you talk about the attributes of laundry detergent, after all?), they associated all with a charitable cause through viral marketing. *Celebrity Apprentice* viewers saw a 30-second TV ad directing them to a Web site to watch videos that featured *Celebrity Apprentice* contestants Joan and Melissa Rivers (they could alternatively watch the video clips on YouTube). The videos featured them using all in ridiculous settings. Each time viewers forwarded the videos, all donated 50 cents to charity. This was a SIM campaign that entertained the customer, encouraged him to share elements of it with his friends, and rewarded the customer for sharing. Success of the campaign was defined by the number of visits to the Web site, the number of unique visitors that registered for a coupon, the number of e-mails sent, and the amount of money raised for the charity.

Give participants equal status

Many marketing campaigns are designed to make the consumer feel special — more special than everyone else around them. That's a good thing. They feel special, and they end up having favorable feelings for your product and go out and buy it. Apple and Harley-Davidson are two brands that personify this philosophy: They make their customers feel special and different than everyone else. That's wonderful, but it doesn't apply to the SIM realm in the same way. People across the social Web like to believe that they're as special and as unique as the next person, as they should. If someone is doing something special, they want to do that as well. If a person does something interesting, others want to access to it as well. That's human nature, and the social Web encourages behavior through the voyeurism it allows for.

One example of giving everyone the ability to participate in status is the virtual gifting programs offered by some of the social networks. Facebook, for example, allows advertisers to sponsor virtual gifts, such as a drink or flowers, that are made available to users. (See Figure 4-5.) A user sees the sponsored gift and gives it to his friend. The friend in turn either reciprocates or gives a new gift to someone else, having been made aware of the program when he first received the gift. Other friends who may have viewed the gift exchange through their Facebook newsfeed are motivated to give gifts to others as a result. And it goes on and on from there. It is easy to reciprocate and extend the virtual gifts to others. As a result, virtual gift programs on Facebook are successful.

Figure 4-5:
Facebook
Gifts.

Let go of the campaign

By virtue of starting the campaign, you probably feel that it is your responsibility to moderate and shape it. That doesn't have to be the case. Successful SIM campaigns are the ones in which the brand advocates take the campaign in new directions. As you develop the campaign, think of yourself as a participant and not just the owner of the campaign. You make better decisions regarding its evolution that way, and, by letting go, you allow others to take it new and much amplified directions. And as always, remember your consumers will be in control of the campaign. That's what makes social influence marketing different. However, you will always be in control of your own response to the consumer participation. And that always presents exciting opportunities.

Killing the Campaign Expiry Date

You're probably used to thinking of campaigns as having a start date and an end date. And they usually need that. You have a finite marketing budget; the campaign is geared around a series of events (like Christmas sales); the fact that new products replace old ones several times a year forces you to end campaigns and launch new ones. However, SIM campaigns are unique in that after they start, they may not stop when you want them to. It's like turning off the lights midway through a dinner party. If you have a conversation going and have gotten a community of people to come together around your brand, product, or campaign, the last thing you want to do is to suddenly disown them. It is very important that you plan for migrating that community of people to a broader purpose or goal.

Here are four ways to do that successfully:

- ✔ **Give participants new reasons to engage with your brand.**

  Your original SIM campaign has a set purpose and objectives. After they're accomplished, don't turn off the lights. Instead, think of the next campaign that you have planned and how you can customize it to this community of people.

  In fact, try to weave the campaigns together into a program that benefits these people. As you do this, remember the four rules of participation I outlined previously: authenticity, quid pro quo, equal status, and disowning the campaign.

- ✔ **Encourage participants to coalesce into communities.**

  Often the people who participate in your SIM campaign all share something in common. This may not always be the case, but depending upon the campaign type, they may indeed be interested in forming a community. If you believe that to be the case, encourage them to coalesce into self-supporting communities. It only helps you in the long run and gives new life to the campaign. Campaigns that have generated goodwill transform into customer communities that you can tap into for future marketing and business efforts.

  A good example of this is the Walmart Elevenmoms, which is shown in Figure 4-6. Walmart tapped eleven mommy bloggers to go shopping at Walmart stores (they were given a budget) and then blog about their experiences. They did so successfully (at least from the perspective of Walmart) and are now organized into a social network.

Figure 4-6:
Walmart's
Elevenmoms.

✔ **Treat participants like existing customers.**

Someone who's participated in your SIM campaign may not have bought your product, but he has given you his time and probably has shared a bit of himself with you in the process. This may have taken the form of commenting on a blog post, participating in a contest, sharing your viral video clip with friends, or testing a product and writing a review about it. Because he's done more than someone who experienced a traditional marketing campaign, you owe him more. Treat him like an existing customer, whether that means sending him special offers, inviting him to participate in focus groups, or beta testing new products. But as you do this, always remember that when you send your customers a special offer, it must be opt-in. Don't spam them if you don't have the permission to do so.

✔ **Extend the campaign to the Web site.**

Many a SIM campaign has failed because it was kept separate from the corporate Web site. The campaigns are traditionally built off of micro sites with display advertising promoting them. When the campaign has run its course, the micro site is shut down and the advertising is stopped. In the case of a SIM campaign, don't shut down the micro site. Instead, promote the SIM campaign on the company Web site and, when the campaign winds down, find a place on the Web site for it. That way, your customers can always find it, and, if they coalesced into communities during the course of the campaign, they always have a place to return to. (See Chapter 9 for more information.)

Often, your participants may know better than you how to create greater meaning from the SIM campaign in the form of a community. Ask them what you should be doing if anything at all. You'll definitely get strong advice from the people who care the most.

Monitoring Brands and Conversations

It's no use running a SIM campaign if you can't measure it. You should always measure your SIM campaigns. Depending on the SIM campaign, different measurements may matter more than others. The brand and conversation monitoring tools help you measure the success of your SIM campaign and your ROI (return on investment). But they do a lot more than that. These tools help you plan and design your SIM campaigns. They give you a peek into actual user behavior on social platforms telling you what people are discussing, whether those conversations are positive or negative, and where they're taking place.

Anytime you're planning to launch a SIM campaign, you must begin by knowing what your target audiences are doing across the social Web. These tools help you do that. They can be classified into three groups:

✔ **High-end tools and services** that use linguistic analysis and deep data mining to provide insights into the conversations, who is having them, and where. These tools can cost anywhere from $5,000 a month to $50,000 a month, based mostly on the number of topics mined and the frequency. Included in this category are Cymfony, Neilsen BuzzMetrics, and Motivequest.

✔ **Low-end tools** that primarily focus on the volume of the conversation over a period of time and only cover positive and negative sentiment. Many of these tools are free or dirt-cheap. Included here are Radian6 and Scout Labs.

✔ **Middle of the road tools** that do some analysis but don't always have the breadth of sources or the depth of analysis that the high-end tools have. Tools in this category are Crimson Hexagon and J.D. Power and Associates. Visible Technologies and Converseon straddle the high and low ends with different service levels and capabilities, including work-flow and the ability to identify influencers.

When choosing which tool to use, keep the following factors in mind:

✔ **Your audience:** If you don't know your audience and aren't sure what their motivations are, where they are participating, and how, you want one of the high-end tools.

✔ **The length of your SIM campaign:** If you're running a short campaign targeting a small population of users, you probably don't need to use one of the high-end tools. It won't be worth your dollars.

✔ **The size of the campaign:** If your campaign touches lots of people, you need a higher end tool that can help you track the activity and manage responses too.

✔ **Influencer identification:** If you're planning to focus on influencers rather than the mass population, choose a tool that's strongest at *influencer identification* (the ability to assist you in identifying influencers who influence customers about your brand). Not all tools do this equally well.

✔ **Regulatory considerations:** If you work in a highly regulated industry, you want a tool that lets you view commentary and glean insights anonymously. Higher/mid-level tools have this capability.

✔ **Dashboard functionality:** Some marketers require interactive dashboards through which they can view the conversation in real-time. If you're one of them, be sure to look for a tool that allows for that.

Lots of free tools for brand and conversation monitoring are out there. Regardless of the complexity of your SIM campaign and tracking needs, there's never any harm in beginning with the free tools. It'll only cost you the time in setting up the domain names. Also keep in mind that these tools are valuable to departments like public relations and customer research, too. They may be willing to share the costs of the tool or service with you.

Responding to Criticism

No SIM campaign is a complete success. It never is. Although you may reach many more people than you could have ever imagined, more likely than not, you're still bound to upset some people and even potentially spark an inflammatory response among a few others. On the outset, before you launch your SIM campaign, you need to plan for the potential criticism that may come your way. There's no perfect way to respond and the answer usually depends on the type of criticism, how widespread it is, and where it is coming from. Your PR department is usually more versed in responding to criticism (and crisis management more broadly) than anyone else, so you should be sure to bring them into the process early.

Regardless, here are some guidelines to keep at the back of your mind as you launch your campaign and prepare for the criticism that may come your way:

✔ **Respond early and often.**

There's no greater insult to people criticizing your SIM campaign than to be ignored. Ignoring criticism results in greater anger and more vitriolic responses that can snowball into a full-fledged crisis as the anger percolates across the social Web. Before you know it, your CEO is calling your desk — or maybe the *New York Times* — so respond quickly.

✔ **Respond honestly and clearly.**

Be sure to use your own name when you respond. Just as you have to be authentic with your campaign, you need to with your response too. Be clear about your rationale for why the campaign is designed the way it is, admit mistakes when the fault is yours, and be inclusive in your responses.

✔ **Be prepared to change based on the feedback.**

It's easier to be stubborn and not to change your SIM campaign. But if there's valid criticism about the campaign, whether it's of the structure, the creative aspect, or the rules regarding the type of conversation, you should incorporate the feedback and make the appropriate changes. You'll win back trust quickly.

✔ **Don't hesitate to bring humor to the situation.**

Some of the best responses have been those that included a touch of self-effacing humor. Brands aren't above people and neither is yours. Humor goes a long way in the social Web and sometimes the response becomes the new SIM campaign.

✔ **Use the same channels for the response.**

This may seem obvious, but it really isn't. Respond to people in the way they've criticized you. Don't go on national television to respond to a YouTube outburst. You'll become the laughingstock of the social Web.

Chapter 5

Developing Your SIM Voice

- -

- -

A social influence marketing campaign, program, or strategic approach won't be successful if no observable people are behind it. Consumers want to know who the people behind the brand are. Being a trusted brand is not enough. Putting your CEO's name on the About Us page of your Web site isn't either. When consumers engage across the social Web, they want to engage with real people who have personalities and opinions. In other words, the people representing the brand need to be SIM voices that people can search on Google or Bing to find out more about. That means the consumer should be able to search the person representing the brand and see via the search results that the brand has put forth a real person to talk on its behalf. That's why you need a SIM voice.

Having voices that can be researched through the search engines is instrumental to establishing credibility and being authentic. This chapter discusses why you need a SIM voice, how it differs from a brand voice or personality, where it gets manifested, and who can play that role. I then discuss using that person's relationships to help with *crowdsourcing* (outsourcing a task to a large group of people or community in the form of an open call).

Figuring Out Why You Need a SIM Voice

As I write this chapter, the U.S., and indeed the entire world, is in a major economic downturn. Practically every major corporation has had to lay off employees and ask their remaining employees to take on more responsibility. In this economic environment, does it make sense to introduce a new type of role into your organization with potentially overlapping responsibilities?

On the surface, it may not appear so, but it's actually more important than ever. If the economic downturn has taught us one thing, it's that consumers are tired of engaging with large, impersonal brands and often turn against them in the social Web. They simply do not trust big brands anymore. In fact, half of the respondents to a survey conducted recently by *The Economist* magazine said that the economic crisis has intensified their distrust of big business. The magazine went on to say that the downturn is accelerating the use of social media because people are placing more value in the recommendations of their friends than they are in big business. According to the 2009 Edelman Trust Barometer, trust in business collapsed in the last year by 20 percentage points from 58 percent to 38 percent. This is just another point on how trust in big business has plummeted.

As a big business or even a medium-sized or small business trying to reach consumers in the social Web, this distrust presents a problem. Those consumers don't want to listen to you anymore. They'd much rather listen to their friends. This means that they're not paying attention to all the advertising that you're pushing at them and certainly aren't making product-purchasing decisions based on it. This means that you have to change your marketing strategy and, because you purchased this book, you've probably already realized that you need to. It also means that if your consumers trust their friends more than big brands, you have to become more like their friends to earn their trust. And at the heart of becoming more like their friends is developing a SIM voice that's associated with a single person in your company through whom you reach out to those consumers. It can't just be your brand name, your logo, or your witty copy that does it. It has to be a *real* person within your company who's reaching out to your consumers.

Sometimes the best way to discover whether you need a SIM voice is by scanning the conversations about your brand across the social Web. You'll probably find people talking about you or your product category at the very least. That'll give you a sense of how important it is and the volume of conversations may serve as a guide to how quickly you need to establish your SIM voice.

Defining SIM Voice Characteristics

The SIM voice is fundamentally the voice through which you engage with your consumers in the social Web. Every conversation touch point on any social platform from YouTube (www.youtube.com) and Facebook (www.facebook.com) to Twitter (www.twitter.com) and your own discussion forums needs to be in the SIM voice. This strategy can take the form of one voice or it can be several. But all SIM voices share certain characteristics in contrast to a brand voice. In the next few sections, I look at some of the key characteristics.

Multiple and authentic

Most companies have multiple, authentic SIM voices. The reason is obvious. They are generally too large to have one person representing them in all the conversations digitally. There are multiple people who focus on different conversation areas, whether it's customer support, industry insights, product information, or awareness building. In some cases, each person represents the company on different social environments. Each person talks in his or her own voice and loosely follows centralized guidelines. Zappos (`twitter.zappos.com`) is a good example of a company with multiple SIM voices. The company is proud of its multiple SIM voices and trusts those employees to represent the brand effectively without losing their own authenticity. My own company has its SIM voices represented at `razorfish.alltop.com/`. We have social influence marketing guidelines that the employees adhere to but beyond that it's all in the hands of those SIM voices.

Transparent and easy to find

Your SIM voices can't be anonymous voices. They have to be real people who are traceable; otherwise, they won't be taken seriously. Now this may seem to be a bad strategy because so much is invested in the one person who's playing the role of the SIM voice, but it's necessary. When making these decisions, think about celebrity endorsements. People recognize that a celebrity may not be the permanent SIM voice, but they would much rather be talking to someone with whom they can form a relationship and relate to even if it's only for a finite period than an anonymous brand voice. For a SIM voice to be real, it has to be someone people can find through Google: There's no question about that.

Engaging and conversational

Some people know how to have a conversation and some *really* know how to. Your SIM voice, whoever she is, needs to be truly conversational. She needs to be a person that can start a conversation, build trust, and be responsive. The person needs to have more of a customer service mentality than an on-message marketing or PR mindset. This is not about marketing or PR, but about more genuine, deeper conversations.

Social Web savvy

Your SIM voice needs to be someone who knows the social Web intimately: the rules, social norms, and the best practices of participating in the social Web. This person ideally should have individual credibility that extends beyond the brand that he works for and must be easily accessible on all the major social platforms. Keep in mind that your SIM voices will make mistakes and they will probably get flamed at times too. You have to allow for that to happen. It is all part of the learning.

Unique to the person

In contrast to a brand voice, this SIM person's voice must be unique to him and not unique to the company. This is incredibly important for the trust to develop. Otherwise, the whole effort will be a waste of time. Furthermore, this voice should be irreplaceable. When the person goes on vacation, the voice cannot continue to participate and be responsive to customer queries. Someone else has to take over and introduce herself first. Think of it like a news anchor in a major television channel who takes the night off. The replacement is a different person and that's not hidden from the viewer.

Distinguishing Between SIM Voices and Brand Voices

At this point, you're probably thinking that your SIM voice is similar to your brand voice or personality. Whether they're representatives from public relations or corporate marketing, you're probably already thinking of people in your organization who can be your SIM voice. Before you jump into this decision too quickly, check out Table 5-1, which compares brand and SIM voices. Use this table to explain to team members why the two voices are different and why this effort may not be best relegated to the public relations department.

A SIM voice is very different from a brand voice. Someone who's spent a lifetime representing your brand and keeping everyone else around on brand message is probably not the best person to be the SIM voice.

As you compare the two voices, ask yourself whether you have a SIM voice and, if so, how does it relate to your brand voice? It can be closely associated with your brand voice, but it doesn't have to be. In some cases, the SIM voice may be closer to the product brand than the corporate brand. That doesn't matter as long as it is driven by an individual or several individuals and is truly authentic.

Table 5-1	Brand versus SIM Voice
Brand Voice	**SIM Voice**
Singular, anonymous company voice	Multiple, authentic individual voices
Reflects the brand personality and attributes perfectly	Transparent, easy to identify online, and only loosely on brand
Everybody follows the brand voice strictly	Engaging, conversational, and responsive
Designed to appear across all brand touch-points	Mostly relevant only where the conversations are
Usually unique to the company	Usually unique to the person
Sometimes manifested in a person but not always	Always manifested in a real person or many people
Used everywhere from signage to ad copy	Used only in real conversations by real people

Establishing a SIM voice may appear in conflict with brand and public relations objectives. The best way to avoid this conflict is to include your brand marketers and your PR team in the early conversations about your SIM voices. It'll prevent an adversarial relationship from developing because they'll truly understand why you're creating it. They'll also have a lot of valuable advice for you based on their experiences in dealing with the mainstream press and customers through other channels. It is worth noting that you can have multiple SIM voices, some of which can be people who currently are your brand marketers and PR representatives. For them to be successful though may require a change in how they're used to talking to the outside world but that will only be discovered in time.

Outlining SIM Voice Objectives

When you're defining your SIM voice and determining whether you even need one, it's important to consider what you'll be using the SIM voice for. Knowing the objectives it serves and how it supports your marketing and business efforts more broadly is instrumental. If you haven't defined the objectives for the SIM voice, don't take up valuable time (and potentially resources too) in identifying those voices and putting a program around it.

Some of the more common objectives served by having a SIM voice include the following:

- **Providing industry and company insights to all stakeholders.**

  A lot of people are probably talking about your brand in the social Web. Many of them are probably forming strong opinions about your industry, your company, and your brand, too. Some of these people may be very influential. They could be key influencer bloggers, shareholders, customers, competitors, or market analysts. An important objective for having a SIM voice is to share your company's own take on industry and company issues with the broader world and negate any false or unfairly biased perspectives.

- **Building awareness for your products and services.**

  Every month there appears to be a new social platform on which your brand needs to have a presence. This may be Facebook, MySpace, CafeMom (www.cafemom.com), LiveJournal (www.livejournal.com), Twitter, or FourSquare (www.playfoursquare.com). Your customers may be gravitating to that service and could be discussing your brand and forming opinions about your product there. Your SIM voice is needed to simply build awareness for your products and services, communicate accurately about the products, and dispel any myths about them on these social platforms.

- **Forging deeper more trusted relationships with your customers.**

  Sometimes your SIM voice is important to simply deepen your relationships with your customers. It may be focused on giving them category purchase advice, sharing tips and tricks about your product, and helping them through product purchase or upgrade decisions. In other instances, it may be about simply participating in conversations and being a helpful representative of your brand.

- **Customer service and product complaints.**

  When customers are struggling with products, they often complain about them in conversations with their peers or other people who are facing similar challenges. You have a huge opportunity to listen in on these conversations, hear those concerns, provide customer support where you can, and learn from those complaints. Some of the most dynamic examples of companies embracing the social Web successfully have been from companies hearing complaints on platforms like Twitter, responding to them in real time, and providing superior customer service. The ROI (return on investment) of this is easily measurable. The shoe company Zappos (www.zappos.com) does this successfully, as shown in Figure 5-1.

Figure 5-1:
Zappo's
Twitter feed.

🗸 **Discounts and promotional information.**

Most brands offer discounts and special promotions on a regular basis. What better way than to share these than via the social platforms as well? Increasingly, brands are forming micro-communities with passionate brand advocates for the purpose of offering them special discounts and promotions before extending them to the wider public. This strategy builds buzz for the brand in the social Web and deepens the connection between the most loyal customers and the brand.

If you do offer discounts and special promotions, you must be prepared to redeem them. Account for the promo to be successful; when it is, your company won't have trouble redeeming it.

Choosing the Owner of Your Organization's SIM Voice

There's no question that you need a SIM voice for the social Web. It is instrumental to forging relationships with prospects, customers, and expert, positional, and referential influencers in addition to the industry at large. But setting your objectives upfront is as important as knowing the difference between your SIM voice and your brand voice. It's no use participating if you do so in a manner that's in conflict with the fundamental ethos of the social Web. You invariably do more damage to your brand and credibility than you may realize. Remember that whatever mistake you make in the social Web gets quickly amplified, so set your objectives carefully, recognize how different your SIM voice is from your brand, and choose the right people to play the roles.

If you're a small company, either the CEO (chief executive officer) or the CMO (chief marketing officer) will always be your SIM voice or at least one of your SIM voices. Zappos, a shoe company, uses its CEO, Tony Hsieh, as its key SIM voice. Because the company is small, the strategy works well and, given that it's building and establishing the brand primarily through social influence marketing, the question of how the SIM voice conflicts with its brand voice doesn't really arise. The brand and SIM voices are perfectly aligned. That may not be the case for you, so as you wade into the social Web, think carefully about your SIM voice and whether you're even comfortable having one before participating.

Richard Branson, Chairman of the Virgin Group, has his own presence on Twitter (with 154,000 followers) and represents himself and his company (`www.twitter.com/richardbranson`). The airline Virgin America (which is a part of the Virgin Group) also has its own Twitter presence (`twitter.com/virginamerica`) that is used to interact with passengers, share special offers, and announce travel advisories. With 27,000 followers and counting, arguably the Twitter activity makes a difference.

Now that you know what a SIM voice is, how it differs from your brand voice, and have a sense of what business objectives may drive the need for this voice, the only remaining question to answer is, "Who exactly in your organization should serve in this role?"

In the next few sections, I look at the most common types of people who serve as the SIM voice and what they're typically best at doing.

Twintern

Dominos Pizza has recently started a job search for what it refers to as a *Twintern*. This person's primary job is to track conversations across the social Web (not exclusively on Twitter, as the name implies) and join or start conversations as and where appropriate. When you deploy a Twintern (think a junior PR person just out of school), he is usually best at forging deeper relationships with customers, helping with customer service issues, and sharing product discounts and promotion information.

Remember that while more junior staff may know the social platforms the best, they probably also require greater supervision and education. This is because they may not know the culture of the company that they represent or be familiar with what's good practice versus bad practice when representing a company to its customers. This is why the SIM guidelines are so important. Those are discussed later in the chapter.

CEO

At the opposite end of the spectrum, a CEO can also be a SIM voice. In many cases, he is already close to being a SIM voice anyway. He's representative of the brand, but is recognized and noticed as an individual personality with independent opinions that happen to drive the business's direction. This person is best used as a SIM voice providing industry and company insights. After all, he has the credibility and the experience to do so. In many cases, you can use the CEO SIM voice to forge deeper relationships with customers as well. The CEO of Sun Microsystems, Jonathan Schwartz, is actively blogging, and you can tell that it's really him. The CEO participating in the social Web and sharing his insights (and responding to blog comments) has done an immeasurable amount for the Sun Microsystems brand. If your CEO does not have time to truly commit to the online community, do not ask him to. It is better that he have no presence, whether it be a Twitter or a blog presence, than to have an abandoned one.

Never let your CEO, or for that matter any employee, comment about your company on discussion forums anonymously. Although this may seem obvious, the CEO of Whole Foods, John Mackey, was caught commenting on an investor forum about his competitors. He got into trouble for trying to influence the stock price of his competitors.

CMO

Along with the CEO, another good person to play the SIM voice for the company is the CMO (Chief Marketing Officer). Often she is closest to customers along with the actual retail outlet employees, talking to them most often, hearing their complaints, and feeding insights from them into new product development. The CMO, as a result, is also a natural choice to be the SIM voice. CMOs are typically useful for providing industry and company insights, building awareness for products and services, forging deeper relationships with customers, and, in some cases (but rarely), sharing special discount and promotional information. At Best Buy, Barry Judge, the CMO, has his own blog and Twitter account; see Figure 5-2. He's very much a SIM voice and a very vocal one, too.

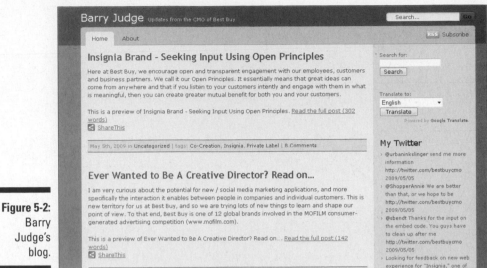

Figure 5-2:
Barry
Judge's
blog.

Social media lead

The social media lead is becoming a more common role within many large organizations. This person coordinates all social media activities across the company between all the different departments and out to customers as well. She is of course the most natural choice to be a SIM voice or one of the key SIM voices. This person knows the social Web well, often has independent credibility within it, and understands how to strike the right balance between representing the brand and speaking authentically as an individual. This person can accomplish practically any of the objectives with the exception of company and industry insights, which may need to come from the CEO or CMO to carry credibility. In some organizations, this person has the title of community manager, social media manager, community evangelist, or outreach coordinator. Ford Motor Company (with Scott Monty as its social media lead) best exemplifies this approach. Figure 5-3 shows Scott Monty's Twitter feed.

PR manager

The PR manager typically manages relationships with the mainstream press. Arguably, managing mainstream press relationships and being a brand voice can and does conflict with the SIM voice, but that doesn't mean that an enterprising PR manager can't play the role of the SIM voice. He may need to choose to take on the responsibility at the cost of being the brand voice to do this authentically, however. After he does, he, like a social media lead, can accomplish all the major SIM objectives with the exception of the industry and company insights.

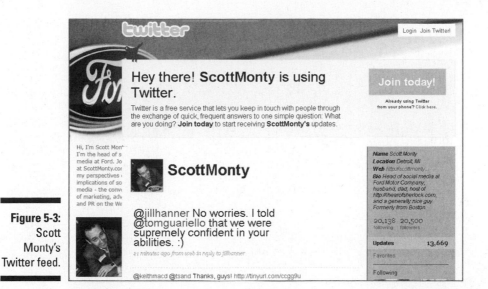

Figure 5-3:
Scott
Monty's
Twitter feed.

Agency

A social media, digital, or advertising agency can also represent you in the social Web as your SIM voice. At the outset, having a SIM voice outside your company may seem inauthentic, but as long as the agency representative is transparent about it and is only building awareness for your product and sharing discount information, it's not a problem. Sometimes, the agency can monitor conversations and provide recommendations on how and where to participate. But the actual participation with the objectives of deepening customer relationships, addressing customer complaints, and providing industry and customer insights must be conducted by someone within your business. The agency can also be used to help with training the internal representatives, monitoring conversations, creating reports for senior management, and providing strategy and insight.

Other external voices

Outside of your agency, spokespeople for your company can serve as SIM voices. For example, if your company uses a celebrity or a series of celebrities to promote products and services they too can serve as SIM voices. These celebrities can engage with your customers and build enthusiasm for your products and services. But each time you use an external SIM voice keep in mind that they may not be as loyal to your brand as you may like them to be. They could be representing other brands as well as your own.

If you have an independent expert serving as a SIM voice, keep in mind that she may not always be available to participate on your behalf when you need her to. Often when external SIM voices are used, they're used in conjunction with internal ones and not in isolation.

Crowdsourcing SIM Voices with Guidelines

For all the strategies that you may put into place to support your SIM voice, you need to do still more. If you're a large company with hundreds or thousands of employees, you can't stop your employees from participating in the social Web. Just as you cannot stop an employee from talking about your company at a dinner party, you can't prevent him from talking about you online. That's not necessarily bad: The more people who know your brand and talk about it favorably, the more it can help you. But it is important to establish some guidelines so that your employees know how to talk about your company online.

Employees care about their companies and they'll welcome the guidelines. They'll see it as a way for them to better represent the company in the public domain. That is, of course, as long as you don't make the guidelines too restrictive and do incorporate feedback. If you develop the guidelines in isolation from your employees, ignoring how they typically participate online and want to represent your company, you're sure to face backlash. It is also important to design the guidelines to be adaptable based on how the social Web is evolving and how behavior is changing on the different social platforms.

Before you write the guidelines, be sure to check whether your organization has any existing guidelines and policies that can serve as a starting point.

Here are elements that you can incorporate into your SIM policy.

- ✔ **Purpose:** Start with the objectives. You need to explain why the guidelines are being established, what they hope to accomplish, and how they help the employees.

- ✔ **Declaration of trust:** Just as important, you must establish that the goal of the guidelines isn't to restrict employees or to sensor them, but to encourage them to be better ambassadors of the company. Similarly, it's important to establish that no one will monitor employees, nor will you ask them to edit or delete posts.

- ✔ **Statement of responsibility:** Make clear that employees are personally responsible for all the content that they publish online, whether it is on a blog, a wiki, on YouTube, or any other form of social media. They should do so in a manner befitting their identity as an employee of the company, recognizing that whatever they publish may be attributed to the company.

✔ **An identification of themselves as employees:** Employees must know that although they do not have to always identify themselves as employees of a company, they must do so when discussing company or industry matters. In those instances, they should either speak as a representative of the company or include a disclaimer emphasizing that they are sharing their own personal opinions. Similarly, employees should declare any conflicts of interest when discussing professional matters.

✔ **A SIM voice:** Employees should speak as a SIM voice by being engaging, conversational, and authentic, but recognizing that they aren't the official brand voice of the company. And furthermore, it is important to do so in one's own name and not anonymously. The CEO of Whole Foods commented on discussion forums about his competitors anonymously and it hurt him and his company.

✔ **Engagement principles:** Being a good SIM voice also means following certain engagement principles. These include responding to comments immediately, providing meaningful and respectful comments, being transparent in all social interactions online, and always looking to add value.

✔ **No unauthorized sharing of business information:** Employees should not share client, company, partner, or supplier information without express approval from the appropriate owners. When referencing somebody, link back to the source.

✔ **Respect for the audience:** As with any other form of communication, by virtue of being associated with the company, the employee is an ambassador and a SIM voice. He can easily tarnish the brand without meaning to do so and without even realizing it. It is therefore important to avoid personal insults, obscenity, or inappropriate behavior that is outside of the company's formal policies. This is especially important because when something is expressed in the social domain, it's easily amplified by others. Just ask Dominos about the crisis it faced when two employees published obscene videos online.

✔ **Respect for copyright, fair use, and financial disclosure laws:** Regardless of the media being published, employees should still respect all local, state, and federal laws especially in the realms of copyright, fair use, and financial disclosure.

✔ **What to do when they make a mistake:** Regardless of what an employee publishes, at some point, he is going to screw up. We're all human, after all. The guidelines must address what employees should do if they make a mistake. That means being upfront about the mistakes, correcting the errors immediately, and accepting responsibility.

These guidelines are culled from an analysis of several social media guidelines, with the IBM guidelines, shown in Figure 5-4, serving as the primary source of inspiration, as they represent the most complete set. If you'd like to see the complete set, go to www.ibm.com/blogs/zz/en/guidelines.html.

SIM guidelines can get long and unwieldy. You may not need every element mentioned in the preceding list. If you're a small company, these guidelines may fold into broader employee guidelines and may not need to be a stand-alone document. But you definitely need them in some form. They provide direction to your employees without hampering their enthusiasm for social influence marketing. And with the right excitement around SIM, you may find yourself turning every employee into a marketer who is representing the company in her own SIM voice, authentically and convincingly. You can't ask for more than that from your employees. Invariably, these spontaneous, natural grassroots efforts complement your more formal brand and SIM voices. They don't contradict but rather strengthen each other.

Be sure to invite employees across your company to provide feedback on the guidelines. It is no use creating and publishing guidelines in isolation. Your employees provide you with valuable feedback. By being included in the creation process, they're more likely to follow the guidelines.

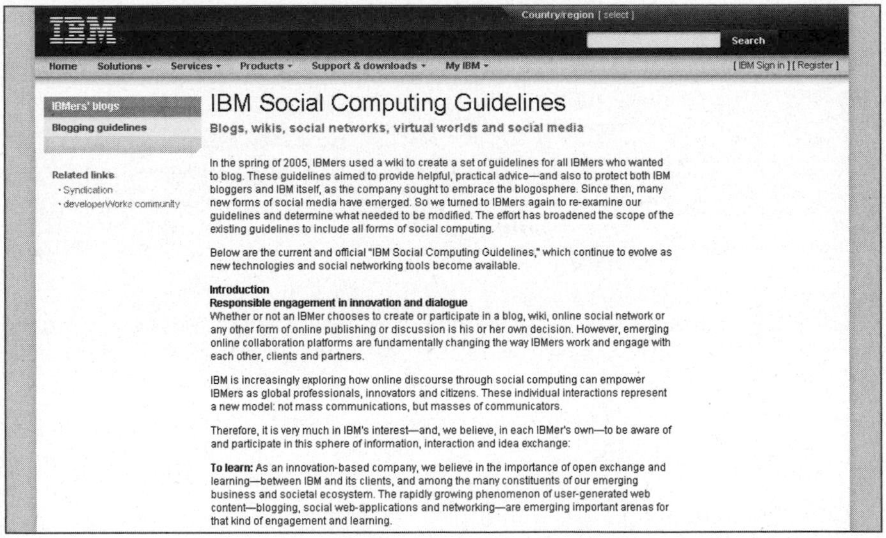

IBM Country/region [select] Search

Home   Solutions ▾   Services ▾   Products ▾   Support & downloads ▾   My IBM ▾   [IBM Sign in] [Register]

IBMers' blogs
Blogging guidelines

Related links
• Syndication
• developerWorks community

IBM Social Computing Guidelines
Blogs, wikis, social networks, virtual worlds and social media

In the spring of 2005, IBMers used a wiki to create a set of guidelines for all IBMers who wanted to blog. These guidelines aimed to provide helpful, practical advice—and also to protect both IBM bloggers and IBM itself, as the company sought to embrace the blogosphere. Since then, many new forms of social media have emerged. So we turned to IBMers again to re-examine our guidelines and determine what needed to be modified. The effort has broadened the scope of the existing guidelines to include all forms of social computing.

Below are the current and official "IBM Social Computing Guidelines," which continue to evolve as new technologies and social networking tools become available.

Introduction
Responsible engagement in innovation and dialogue
Whether or not an IBMer chooses to create or participate in a blog, wiki, online social network or any other form of online publishing or discussion is his or her own decision. However, emerging online collaboration platforms are fundamentally changing the way IBMers work and engage with each other, clients and partners.

IBM is increasingly exploring how online discourse through social computing can empower IBMers as global professionals, innovators and citizens. These individual interactions represent a new model: not mass communications, but masses of communicators.

Therefore, it is very much in IBM's interest—and, we believe, in each IBMer's own—to be aware of and participate in this sphere of information, interaction and idea exchange:

To learn: As an innovation-based company, we believe in the importance of open exchange and learning—between IBM and its clients, and among the many constituents of our emerging business and societal ecosystem. The rapidly growing phenomenon of user-generated web content—blogging, social web-applications and networking—are emerging important arenas for that kind of engagement and learning.

Figure 5-4:
IBM's social media standards.

Some SIM guideline resources and examples

Here are some of the most helpful online resources for creating SIM guidelines:

- ✔ **Disclosure Best Practices Toolkit:** `http://blogcouncil.org/disclosure/`

- ✔ **IBM Social Computing Guidelines:** `www.ibm.com/blogs/zz/en/guidelines.html`

- ✔ **HP Blogging Code of Conduct:** `www.hp.com/hpinfo/blogs/codeofconduct.html`

- ✔ **Intel Social Media Guidelines:** `www.intel.com/sites/sitewide/en_US/social-media.htm`

- ✔ **Sun Guidelines on Public Disclosure:** `www.sun.com/communities/guidelines.jsp`

- ✔ **BBC Editorial Guidelines:** `www.bbc.co.uk/guidelines/editorialguidelines/advice/personalweb/index.shtml`

- ✔ **U.S. Navy Web 2.0: Utilizing New Web Tools:** `www.doncio.navy.mil/PolicyView.aspx?ID=789`

- ✔ **U.S. Air Force New Media Guide:** `www.af.mil/shared/media/document/AFD-090406-036.pdf`

Chapter 6

Reaching Your Audience and Their Influencers on the Major Social Platforms

● ●

In This Chapter

▶ Choosing the right social platform

▶ Exploring marketing strategies for Facebook

▶ Harnessing MySpace for marketing

▶ Using Twitter and YouTube to achieve your objectives

● ●

*I*f you have been an Internet user since the mid 1990s, you probably know that the popular social platforms today are not the first to have been launched. Many came before Facebook and MySpace. In some cases, those early social networks and online communities were extremely successful too. For example, back in the mid 1990s, the Well was considered the most influential online community. It wasn't the largest, but it was the most influential. GeoCities, which rose to fame in the late 1990s and was bought by Yahoo! for a whopping $3.57 billion at its peak, boasted millions of active accounts. Friendster, which was the darling of the social networking world in 2003 and 2004, fizzled when its technical infrastructure and lack of new features pushed people in America away from it. (More than 90 percent of its traffic comes from Asia today.) And even in the last two years, users have moved away from MySpace, which was the largest social network in the country, to Facebook, in what appears to be an unstoppable and extremely worrying trend for MySpace.

The point is that customarily social platforms such as online communities, social networks, and loosely connected personal spaces online have periods of immense growth, a plateau, and then a slow, painful decline. It appears hard for a social platform to avoid this evolution. I've seen this happen time and again. This poses a difficult challenge for marketers. Where do you invest your marketing dollars if you don't know whether a specific social platform is going to be around in a year or two? Similarly, how do you know which up-and-coming social platform your users are going to gravitate towards after a major social platform starts fizzling? Knowing which social platform is going to have explosive growth next and where your customers will spend their time is not always easy. Nevertheless, you must try to answer those questions.

This chapter helps you identify which of the four major social platforms — Facebook, MySpace, Twitter, and YouTube — on which to launch, sustain, and promote your brand. I also discuss here the various marketing opportunities on each of these major social platforms.

Before marketing on these social platforms, you need to figure out your social voice. See Chapter 5 for more information on how to do that.

Finding the Right Platforms

The first step is to recognize that no *single* social platform is going to be enough for your SIM activities. It's extremely unlikely that your potential customers use only one of the social platforms exclusively. In fact, research shows that a user is rarely only on one platform. It is far more likely that your customers have profiles on two or three social platforms and use some of them more than others. You've probably also noticed that marketing on several social platforms isn't that much more expensive than marketing on one, as long as most of your energies are focused on a few. It makes sense to choose several platforms versus just one to do your marketing.

Still, that doesn't answer the question of where to market. You can't be marketing on MySpace, Facebook, Friendster, LinkedIn, YouTube, Hi5, Bebo, Orkut, Flickr, Twitter, and Classmates all at once with the same amount of effort. Although SIM is considered cheap, it still takes time, money, and effort when you're doing so on many social platforms at once. Not to mention the fact that you're probably going to confuse customers who have presences on several of the social platforms. The answer is to put a lot of effort into marketing on a few social platforms where your customers are participating the most and to have lighter presences on the other platforms.

Choose where to practice SIM by researching and understanding where your customers are spending most of their time. This doesn't mean identifying where most of your customers have registered profiles, but instead researching where the customers have the highest levels of engagement. This means

✓ **Finding out what amount of time that they spend on the social platform, what they specifically do, and how they use it to interact with each other.**

Tools like Quantcast (www.quantcast.com) can you help you understand engagement, but you may need to reach out to the social platforms themselves to understand the details of the engagement. Keep in mind that with Quantcast, only if the site has been Quantified (which means that only when the site owner has added Quantcast code to his site) are the statistics the most accurate. comScore (`www.comscore.com`) is a paid solution that can provide more accurate numbers for the non-Quantified sites. Figure 6-1 shows the Quantcast home page.

✔ **Understanding the user behaviors on the social platform.**

For example, if you're a business to business (B2B) solutions provider and your customers use LinkedIn to ask each other for advice when making business-related purchasing decisions, but spend a lot more time on Facebook, LinkedIn may still be a better place to practice SIM. That's where they're making the purchasing decisions that matter to you. It doesn't matter if they're spending more cumulative minutes on Facebook.

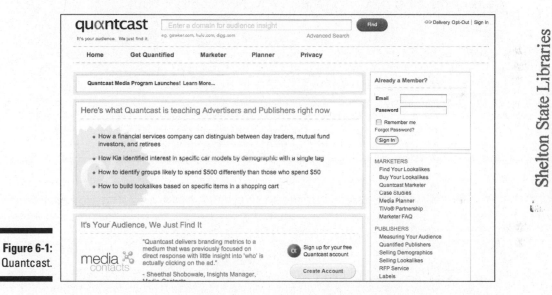

Figure 6-1:
Quantcast.

Invariably, you discover three to four social platforms match your customers' demographics, have high engagement levels for them, and are what I loosely call *locations of influence* as far as your product category is concerned. That's where your customers make their decisions, get influenced by others, and observe how their peers are purchasing or discussing their own purchases. These three factors together tell you where to practice SIM. And as you do so, recognize that you must also consider two broader aspects:

✔ **Think about the macro trends of the social platform.**

For example, does the platform look like it's emerging, has it settled into a plateau, or is it fizzling? Accordingly, you may want to devote more or fewer dollars and effort to it.

> ✓ **Whether the social platform is a place where your brand will have permission to participate and one in which you will want to participate.**
>
> Participating in some social platforms may hurt your brand. For example, if you are a high-end exclusive brand like Chanel, it may not be appropriate to engage in conversations in a casual, music-oriented social environment like MySpace.

Your customers move between platforms as time passes. As a result, be prepared to adjust your social influence marketing campaign significantly. Your customers may not always stay on the platforms that you're targeting them on currently. This matters especially with small business marketers.

Each social network has a reputation. Make sure that your brand is in alignment with that reputation. For example, MySpace is known to be more music-oriented and has a reputation for attracting a young, less affluent audience. Keep that in mind as you choose where and how to market.

Looking at Marketing Strategies for Facebook

As you do your analysis, you'll more likely than not discover that Facebook (www.facebook.com) is one of the social platforms on which you have to practice SIM. It has had explosive growth in the last two years (Facebook now has more than 200 million users) and is the largest social network in the United States. Approximately 70 million Americans are on Facebook in some capacity or another, so it is fair to assume that at least some of your customers are going to be on Facebook. As such, I want to spend a few minutes explaining what SIM on Facebook is like today and provide a few pointers too.

First and foremost, you can market on Facebook in different ways. I start with the paid advertising tactics and then move on to discuss the unpaid or earned tactics. On the paid advertisements side, you can market in one of four ways, which I cover in the first four sections.

Facebook is still in the process of evolving its social platform. As a result, new ad unit formats may appear and some may be removed from the Web site, too. Rumor has it that Facebook is planning to launch an ad network as well, through which it will run advertisements on third-party Web sites. The advertising industry feels that Facebook still has a lot to do to monetize its traffic and become more advertiser-friendly. So, expect more changes from Facebook. Outside of the guidance highlighted in the sections that follow, I recommend visiting Inside Facebook (www.insidefacebook.com) and All Facebook (www.allfacebook.com) to keep pace with the evolving marketing opportunities and advertisement formats on the platform.

Traditional banner advertisements

Banner advertisements are the traditional display advertisements that you see on most Web sites. These get very few click-throughs because with such engaging content on a social network, few users notice the advertisements and click them. Banner ads on social networks have been universally panned as being ineffective and aren't recommended. Facebook currently has an agreement with Microsoft to provide Facebook with the traditional banner advertisements, as shown in Figure 6-2. These advertisements are bought through the Microsoft Advertising adCenter (https://adcenter.microsoft.com) but are viewed on Facebook.

Figure 6-2: Facebook advertising.

Social advertisements

Social ads are a unique ad format from Facebook in which demographics, user interests, and other keywords that are listed in profiles target the advertisements. When you set up the advertisement, Facebook tells you how much you're narrowing your audience with each additional criterion you specify. You can also add social actions to those advertisements that include asking the viewer to rate the advertisement and become a fan of the brand directly through the advertisement. When you create the advertisement, you can also have friends of the viewer who have endorsed a brand appear in the advertisement itself as an endorsement. It's a clever way to capture your attention and tell you that a friend likes the brand, so maybe you should give it serious thought too. These can be bought on a cost per click (CPC) or a cost per impression (CPM) basis and have been very popular with small businesses because of their low cost and the ability to pick a daily budget for how much to spend. You can learn more about these ad formats at `www.facebook.com/advertising`.

Sponsored stories

As the name implies, sponsored stories appear with a title, body copy, and images, and they look and feel like stories. They appear in the user's newsfeed and may link to a Facebook page or even to an external site. (It is usually recommended to link to a Facebook page and keep the user within Facebook itself.) The sponsored stories are targeted through profile data like the social advertisements and are popular because they're highly visible. The newsfeed is what a user first sees when he logs into Facebook. The ads appear on the right side (not in the news stream) but are easily noticed. A variation on the sponsored story is the sponsored video, which functions in a similar fashion. The sponsored videos are popular because they don't require the user to leave the newsfeed to view them. You can learn more about these at `www.facebook.com/advertising` or by contacting the Facebook sales team.

Gift sponsorships

Sponsored gifts work in addition to the gifting application within Facebook, which lets users buy gifts and give them to friends and family. Advertisers have the option to sponsor branded gifts and give them away for free to users targeted through profile data. The gifts appear in the newsfeed and, because they are rare, carry more stature than other gifts. Gift sponsorship is popular because the giver, the receiver, and anyone who visits the receiver's profile page all see the branded gift. This extends the life of the gift and the branding too. Figure 6-3 shows the Facebook Gifts page.

As an example, in April 2009, Honda provided 750,000 free virtual gifts for Facebook users to gift to each other. The gifts, which were fuel gauges shaped like hearts, were all given away within four days. As a result, 1.5 million people directly interacted with the gifts through the promotion. This doesn't include the number of other people who may have seen those fuel gauges in the profile pages of their friends. The best way to learn more about the fit sponsorships is to contact the Facebook sales team at www.facebook.com/business/contact.php.

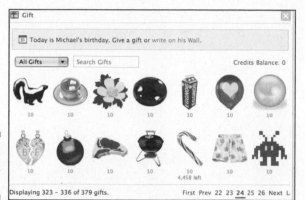

Figure 6-3:
Facebook
gifts.

Facebook pages

Think of Facebook pages as company profiles on Facebook. You can set up one for your brand and encourage others to become a fan of the page. It doesn't cost anything to create a fan page, but it does take time and effort to make it relevant and worthwhile. This can be a public page through which you share business and product information. On your Facebook page, you can publish blog posts via RSS, host conversations, and publish photos, Twitter feeds, event information, coupons, and other promotional items. You can also add Flash widgets to these pages. Keep in mind that you have the ability to send all of your followers messages that appear in their Facebook inboxes. Victoria's Secret Pink, shown in Figure 6-4, has one of the most popular Facebook pages.

Facebook events

If you're holding an event for your customers, employees, or business partners, you can promote it on Facebook by listing it as an event. This can be a virtual or a physical event supporting your company, its products, special promotions, or milestones. People can be invited to attend the event (you invite them from within Facebook) and the event page can include content about the event, your brand, and your products and services. (See Figure 6-5.) Conferences, product previews, and special promotions are popularly highlighted through Facebook events. Once the event is complete, you can share photos and write-ups of the event on the event page.

Figure 6-4:
Victoria's
Secret
Pink on
Facebook.

Figure 6-5:
A Facebook
event.

Facebook applications

Creating pages and events that are supported by advertisements, sponsored stories, and gift sponsorships may not be enough. Some companies choose to build applications that can be installed in a user's profile or on a Facebook page. For a branded application to be a success, it must engage users in a meaningful fashion whether that is utility- or entertainment-driven. The most successful applications can take weeks to build and promote within Facebook, so don't expect this to be a simple endeavor. Popular applications include games, quizzes, badges, calculators, and tools that analyze a person's social graph. For example, TripAdvisor's Cities I've Visited application lets you show your friends which cities around the world you've visited. It has been an extremely popular application. For more information on building Facebook applications, visit the Facebook Developers Home (`www.face book.com/developers`). For a list of the top Facebook applications, visit `http://statistics.allfacebook.com/applications/leaderboard`.

Facebook groups

In addition to applications, events, and pages, your brand and product category could well be a part of one of the hundreds and thousands of conversations in the Facebook groups. These groups are set up by users and are for them to use to discuss topics of interest and express their points of view. You can't market directly in the Facebook groups, but you can certainly identify the ones in which your brand is being discussed extensively. In some cases, groups may be dedicated solely to the discussion of your brand. In those cases, you may want to observe the conversation, learn from it, and maybe participate as a SIM voice when and where appropriate. You may want to also contact the group administrator to see whether they'd be open to doing a joint promotion with you. If your brand has an official group, Facebook will help you move it to a page. As a brand, it's better for you to have a page than manage a group, which is really designed for user-to-user interaction only. Figure 6-6 shows a Facebook page.

Facebook Connect

Facebook Connect allows a user to bring her Facebook social graph to a third-party Web site. (A *social graph* is a global mapping of people and how they relate to each other.) More and more Web sites are supporting Facebook Connect. This means that when users log into those sites with their Facebook credentials, they can see which of their friends have participated on that Web site in some fashion, whether it be by commenting, rating, or writing a in the newsfeeds of all their friends. This allows users to share their activity on third-party Web sites with their friends in Facebook, which inadvertently gives the site more exposure. Facebook Connect is discussed in more detail in Chapter 9. Figure 6-7 shows the home page for Facebook Connect. For more information about Facebook Connect, visit the Facebook Connect Developers page (`http://developers.facebook.com/connect.php`) or view this SlideShare presentation that I put together with a friend on its potential (`www.slideshare.net/shivsingh/portable-social-graphs-imagining-their-potential-presentation`).

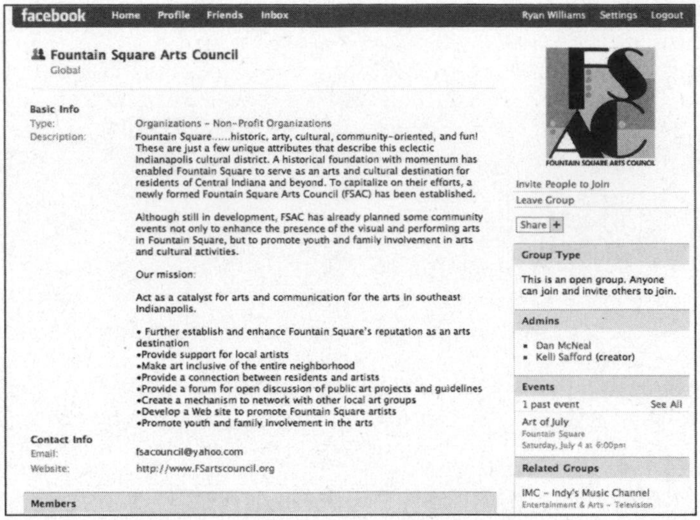

Figure 6-6:
A Facebook
page.

Figure 6-7:
Facebook
Connect.

Discovering Marketing Strategies for MySpace

Another social network with a large presence that you will invariably want to do some advertising on is MySpace (www.myspace.com). It is not the largest social network in America — Facebook recently overtook it — but it's still a force to be reckoned with. As a result, the MySpace advertising tactics warrant explanation here too. I start with the paid advertising tactics on MySpace.

MySpace ads

The most common form of advertising on MySpace is the more traditional banner advertisements. These are in either the 728 x 90-pixels leaderboard size, the 350 x 250-pixels medium rectangle size, or the 160 x 600-pixel size. These are cost per click (CPC) advertisements, which means you only pay when someone clicks the advertisement. The hyper-targeting capabilities of the MySpace ads let you target the advertisements based not just on demographics but on user interests too. These work like the Facebook advertisements — with each additional interest added, you're told by how much you're narrowing your audience population. A user-friendly ad builder lets you upload the creative, modify it online, and then track the campaign progress through a dashboard. For more information on MySpace advertising, visit the MySpace advertising page (https://advertise.myspace.com).

MySpace Apps

In addition to the MySpace Ads, you can also advertise MySpace applications. The MySpace Apps advertising program is targeted at developers of applications and allows them to promote their applications on category pages and across the MySpace social network. If you're a brand with an engaging application, you may wish to promote it through the MySpace Apps program (shown in Figure 6-8). It lets you promote the application in certain interest categories as well as the applications home page. You can learn more about MySpace Apps at http://apps.myspace.com.

Figure 6-8:
MySpace
appli-
cations.

MySpace Music

MySpace has its roots in music, and music is very much in its DNA. Its ability to give unsigned musicians a voice drove its early adoption and usage. To this day, MySpace has a leadership position in music. MySpace Music (shown in Figure 6-9) allows you to sponsor free music downloads, skin the music playlists (which means putting your brand's look and feel on top of the playlist), and provide song recommendations. MySpace Music also sells ringtones that you can sponsor. With more than 65 percent of MySpace users streaming music in their profile pages and six billion songs being played each month, advertising through the various MySpace Music offerings presents you with a viable alternative. You'll find more information on MySpace Music at `http://music.myspace.com` and on the page for Musicians at `https://advertise.myspace.com/musicians.html`. Also, get in touch with the MySpace Advertising team for custom packages (`http://adsupport.myspace.com/index.cfm?fuseaction=advertiser.sales`). Vendors like TrueAnthem help connect your brand to fans on MySpace, too (`www.trueanthem.com`).

MySpace profile

Through a MySpace profile, you can encourage people to become "friends" of your brand and join a conversation. This can be jumpstarted with media contributed by you, such as questions for the community, video clips, advice, or factoids. You can publish photos, RSS feeds, tweets, event information, and product announcements. You can also install applications. A profile doesn't cost you anything to set up, but, like the Facebook pages, it takes time and effort to make the profile relevant. Weight Watchers has an interesting MySpace profile that's used primarily to encourage conversations about weight loss. Hosted by a video blogger with featured guests, it encourages participation. You can register to set up a MySpace profile from the home page (www.myspace.com).

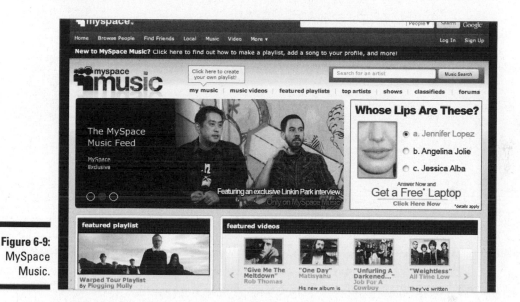

Figure 6-9: MySpace Music.

MySpace & OpenID

OpenID (http://openid.net) is Facebook Connect's competitor, although, unlike Facebook Connect, it is built on open standards. With MySpace's implementation (called MySpace OpenID and shown in Figure 6-10), it lets users log in to third-party Web sites using the same usernames and passwords. When they do so, their friends (or social graph) travel with them from MySpace. It also allows the publishing of activities on the partner sites back to MySpace profiles, just as Facebook Connect does, and in turn syndicates MySpace activity to the partner sites as well. MySpaceID works with Google Connect (are you confused yet?), which lets you add social features to any Web site.

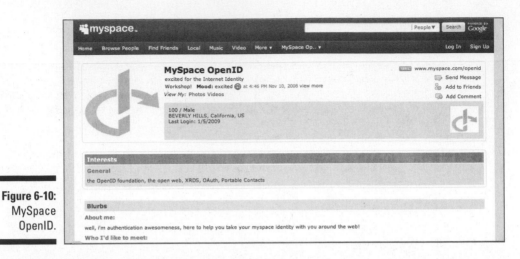

Figure 6-10:
MySpace
OpenID.

Marketing on Twitter

No social platform has had more explosive growth in 2008 than Twitter, the microblogging service. Twitter (www.twitter.com) is similar to a blogging service, except that you're limited to 140 characters per message or *tweet*. Also, only people who "follow" you on Twitter see your tweets. You reply to other people's tweets, forward their tweets, or send them direct messages. All of your followers see anything that you tweet.

According to Nielsen Online, Twitter grew by a staggering 1,382 percent from February 2008 to February 2009, and every month, the growth rate increases. Every day, more people create accounts on Twitter than they do on any other social platform. Unlike the other fast-growing social platform, Facebook, Twitter users are typically older. Although the total number of Twitter users is still small (less than 20 million as of May 2009), it is growing so rapidly and has such an influential user base that marketing on Twitter requires a specific discussion.

At the moment, there are only unpaid marketing tactics on Twitter. You can't buy any advertising units or harness any innovative advertising programs like virtual gifts. At least so far, that's the case. Industry insiders expect Twitter to develop sponsorships and advertising formats within the next 12 months. In the meantime, you should explore some of the unpaid tactics. And as you do, remember that Twitter is most powerful for building and nurturing relationships between people even more so than Facebook. It's simply because you're limited to 140 characters. When marketing through Twitter, focus tightly on building the relationships, and everything else will follow. Don't worry too much about pushing messages to the community.

Twitter handles

It is very important to take ownership of your brand on Twitter. Sign up for Twitter with your brand or company's name as the Twitter handle. If you're lucky, no one has already taken it. Use this account to communicate company or brand news, special promotions, product offers, respond to questions, and resolve customer service issues.

TIP

Follow every person who follows you: It's good Twitter protocol to do so if you're looking to build relationships with lots of people. But if your goal is just customer service, don't feel the need to follow everyone.

WARNING!

If you do not take ownership of your company or brand name on Twitter, someone else may do so on your behalf. This could be a competitor, another business with a similar name, a customer, or a fan. If that happens, you'll probably have to spend a lot of time (and maybe money, too) to get back the username. Most Twitter users automatically associate your brand name on Twitter with your company. Many may not realize that the person behind the Twitter account is not from your company.

Searches

The first step on Twitter is to monitor the conversations for your company, brand, and product mentions. You want to know how people are talking about you. You can set up these searches easily within Twitter itself or by using a separate application like TweetDeck (www.tweetdeck.com), which is shown in Figure 6-11. Make sure you track not just your company brand but also your competitors too. You'll probably learn more from people talking about your competitors than from their conversations about you. You can use the Twitter search engine (http://search.twitter.com) or one of the real-time engines like OneRiot (www.oneriot.com), Tweetmeme (www.tweetmeme.com), Twazzup (www.twazzup.com), and Scoopler (www.scoopler.com). You could also try Tweetbeep (www.tweetbeep.com), which gives you Twitter alerts via e-mail on an hourly basis.

Responses

It's not enough to just listen in on the conversations. It is important that you participate in the conversations too. This means responding to questions directly addressed to your Twitter user name, whether the questions are customer service-related or more general. It also means following the brand mentions and correcting misinformation (although don't appear too defensive when you do this as it can backfire), providing helpful advice when and where you can develop relationships with the people who are talking about your company. And remember, part of being a good SIM voice is about allowing your own personality to shine through, which means opening up and being willing to talk about your own life.

Figure 6-11:
The
TweetDeck
Web site.

Following and followers

The core of activity on Twitter is following other people and getting followed yourself. First and foremost, make sure you follow anyone who follows you. Second, consider following all the employees at your company who have Twitter accounts. You'll build goodwill with them and they'll generate followers for you. Next, identify influential tweeters who have large followings to follow and establish relationships with. These people are similar to influential bloggers. They're the experts in a specific domain with large audiences who can encourage people to follow you and who can influence others. Different applications can help you identify these users, but one I like that measures a user's influence is called Twinfluence (www.twinfluence.com). You may want to also try WeFollow (www.wefollow.com), which is a popular Twitter directory that helps you find interesting and influential people and brands to follow. When deciding who to follow and who not to follow, think about it like a cocktail party. First, start with the people you know, then the people that they know, then people talking about subjects important to you, and finally, random (or influential!) people and those that approach you.

Sponsored tweets

One current advertising opportunity that blends into the paid tactics domain is sponsored tweets. In a similar fashion to sponsored posts on blogs, some Twitter users with very large followings are open to publishing sponsored tweets. This means that you would discuss the marketing campaign with those users and they would tweet about it in their language and style to their audiences. Typically, Twitter users would only do this if they can declare that these are sponsored tweets and if the marketing messages are in sync with their own personal brand and the type of information that they like to share with their followers. This is an emergent marketing tactic and currently very few examples exist, so there's no single source for information on sponsored tweets. But do take a look at Twitter Sparq (`http://sparq.socialmedia.com`), which is an innovative platform for sponsored tweets.

Creating a YouTube Strategy

YouTube (`www.youtube.com`) is another social platform that has had explosive growth in the last few years. It is the number one Web site for online videos and, whenever marketers think of viral marketing, they think in terms of YouTube. Today, YouTube has approximately 81 million people visiting each month, with each visitor spending 54 minutes on the site in a month. More than 150,000 video clips are uploaded every day and, in March of 2009, YouTube streamed 5.9 billion videos. Knowing how to publish and promote your marketing video clips is essential to getting them the attention that they deserve. The following are some recommendations for promoting your video clips on YouTube.

Always create a customized channel

Having a YouTube channel just for your company or brand is important because it allows you to showcase all the related video clips in one place. A YouTube channel is your brand's account home, where clips that you have published can appear. Setting up a channel is very easy, so don't hesitate to do so. A channel also allows you to create a profile for yourself and have a place to link your Web site. Make sure that you customize the channel to match your company's or your brand's visual identity. You do not need to manually create a YouTube channel. As soon as you sign up for an account (using the Sign Up link in the top-right corner of the home page) and upload a video clip, a channel is created for you. To reach your YouTube channel, just click your username after you log in. Figure 6-12 shows one channel.

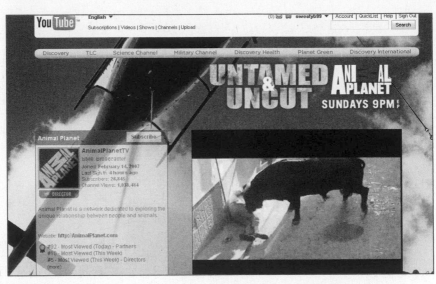

Figure 6-12:
The Animal
Planet
YouTube
Channel.

Create custom content for YouTube

It is not good enough to simply add your TV advertising spots to YouTube. Create custom content that matches the style and format of YouTube. Keep the running time to five minutes or less and stay within the 100MB limit on file sizes. Group the video clips into themed playlists for increased viewing.

Tag and categorize all your clips

Choose the category for your video clip carefully. Start by looking at how popular video clips in your category have been tagged and consider using some of the same tags. Those tags have probably worked for the popular clips and they'll work for you too.

Your content may not fit into a category neatly. Choose your category based on the number of similar video clips that reside in it.

Use tags to make up for the limits of categorization. YouTube does not limit the number of tags that you can add. These tags also make unsearchable data (like photos and video) searchable by adding meta-data to them. Video titles and descriptions can also help with this.

Promote your video with YouTube E-mail and Bulletins

YouTube helps you with the promotion of your clips through the E-mail and Bulletin features. Reach out to other users through YouTube E-mail and tell them about your content and why it is of interest to them. On a similar note, leverage bulletins, which let you post short messages to your channel or on other user pages. You can manage YouTube e-mails, bulletins, subscribers, and friends all through your channel page on YouTube.

Be careful not to spam other users. If someone hasn't asked for e-mail from you, don't send it.

Video responses: The social currency of YouTube

Don't ignore the fact that you can build goodwill with other users by leaving video responses to their clips. This matters, especially with the extremely popular clips in your category. So don't hesitate to create YouTube video responses. When you do, make sure that your responses are civil and relevant.

Joining YouTube Groups

Consider joining a YouTube Group that matches your category or interests. You'll learn about people who share common interests (maybe customers) and will be able to target your clips towards them more effectively down the road. You can find YouTube Groups by clicking Community in the main navigation or by going to this Web address: www.youtube.com/groups_main.

Have some fun, too

Your customers are typically looking to be entertained when they're on YouTube. Have some fun with the clips that you post. Even if they're educational in nature (which can be very valuable and popular on YouTube), don't shy away from injecting a bit of humor into them. Keep in mind that the clips should be engaging enough that they encourage the user to share the clip with others.

If you're a marketer at a large brand, you may have the dollars to invest in some paid advertising tactics. YouTube offers primarily two kinds of paid advertising. Self-service advertisements that function similar to a Google AdWords program (you can also run Google AdWords campaigns) and more strategic campaign-based advertising that may include a *home page takeover* (which is when you take over all the primary advertising spots on the home page of the site) or something else similar. With these paid tactics, YouTube provides all the standard media metrics such as impressions, click to play, click rate, and quartile viewed in addition to the community metrics (star ratings, views, and comments). These advertisements can also be targeted to run next to select partner content, if you prefer. This matters to many marketers who worry about what their own advertisements (video or otherwise) may appear next to.

YouTube subscribers

People on YouTube who choose to subscribe to your videos are known as YouTube subscribers. Every time you upload a new clip, they're notified and their names and icons are visible on your YouTube channel page. Think of the subscribers as similar to followers on Twitter or fans on Facebook pages. Just as you'd nurture relationships with them on those other social platforms, you should do so here, too. The best way to build subscribers is to publish quality video clips, encourage commenting on those clips, and subscribe to others, as well. Sharing the clips on the other social platforms may also help you build goodwill, increase views, and get more subscribers.

Chapter 7

Marketing via Niche Networks and Online Influencers

*T*hroughout this book, I discuss social influence marketing on the major social platforms: what you can do on the paid side of the equation as well as on the unpaid or earned media end. Still, much more social activity is happening online beyond Facebook, YouTube, MySpace, and Twitter that needs to be accounted for. Industry insiders believe that in the coming years, greater fragmentation will happen as user-generated content flows more seamlessly between the major social platforms and the rest of the Internet.

In this chapter, I discuss the social platforms beyond Facebook, YouTube, MySpace, and Twitter. I introduce these other social platforms, help you identify which ones are most appropriate for your marketing needs, and guide you through the process of determining how best to market on them.

Exploring the Niche Social Networks

So what are these niche social platforms that I'm talking about? Table 7-1 outlines the top 20 social networking platforms as of February 2009 from comScore, a marketing research company. Keep in mind that although this categorization uses the term *social networks* very loosely, it still excludes user-generated content (UGC) video sites such as YouTube and community platforms like Ning (www.ning.com).

Table 7-1	The Top 20 Social Networking Platforms	
Social Networking Platform	Feb 2009 Unique Visitors (000)	Year Over Year Percentage of Change
MySpace	70,303	3
Facebook	57,375	77
Classmates	16,247	24
MyLife	15,345	N/A
Buzznet	8,661	66
Yahoo! Buzz	7,955	169
AOL Community	7,261	9,513
LinkedIn	6,948	110
AIM Profiles	6,928	−13
Digg	6,917	25
Bebo	5,789	N/A
Tagged	5,396	217
deviantART	4,770	29
Twitter	4,033	1,085
Hi5	3,670	35
CaringBridge	2,483	45
BlackPlanet	2,381	17
Gaia	2,325	38
AddThis	2,020	396
SodaHead	1,801	132

Arguably, by studying the monthly unique visitors and growth rates of these social platforms, you may wonder whether calling them niche platforms is even appropriate. They still have millions of unique visitors each month and, barring few exceptions, appear to be growing at a relatively brisk pace. For many people, these social platforms are more valuable and personal than MySpace, Facebook, Twitter, or YouTube.

Here's why I categorize them as niche platforms: Their size or growth rate still pales in comparison to that of the four major social platforms. These networks are typically more narrowly focused (LinkedIn is for professionals, Sermo is for physicians, and Classmates is for alumni relationships) and, in some cases, they serve as platforms only for the aggregation and distribution of social media and are less focused on the social graph.

But here's a tricky fact: When you look at the major social platforms through the lens of your target customers, you may discover that they're not spending that much time on them. It is even possible that their time spent on a niche platform or cumulatively on several niche platforms exceeds time spent on the major platforms. It becomes apparent that you need to be focusing as much attention on these niche platforms (even though there are many more of them) as you do on Facebook, YouTube, MySpace, and Twitter.

Finding the Right Social Platforms

If I were to start a new business, it would probably be a business that, through some magic formula, would tell marketers which social platforms their specific customers are spending most of their time on in a given month, with guidance on how to reach them. I would probably make a fortune for the simple reason that it's hard to find these customers beyond the major social platforms.

It's easy to learn the paid and unpaid marketing solutions on the second rung social platforms. (They're listed in Table 7-1.) What about the rest? How do you as a marketer beginning to apply social influence marketing know where your customers are spending their time? Making your job even harder is the fact that you can't just focus on the social networks: You need to look more broadly at the video Web sites, the mainstream media Web sites, the blogger networks, and social media publishing tools that are all beginning to incorporate social functionality.

To help you identify the social platforms, I'm going to share a four-step process for identifying the right social platforms on which to find your customers. But before I do that, I'd like to classify the social platforms into a more meaningful segmentation.

Classifying the social platforms

As of this writing, there are four *major social platforms*:

- ✔ Facebook
- ✔ MySpace
- ✔ YouTube
- ✔ Twitter

I classify them as the four major platforms based on their overall size and the growth rate. When you're marketing to a mass-market audience, you simply cannot ignore these platforms.

It's just a matter of time before the major media and entertainment sites incorporate so much social functionality that they'll be considered social platforms too. In fact, the *Wall Street Journal* already includes a community section and *BusinessWeek* runs Business Exchange (`http://bx.businessweek.com`), an online community to share relevant content among like-minded professionals.

Next come the *niche social platforms*. These are the ones that have a narrower focus, whether that's driven by the subject matter, the audience reached (Facebook, for example, only reached college students once upon a time), their overall size, or their core focus. LinkedIn, CafeMom, and deviantART are good examples. These platforms succeed by defining a sharp niche and owning it.

The *social platform infrastructure providers* are a separate category too. These infrastructure providers allow users to create their own social networks or blogging environments on them. Ning (`www.ning.com`) and Gather (`www.gather.com`) are among the most popular of these platforms, allowing people to set up social networks that behave similar to the way a MySpace or Facebook behaves, with member pages, community areas, and activity streams. Vox (`www.vox.com`) and Blogger (`www.blogger.com`) are other successful infrastructure providers too.

Finally, you have the *blogosphere*. Blogs rarely have any formal or technical relationship with each other, but they behave cohesively from time to time thanks to trackbacks, commenting, and the reciprocal linking that goes on between them. Blogs received 77.7 million unique visitors in the U.S. in August 2008 alone, according to comScore, and traffic to them continues to increase. In fact, four of the top ten entertainment sites are blogs.

You need to look for your customers on the major social platforms, the niche social platforms, the social infrastructure providers, and across the blogosphere, too.

Understand your customers

To discover where your customers are spending their time online, you need to begin by understanding them better. Depending upon their *sociotechnographics* (which means how your customers engage on the social platforms), they might be spending a lot of time on the major social platforms or very little. The first step in understanding them is to determine their participation levels in the social Web.

The freely available Forrester Social Technographics Tool allows you to profile your customers' social computing behavior. All you have to do is select the age range, country, and gender of the people you want to research. The tool then returns an analysis of your customers, dividing them up into creators, critics, collectors, joiners, spectators, and inactives. The tool currently includes only 11 countries, but that number is sure to increase over time. It is a useful starting point for understanding your customers. You can find the tool at `www.forrester.com/Groundswell/profile_tool.html`.

Quantcast (`www.quantcast.com`) is useful to understand the audience profile of someone using a social platform. Just type the Web site address of the social platform, and the tool returns demographics information for that Web site. In some cases, it may even go deeper and include user segmentation responses as well.

The third form of research (and my favorite way) is to actually talk to your customers. Conduct social influence research to discover how they use the Web, whether they socialize online, where that takes place, and how their friends and networks influence them. Even a small sample of users can yield a lot of valuable information about their online behaviors and the social platforms that they're engaging on. Often, the best way to do that is to ask interviewees to come in for the interviews with a few friends and observe them interact with each other. You can then supplement this in-person form of research with site surveys to get statistically significant results.

And then of course, you can also research what consumers are saying online about the product, company, or brand. Using the research tools discussed in Chapter 2, you can understand where these conversations are taking place and how your customers think. Don't ignore peeking into these conversations, as sometimes it's more insightful than any other form of research.

Social behavior online is changing at a rapid pace, so consider putting an ongoing social research program in place. The ways your customers use the social Web probably change every three to six months. You want to be ahead of those changes, so ongoing research is important.

Research the platforms

Just as it is extremely important to understand your customers and where they're spending their time online, and with whom, it's extremely important to research the social dynamics of the various social platforms. It's no use proposing a social influence marketing strategy that covers YouTube if you don't really know how marketers can and are allowed to use YouTube. Nor will your marketing efforts be a success if those marketing efforts, even if YouTube allows them, are out of sync with how users expect to use that social platform.

I've discussed how you can market on the major social platforms, covering Facebook, MySpace, YouTube, and Twitter, but there's more to the social Web than those platforms. Knowing what is permissible and appropriate for the other social platforms can be a tricky. There aren't any hard and fast rules and the advertising industry is just beginning to establish guidelines, advertising formats, and best practices.

Keep an eye on the Social Media Subcommittee of the Interactive Advertising Bureau (`www.iab.net/member_center/councils_committees_ working_groups/committees/social_media_committee`), which is currently working to define best practices for advertising in social media. Expect to see valuable recommendations from them in the near future. Also watch the Social Media Advertising Consortium (`www.smac.org`), which includes representatives from agencies, brands, and publishers. It's focusing on defining standards for ad units, a common vocabulary, and best practices.

Although a lot of the marketing tactics on the social platforms are still in their infancy, a few practices and standards are starting to emerge. These can be classified as follows:

- ✔ **Traditional display advertising:** Think of these as display banners that you see elsewhere across the Internet. These banner ads generally have cookie-based behavioral and other forms of targeting overlaid on top of them. They're sold and measured as traditional display banners are (primarily through CPMs, or cost per impressions, and CTRs, or click-through rates).

- ✔ **Social advertisements:** These ad formats bring a person's social graph into the ad unit itself, encouraging engagement (imagine if you saw a friend's photograph in an advertisement) or pushing similar advertisements to friends of a person who clicked a specific advertisement. Sometimes these social advertisements include user-generated content and are targeted based on browsing patterns of friends in a network.

- ✔ **Sponsorships:** Drawing inspiration from the advertorials of print publishing, these ad formats encourage bloggers specifically to discuss certain topics. You can establish specific rules governing what can be blogged about, but the bloggers have a lot of freedom too. When you see these posts, they're typically marked as sponsored ones. Sponsorships are becoming more popular on Twitter, too, although, keep in mind that some bloggers find pay per post formats and incentives distasteful.

- ✔ **Influencer marketing:** Social platforms like CafeMom give you access to influencers who are given assignments to perform and then discuss the results on their blogs or their social platforms. For example, Kohl's gave CafeMom influencers gift cards and opportunities to explore their favorite colors at Kohl's stores. Each mom then returned to the site and wrote about their shopping experiences.

- ✔ **Widgets and applications:** Several social platforms allow the creation, launch, and seeding of widgets and applications on their platforms.

read the small print you'll see that directory compilers do not guarantee the truth of the information agencies send them. They have no way of doing so.

When researching agencies, always consult the most recent directories you can find, and compare listings between different directories. (Some agencies will be listed only in the NAIC Directory.) This way you won't accidentally miss a good prospect because it wasn't in the one directory you looked at.

8

INDEPENDENT ADOPTION

a. A CONSUMER'S LOOK AT ADOPTION FACILITATION SERVICES

Two-thirds of infant adoptions in the United States are carried out independently. International adoptions are often independently contracted. The primary appeal of independent adoption is that it allows adopters to make an adoption plan directly with birth parents and/or their representatives, bypassing agency gatekeepers. Issues such as age, sexual orientation, marital status, and religion are not barriers. Adopters must merely meet their state's legal definition of who may adopt, find birth parents who agree to place a child with them, obtain a home study, and, if everyone is satisfied with the plan after the child's birth, petition a court to approve the adoption. With the exception of the six states discussed in section (e) below, independent adoption is permitted in the U.S. as long as it is carried out lawfully.

The boom in independent adoption has led to the development of sophisticated adoption facilitation services. Today, some are provided through licensed adoption agencies. Others are independent businesses. Adoption attorneys have law practices that are — in essence — facilitation businesses spanning the country. Some independent facilitation services are volunteer operations, staffed by adopters who wish to share their experience with other hopeful parents. Like adoption attorneys, these facilitators are not usually licensed as agencies, since they don't acquire custody of the children, do home studies, or make placement decisions. Facilitators may help adopters locate birth

144

parents and advise them how to present themselves in order to interest birth parents in placing with them. A facilitator may do as little as bringing an adopter to the attention of a pregnant woman or as much as shepherding adopters through the full process and representing them in court.

Today, birth parents are more likely to choose independent adoption because it allows them to exercise more control over who parents their child and the degree of contact with the adoptive family. It allows them to minimize contact with social workers they may perceive as judgmental and intimidating. Birth parents with prior experience of social service bureaucracy may be reluctant to place themselves in agency hands. Unfortunately, this sometimes leads to their being taken advantage of by unscrupulous facilitators whose interest is to provide a newborn baby to adopter clients, not to help birth parents make an important life decision.

When evaluating facilitators, try to compare fees between services which are roughly equivalent. Independent adoption has the most fee variability of all adoptions. If you use a volunteer facilitator, do a lot of the work yourself, and your birth mother has full medical coverage, your entire adoption could cost as little as $2,000. On the other hand, if you use a nationally known attorney, do little work yourself, and pay all medical expenses, if the process of obtaining birth parent consents is complicated, and if the birth mother has a difficult delivery such as a caesarean section, your fee could be $20,000 or more. Some expenses can be anticipated, but you will need to allow for unforeseen contingencies. Adoption insurance might be worth investigating.

In planning an independent adoption, it is important to use an ethical, competent facilitator. You will be responsible for the adoption and your family will have to live with the results. While national adoption advocacy organizations have collected statistics on agencies, no complete compilation of facilitation services has been made. A few books list adoption attorneys, but since many facilitators are part-time businesses or off-shoots of other professions such as law and social work, it may be difficult to identify services for the purpose of comparison.

Although your state licensing authority may not directly regulate a facilitation service, they may be able to tell you if they know of or have received complaints about it. Some facilitators are adoption professionals who worked in adoption agencies first and have a reputation within the adoption community. The agency, usually the attorney general's department responsible for consumer protection, may also have information. And while it's a long shot, don't forget to check with the Better Business Bureau.

Choosing a new, unlicensed facilitation service is risky. If it has no track record, it may be difficult to evaluate. That doesn't mean that the service will be bad, simply that you will have little information to go on.

Facilitation services offered by attorneys are easier to evaluate. Adoption is a legal subspecialty. Lawyers who specialize in adoption or devote a considerable percentage of their practice to it, are usually members of the adoption bar. You can check with your local or state bar association to ascertain the experience of your attorney.

Social workers are also subject to regulation. Check with a professional social work organization, such as the American Council of Social Workers and/or the state adoption specialist. Don't assume that because an adoption facilitator advertises in an adoption periodical such as *Ours,* it is a good source. No adoption periodical has resources to investigate the credentials of its advertisers. While they would not knowingly accept advertising from an illegal facilitator, they have no way to verify that a facilitator is operating legally.

b. LOCATING FACILITATORS

Contact adoption agencies and ask if they facilitate independent adoptions. Some offer programs in which they help

You can either sponsor popular widgets or create new utilitarian or entertainment ones that fulfill a specific purpose for the users and have a tie-in with a brand. When launched, these widgets are promoted by the social platform and typically include a media buy as well. Sponsored music players on MySpace and myYearbook (www.myyearbook.com), for example, are becoming quite common.

✔ **Brand pages:** Just as the major social platforms allow for the creation of brand pages, so too do the other social platforms. These may differ in functionality and purpose based on the platform, but they're all virtual homes where you can promote your products, showcase your latest advertising, and launch promotions and contests. They can often include games, screensavers, desktop backgrounds, iconography, and the ability to recruit fans.

✔ **Gifting:** Mimicking Facebook's extremely successful gifting program, more and more niche social platforms offer gifting-related advertising. You can offer users gifts, such as a virtual birthday cake or chocolates, that they can share with their friends. The gifts are extremely viral, and the advertising buy runs out once the gifts have.

✔ **Other promotional opportunities:** Most niche social platforms offer other similar related branding opportunities. These include sponsoring different parts of the social platform, sponsoring applications, polls, and contests. Other opportunities include pairing members together to accomplish tasks, sharing database information for remarketing and customer research purposes, and social merchandising.

Advertising formats for the social Web are in a state of flux. New ad formats are emerging just as old ones are being retired. The rules for advertising on the Internet are changing too as a result. The advertising formats by definition cannot be totally comprehensive.

If you're looking for guidance on blogger outreach and are worried about harassing bloggers and losing their support, take a look at The Ogilvy Blogger Outreach Code of Ethics (http://rohitbhargava.typepad.com/weblog/2007/09/the-ogilvy-blog.html). It includes some excellent recommendations.

RFP the vendors

After you've decided which social platforms are appropriate for your target audience and have a sense of what can be accomplished on them, consider issuing requests for proposals (RFPs). It may become a time consuming effort but it helps you in the long run. The RFPs matter if your marketing effort is going to exceed $7,500. If you're planning on spending less on your marketing efforts, it may be better to use the cheaper, less sophisticated, self-service tools provided by the major social platforms. Here are some pointers to consider when issuing RFPs:

✔ **Describe your objectives explicitly.**

The social platforms are vying for your business. The more explicit and specific you can be about your marketing and campaign objectives, the more the social platforms can provide a response that meets your needs. Don't shy away from telling them exactly what they need to know. This means describing your audiences in incredible detail too. You're fundamentally looking to match your audiences with theirs and build engagement around it. Some social platforms are invariably a better fit than others.

✔ **Be clear about your benchmarks for success.**

The social platforms need to understand how you're going to measure the success of your marketing efforts. It's important to be very clear about those benchmarks, as you'll probably be holding the platforms to them as well. Most social platforms (as well as other publishers on the Internet) would rather know how they're going to be measured before participating in an RFP. Accordingly, a few of them may even choose to drop out of the process. They're always more interested in a long-term mutually beneficial relationship than a one-off partnership that hurts their credibility.

✔ **Recognize that you're getting free advice.**

When you're issuing a request for proposals you're asking the social platforms to prove why they're the right places for you to market. But not only are you getting their credentials, you are also getting a lot of great ideas too. As a result, it's important to be completely fair and transparent during the RFP process. Even if you do not choose a specific platform, you're going to learn a lot from them while going through the RFP process. Furthermore, they'd have put a lot of time and effort into responding to the proposal. You owe it to them to be transparent, clear, and appreciative of their efforts. Providing feedback on why you didn't choose them when you can is also important.

✔ **Beware that you can be limited by who you RFP.**

When issuing RFPs, it's easy to forget that you're limiting yourself by whom you ask to participate in the RFP process. Therefore, choose who you invite to participate in the RFP process carefully. Make sure that you're casting a wide net and are including all the different types of platforms that may be able to help you achieve your marketing objectives.

For example, social platform vendors that provide appvertising solutions on Facebook, like Buddy Media (www.buddymedia.com) or Context Optional (www.contextoptional.com), may get left off of the RFP process because they're neither social platforms or social platform infrastructure providers. They sit somewhere in between. The same applies to a social gaming company like Playfish (www.playfish.com), which provides some exciting opportunities for advertisers reaching specific audiences.

Evaluate and plan strategically

Planning is, of course, the most important step. As you plan your SIM campaign on a niche platform, you want to make sure that you're reaching the audiences that you want to and are engaging with them in an authentic, transparent, and meaningful fashion. Choosing the niche platform is always part art and part science. I've spent time discussing the science part of the question — how you find where your audiences are, what they're doing, and what tactics are most appropriate.

So now I want to look at the art piece of the equation. This means having an intuitive sense for the following items:

- **Knowing which social platforms can extend or strengthen your brand.**

  You don't want your brand to be tightly associated with a social platform that has a mixed reputation.

- **Having a sense of which social platforms are on the verge of breaking out and growing in size and scale.**

  Victoria's Secret Pink practiced SIM on Facebook in its early days and those efforts have paid off today. What's the next Facebook?

- **Being able to separate the wheat from the chaff.**

  This matters especially with the niche social platforms. Because hundreds of them are out there, many of which have a lot of traffic, knowing which ones have meaningful social engagement and can help you achieve your marketing objectives can be tricky.

- **Thinking beyond audiences and reach.**

  Traditional advertising online has always focused on audiences and where they are. But with social influence marketing, you have to think in terms of the influencers and the exponential value of their participation and engagement. Don't just use the traditional display banner metrics.

- **Being in it for the long run and not getting impatient.**

  Social influence marketing requires patience: the patience to build relationships, to test, to learn and optimize, and to think beyond the confines of a campaign. These philosophies apply all the more when you're practicing SIM on the niche platforms. They may not give you the results that you want on the first day or the first month or the first quarter, but they've been proven to showcase strong results over the long term.

- **Thinking holistically and strategically.**

  Most importantly, think holistically about your social influence marketing efforts. Think about how you want your marketing efforts on the niche platforms to work with those on the major social platforms and on your own Web site too. Don't treat them all as separate, disjointed marketing efforts. They need to work together. And ideally, these marketing efforts should also be coordinated with offline marketing efforts too where one feeds the other.

Moving Beyond the Platforms and the Blogosphere

A discussion about marketing in the social Web would be incomplete without addressing the role that companies, which create new advertising opportunities on the social platforms, play. For lack of a better name, I call them social platform enhancers. They're not social platforms and do not have their own audiences. Nor are they advertising agencies or public relations firms who can help you market on the social platforms. Some of them function as advertising networks that sit on top of the social platforms, whereas others are more similar to software companies that build applications and widgets for the social platforms and the blogosphere. Regardless of how they fit into the social ecosystem, they play an important role and you can harness them for marketing purposes. In the next few sections, I discuss a few of the types of social platform enhancers.

Social advertising network

The first type of platform enhancer is the advertising network. Many of the most successful applications on Facebook belong to networks of applications that solicit advertising in a unified fashion by aggregating audiences. Sometimes the network is just one application developer who owns and manages a series of extremely popular applications. In other cases, several application providers band together to form a network and solicit advertising. RockYou (www.rockyou.com), SocialMedia.com (www.socialmedia.com), and Slide (www.slide.com) are the leading advertising networks that reside within Facebook and MySpace. Their Facebook and MySpace applications serve as a home for brand advertising. Through them, you can place branded ads, application promotions, and integrated sponsorships next to specific applications on those social platforms.

Appvertisement providers

In conjunction with the advertising network are the platform enhancers who build appvertisements for brands. These *appvertisements* combine the best of advertisements with useful or entertaining applications: hence the name *appvertisement*. These appvertisements harness a person's social graph and are designed to provide meaningful value to users, often by having them contribute and personalize the application. This can be in the form of entertainment, information, or a utility that can sit within a social environment like a Facebook profile page. They're designed to be social in nature, encouraging people to install the application and have their friends install it too. These appvertisement providers work with your advertising agency to define and build the appvertisement and then guarantee a certain number of paid installations by leveraging the social advertising networks. Gigya (www.gigya.com), BuddyMedia (www.buddymedia.com), and ContextOptional (www.contextoptional.com) are all examples of appvertisement providers.

Blogger networks

Approximately 10 million active blogs are on the Internet, of which probably not more than 10,000 have significant traffic. But even reaching these bloggers can be challenging. It's a question of scale. As a marketer, you certainly don't have time to reach out to 10,000 bloggers yourself. This is where blogger networks enter the picture. Every day, more and more bloggers are organizing into blogger networks that represent them. The representatives align marketers with the appropriate blogs, promote the blogger network, manage the relationships with the bloggers, and handle all advertiser relations. Many blogger networks also have dashboards that allow you to choose different advertising options by selecting audiences, specific topics, and blogs through which you want to market. The most important blogger network is probably Federated Media (www.federatedmedia.net), which represents probably 200–300 of the most influential blogs covering most topics. BlogHer (www.blogher.com) is another important blogger network, representing women bloggers. Six Apart (www.sixapart.com) also has a very active blogger network. In the case of Six Apart, as with Technorati, their blogger networks represent blogs that reside on their own platforms. Some of the other blogger networks include PayingPost (www.payingpost.com), BuzzLogic (www.buzzlogic.com), and Adphilia (www.adphilia.com).

Taking Care of the Unpaid Media Basics

No marketing effort on the niche platforms is complete if you ignore all the possibilities on the unpaid side of the equation too. The social platforms, which depend on advertising as revenue, may not always be keen for you to deploy these tactics.

In the following sections, I discuss some tactics to consider in the unpaid realm.

These platforms afford the opportunity and as long as you're not disrupting the platforms, breaking any privacy rules, or irritating the users on them, these tactics are fair game.

Wikipedia

You should always research how your company or brand is represented on Wikipedia (www.wikipedia.org), which is the free encyclopedia that anybody can edit. When you do find your company page, don't pepper it with marketing-speak. The page will just be reedited to the original version. Instead, read the page carefully and correct any misrepresentations. Shy away from promoting your company or products. Instead, point to complimentary articles. In fact, most social media professionals believe that you should never edit your own Wikipedia page, as it may be considered a clear conflict of interest. Those professionals encourage brands to only comment on the discussion tab.

Flickr

This photo sharing Web site (www.flickr.com) is starting to act and feel more and more like a social network. You'll want to search your brand and company name on it to see what photographs are associated with your company. If photographs have been uploaded by someone else and tagged with your company name, you just have to live with them. However, you can also publish your own corporate and product imagery so that users know your own digital photography. I recommend setting up an official company account to share photographs, run contests, and encourage others to publish photographs, too.

Delicious

This bookmarking site (www.delicious.com) is extremely popular: Consumers use it to store their Web site bookmarks and to find other useful Web sites. All that you have to do here is make sure that your corporate Web site and any brand or product sites that you may have are bookmarked and tagged with your company name.

Digg

Here's another site (www.digg.com) that looks and feels like a social network but isn't. Digg is fundamentally a user-powered news aggregator. Each time you have an interesting piece of news to share about your company or product, publish it to Digg. Depending upon its newsworthiness, it may get voted to the top of a category, giving you an immense amount of free publicity.

Message boards

Regardless of how you use the social platforms, you'll want to know what conversations are happening on the message boards about your company and brand. The best way to do this is to use a service like BoardReader (www.boardreader.com) to scan the message boards for you. Here again, how you participate depends on the specific message board, the type of discussion, and whether you have to deal with a factual error, slander, or just category information. You'll have to make the judgment call for yourself.

Chapter 8

Accounting for the Influencers

*I*n Chapter 1, I briefly introduce the social influencers and how they affect purchasing decisions. In this chapter, I discuss social influencers in greater detail and explain why they matter, how you can reach them, and what best practices to deploy in the process of doing so. I focus on the social influencers who reside within the social graphs of your customers and how you can account for them in all your marketing efforts. Some of the concepts in this chapter rightly seem to draw inspiration from influencer marketing, with its roots in the public relations world, whereas other concepts will feel very different.

Knowing the Expert Influencers

How influencers are defined is a controversial subject among marketers. Some marketers' focus on what they consider to be key influencers, whereas others place more emphasis on everyday influencers. Back in the Chapter 1, I introduced the three types of social influencers, which I believe accounts for all the types of influence taking place around a customer. Here's a quick recap of them.

- ✔ **Referent influencers** are in a friend's social graph, but they may not be tightly connected with the user.

- ✔ **Positional influencers** are that inner circle around the user and often have to live with the choices of the purchasing decision.

- ✔ **Expert influencers** are considered authorities in the specific domain or are people whom others depend upon for information advice. They do a lot to build awareness and affect purchasing decisions at the consideration stage.

I'm now going to further delve into the social influencer categories, starting with the expert influencers.

The *Word of Mouth Marketing Association Handbook* explains that there are five types of influencers who you need to account for. When you think of expert influencers, be sure to cover these five types:

- ✔ People in formal positions of authority
- ✔ Individuals or institutions that are recognized as subject matter experts
- ✔ Media elites (journalists, commentators, and talk show hosts)
- ✔ Cultural elites (celebrities, artists, and musicians)
- ✔ Socially connected individuals (neighborhood leaders, members of community groups, online networks, and business networkers)

You can find out more about the Word of Mouth Marketing Association, shown in Figure 8-1, at www.womma.org.

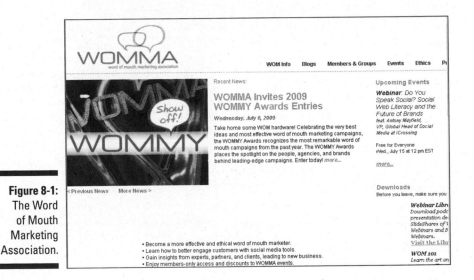

Figure 8-1: The Word of Mouth Marketing Association.

As you scan the preceding list, three thoughts might cross your mind:

- ✔ **Your PR department is already taking care of this.**

   The first is that your public relations department is probably concerned with these expert influencers and is already developing relationships with them. That's good news and it should be encouraged. The question to ask your PR department is whether they're nurturing the relationships with these expert influencers online via all the social platforms on which these expert influencers have set up presences. It's not enough to know what the expert influencers are doing and saying in the physical world — you need to track their activity, commentary, and points of view online too. And most importantly, you need to build relationships with these influencers online as well.

✔ **You're not sure these influencers matter online.**

The second thought that might cross your mind is that you don't know their relative importance to each other. You may also wonder whether you *do* need to track their online activities. If you're a marketer in a small business or maybe a CEO in a small business that doesn't have a formal marketing department, you may wonder whether it is even possible to develop a relationship with these expert influencers online. Will they even care what you think? Will they even respond to your tweets, Facebook friend requests, and prodding e-mails? Those are all valid questions.

✔ **You have the wrong list of influencers.**

The final thing you may wonder about is whether you even have the right list of expert influencers. Thanks to the excesses of several mammoth corporations, we now live in an age where trust in formal authority is at an all-time low. An April 2009 article in *The Economist* emphasized that consumers are increasingly distrusting big business and are turning to each other for advice. The experts that your consumers depended upon when making purchasing decisions two years ago may not be the very same experts that they are looking towards today.

What does all this mean? Quite simply, it means that you must begin by analyzing who are the expert influencers affecting brand affinity and purchasing decisions for your consideration set. They may be all the people that your PR department is currently tracking, but that list of people may have changed too. You need to know who these expert influencers are, where they are active online, whether it is feasible to even develop a relationship with them on the social platforms in which they are participating, and, finally, how much influence they actually have.

Other departments within your company may already have relationships with the expert influencers. That's a good thing. Find out whether existing relationships are in place before knocking on the doors of the expert influencers. They certainly don't want to be harassed by multiple people from one company.

Recognizing the importance of influence

Research published by Harvard Business School professor Sunil Gupta in May 2009 is the latest proof point in a long series of research demonstrating that friends influence purchasing decisions on social networks. Dr. Gupta analyzed user behavior on the Korean social network Cyworld and discovered that there's a significant and positive impact of friends' purchases on the purchase probability of a user. That means that when a user buys something, he influences his friends to make a similar purchase too. But he also saw that this only happened among 40 percent of the users who have middle-status and are moderately connected on a social network.

Other research dissects the social influence on purchasing behavior differently. For example,

on average, 31 percent of online adults rely on friends' recommendations a lot when making purchasing decisions, and 44 percent of adults tell friends about products that interest them, according to Forrester Research. Social influence across the social platforms and on Web sites does impact purchasing behavior; although, how much depends on a variety of factors such as the platform, the type of purchase, and the users involved. How significant the influence is may be quite different for your product versus another. But whatever you do, don't ignore this influence and the social influencers because their role could be significant.

Reaching the Expert Influencers

Different strategies exist for reaching and activating the expert influencers. How you reach them varies based on who they are, what you want them to accomplish, and where you think you have the best chance of establishing a relationship with them. This could be by introducing yourself to them at conferences, replying to their tweets, commenting on their blog posts, or friending them in Facebook. It all depends. The good news is that influencers like to influence and, as long as you have a promising value proposition, they will at the very least listen to you.

Keep in mind that nurturing expert influencers is an investment in the long term and you may not always get the response you want from them immediately. Also remember that influencers draw their strength and importance from being unbiased, independent, and credible. Don't ask them to compromise that position.

Expert influencers like to be in the know. Provide them with exclusive sneak peeks and they'll be grateful for the opportunity to see and talk about your product before anyone else does. You can use that access to information to deepen your relationship with them.

Reaching the expert influencers may be easy depending upon your industry, the size of your business, and the product you are selling. But for other marketers, that may not be the case. For example, if you're a marketer for a small business, reaching expert influencers is going to be even harder because these people may not be high-profile or visible. You'll have to really seek them out. Here are some tips for reaching expert influencers:

- **Ask your customers whom they seek out for advice.**

  There is little in marketing that beats first-hand customer research, and the same applies to social influence marketing. You can identify and reach the expert influencers by asking your consumers who they are and where they spend their time.

- **Pay attention to the media.**

  Keep an eye out for the experts who are quoted frequently by the media when your product or category is discussed. Also keep an eye out for who appears on television. Make a list of these experts and use that list as a basis to research their influence.

- **Look at your competitive environment.**

  Your competitors, suppliers, and business partners probably seek out the experts just as you do. In many cases, these experts sit on the advisory boards of other companies that operate in your space. Understand who these people are. A lot of that information is freely available online.

- **Attend conferences and exhibitions.**

  The expert influencers are often called upon to give keynote addresses to industry conferences, lead seminars, and pass judgment on new products and services at exhibitions. Pay attention to these people at those events.

- **Seek out the industry analysts.**

  The analysts often have an outsized influence on customers in your product category. Their influence increases dramatically in the business-to-business space, where customers depend upon them for advice when making large-scale purchasing decisions. Pay attention to them and to what they have to say.

- **Evaluate their online footprint.**

  Tools like Technorati (www.technorati.com), as shown in Figure 8-2, rank all blogs based on the number of inbound links to them. Search the rankings by your product category and see which independent blogs rank high. Those bloggers are expert influencers to develop a relationship with. Use other professional tools for the rankings, such as the Alexa scores (www.alexa.com), the Google PageRank, the number of RSS subscribers (often listed on the blog itself), and proprietary technology like the influencer identification ones from Collective Intellect (www.collectiveintellect.com).

✔ **Become an influencer yourself.**

Sometimes there's no better way to influence than to become an influencer yourself. Seek out leadership positions in your community and in your industry by joining trade groups and industry associations. You'll become an influencer and will get access to other influencers.

Figure 8-2:
The
Technorati
home page.

Tapping into the Referent Influencers

Until recently, there was no way to reach referent influencers. In fact, in conversations about influencers, there'd be no mention of the referent influencers because they couldn't be identified and therefore were not even thought about. Marketers had no way of identifying them, tracking their behavior, or marketing towards them specifically. For all practical purposes, they did not exist. That's now changed because consumers connect with their friends and make their social graphs available through the social networks.

Social graphs are commonly defined as the global mapping of everyone in the world and how they are related to each other. When I refer to an individual's *social graph*, I'm referring to who is mapped to that individual and how he relates to that individual. Referent influencers are people in your friendship circle, such as your high school friends or people you've become friendly with at work. You may be close to only a few of them, but you probably observe the activities of them all on your favorite social platform.

The holy grail of social influence marketing is increasingly considered the ability to identify which referent influencers are most powerful and have the highest impact on brand affinity and purchasing decisions. After you've identified them, the next question is, how does a marketer reach these referent influencers that surround their customers? They matter because it has been statistically proven that networked neighbors (or those consumers linked to prior customer) adopt the service or product at rates three to five times greater than baseline groups. The research also shows that these network neighbors impact purchasing decisions very directly too.

The referent influencers themselves break down into two categories, which I cover next, and it is important to differentiate between the two.

Anonymous referent influencers

These are everyday people who are extremely active on the social platforms and blog, upload, comment, rate, and share much more than other consumers who share their same demographics. By virtue of the volume of their activity on the various social platforms, the anonymous referent influencers carry weight. Your customers probably don't think of them as experts, but they do notice what these people are doing online.

Known referent influencers

These are the everyday people who reside specifically within the social graphs of your customers and are known to your customer. The best way to think about this group is to consider your high school class. Of the approximately 300 kids who may have been in the class, there were probably 10 or 15 who everyone else looked up to and followed. These are the cool kids who everyone wanted to be like even though they may not have known them well. These are the referent influencers.

Marketing to the referent influencers is all about knowing who they are, the weight they carry, whether they reside within your customer's social graph, and how to reach and activate them to influence your customer.

Reaching the Referent Influencers

Referent influencers are not that easily reached. Most social platforms do not allow marketers to mine the social graphs of their users, so identifying these people and reaching them can be challenging. As a result, it can be difficult to identify these referent influencers and activate them.

But there's good news too. Some enterprising advertising technology companies have been researching ways to reach these referent influencers without compromising the privacy of your customers or their circle of friends. Reaching the referent influencers through these methods is safe and reliable, although it does cost you money, with the amount depending on how many referent influencers you're trying to reach. In the next few sections, I discuss how these companies help you reach the referent influencers.

Not all tactics for reaching referent influencers need to be paid for. Your company's Facebook page can be a great place to build a community and encourage referent influencers to influence your customers by incentivizing them with competitions, coupons, and special offers. Your customers who fan your Facebook page will probably bring their referent influencers to the page too if you give them incentives to do so.

Social graph analysis

Using database technologies, companies can crawl the major social networks in a similar fashion to the way the search engines crawl the Internet's Web pages. These companies can create a mapping of users and how they relate to each other on the major social platforms. They can also capture personality attributes of the users, the number of friends they have, how active they are on a social platform, and whether their friends respond to actions that they take. Companies in this space include Unbound Technologies (www.unboundtechnologies.com) and Rapleaf (www.rapleaf.com), which use metrics like friend count, social persuasion track record, and *influence context measurement* (meaning how the subject matter affects influence) to identify the influencers.

These advertising technology companies map your e-mail database against their social graph database to determine the overlapping customers and to identify the influential ones from the mix. That serves as a starting point for you to then market to the referent influencers and encourage them to talk about a brand.

A place to get started creating your own social graph is with Google's Social Graph API, as shown in Figure 8-3, at http://code.google.com/apis/socialgraph. This lets you add social functionality to your own Web site encouraging your friends and customers to join the mini-social network.

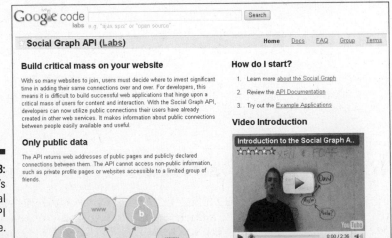

Figure 8-3:
Google's
Social
Graph API
page.

Cookie data

Other technology companies analyze cookie data to infer the relationships between people and target similar advertising to them both. If one set of users responds well to the advertisements, they then present the same advertisements to other similar people or to the friends of the original group in similar social networks, conversations, or Web sites as the original set of users. It allows for your advertising to reach anonymous referent influencers. Keep in mind here that this applies only if you have an advertising budget and are advertising online. Otherwise, you won't be able to take advantage of the cookie data. Two companies that focus on this are 33Across (www.33across.com) and Media6Degrees (www.media6degrees.com).

Web site behavior

You can do a lot on your Web site to allow for the referent influencers to converge and positively influence each other. From the most basic of solutions, like implementing customer reviews, to creating discussion forums where customers can talk about issues of concern, your Web site can be a destination where people congregate and talk to each other. Recent developments like Facebook Connect, which is discussed in the next chapter, address how you can more directly enable your prospective customers to bring their referent influencers to your Web site.

Once you've identified these referent influencers, be sure to give them the best possible service if they're customers as well. Not only will you increase the sales from them but you'll also increase sales among the people that they influence directly. As a recent *Huffington Post* article pointed out, American Express gives its influencers (who they identify by how much they spend) a distinct credit card with special benefits that include a concierge service and first-class upgrades.

Use this group to improve your products and services, too. They're typically people who have strong opinions, care about the products, and want to impact product design. Ask their opinions — or at the very least, share new products with them — before you do so with anyone else. Similarly, also consider giving them special discounts and coupons and cultivate their loyalty by marketing to them with additional care.

Tapping into the Positional Influencers

Finally, there are the positional influencers. These are the people who are closest to your customers and influence them the most at the point of purchase. Because they are the people who have to live with the purchasing decision, they are the most vested in it too. But they're not celebrities, so they're not always noticeable and can be the hardest to find. They're important, but marketing to them can be similarly difficult.

What makes tapping into the positional influencers harder still is the fact that how big a role they play in a purchasing decision varies dramatically by the purchase. For example, if I were to buy a desk for my apartment, my wife (arguably the most important positional influencer in my life) would have a huge impact on the purchasing decision. Her opinions would heavily influence where I shop and what I choose. On the other hand, if I were purchasing a laptop for professional use, she'd play a much smaller role in the purchasing decision. This is because the choice doesn't impact her significantly and the product isn't of interest to her even though it's a high consideration purchase.

Without a doubt, positional influencers are important. Identifying them can be challenging, as can developing an understanding of the weight they may carry.

Sometimes it may be hard to separate the referent influencers from the positional influencers, especially when you're marketing on a social platform. In those cases, it doesn't matter as much. What matters is that your customers should be provided incentives to bring their influencers to you so that you can market to them as well. Focus on that, and the right influencers will get influenced, and then they'll do the influencing for you!

The following sections cover tips to allow for positional influencers to play the role they normally do best.

Understand the circles of influence around your customers

Most important is to understand who will be most impacted by the purchasing decisions of your customers. That alone will tell you who the positional influencers are and how important their influence is. For example, with first-time car purchases, family members are very important positional influencers because they'll be riding in the car and, in some cases, driving it too.

Let consumers shape and share the experience

It may be hard for you to reach those positional influencers, but your customers will reach them for you. Make sure that your e-commerce Web site or even your campaign-centric microsite allows for the sharing of content and posting to Facebook and other social platforms. Let the consumers shape and share the experiences in any format that they want. Make it easy for customers to pluck information off your Web site and carry it elsewhere and to their positional influencers.

Articulate your product benefits for multiple audiences

You probably always assume that you're selling a product to your target customer, ignoring the fact that social influencers play a big role in the purchasing decision. If you know who the influencers are, articulate your product benefits so that they resonate with the influencers too. To go back to car purchases once more: If you're selling a car to a college student demographic, tout the safety benefits because the students' parents will most probably be involved in the purchasing decision. Don't ignore them.

Fish where the fish are

This is becoming a cliché in social influence marketing, but the point holds strongest in the context of positional influencers. As these influencers are the hardest to find yourself, you need to make sure that you're marketing and selling your products where these positional influencers probably influence your customers. So it goes without saying that you need to have a deep presence on all the social platforms where your customers and their influencers are congregating. But it also means that you need to design your Web site or your presence on the social platforms to encourage your customers to reach out to those positional influencers. You need to include the basic ShareThis functionality that lets a user take product information from your Web site and socialize it with her influencers. You can start by allowing users to share your Web site info with ShareThis, as shown in Figure 8-4, at www.sharethis.com.

Badges and promotions

As consumers, we buy products for many different reasons. The product purchase can be a necessity, a comfort, or a luxury. It can also be a status symbol or a statement about your own identity. Whatever it may be, you want to make sure that you give your customers a way to promote their purchase among their peer group. You want them to be able to tell their referent and positional influencers what they've purchased and how it'll benefit them. As a result, it is important to allow for additional *badging*, which is the ability for your customer to announce his affinity with your product by placing a badge of it on his blog, social network profile, or Web site.

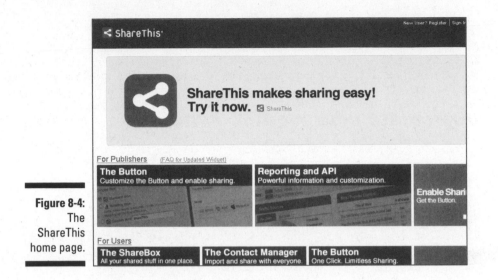

< ShareThis·

Figure 8-4:
The
ShareThis
home page.

Friends and family incentives

When talking about social influencers and the role they play in brand affinity and purchasing decisions, it is easy to forget that many marketers have been practicing these concepts in the physical world for decades. One of the most popular examples of reaching out to social influencers is in the form of "friends and family" incentives. As I write this chapter, AT&T has introduced a special family plan for its mobile phone service. If your whole family uses the service, you get discounts on the monthly plan. The best way to engage the positional influencers around your customers is to have your customers engage them for you. You get them to engage the positional influencers by giving them incentives to do so or by converting the purchasing decision into a group decision.

Translating Influence to the Offline World

For all the discussions about social influencers, I would be remiss if it didn't discuss how this concept ties into influence in the offline space. The online world is not completely separated from how influence works in the real world. The following sections include recommendations for how you can tap into social influencers to affect physical world purchasing decisions.

Put your customer reviews in your stores

If you sell products in stores, consider putting the customer reviews that have been created by customers on your Web site next to the actual products in the physical stores. If there isn't space to place customer reviews, at least include the customer ratings. Staples is one company that has already started doing this. The result is that in-store sales of products with the customer ratings have increased. Along with the customer reviews, consider adding expert reviews and ratings as well. They do a lot to give your customers confidence about the purchasing decision and also help them choose between products.

Marry social influence marketing with events and PR

Here's a tip about social influence marketing that's worth paying a lot of attention to: Marketers who tie together social influence marketing initiatives with traditional events and surround them with PR tactics invariably have immense success. When you're trying to tap into social influencers, consider organizing an event that your customers can bring their social influencers to. Promote the event heavily on the social platforms and use your presence on those platforms as a way to manage invitation lists, reminders, and post event communications. For example, send out invitations through Facebook and encourage your potential customers to RSVP through Facebook itself.

Measure online buzz and offline influence

Even though it may not always be obvious, there's a very direct relationship between online buzz and offline influence. What is talked about on the social platforms often gets translated to real world conversations when people interact with each other at work, in the shopping malls, and at home. Consider tracking how your social influence marketing activities translate into offline influence. How? By using surveys to track conversations about your brand before, during, and after a social influence marketing campaign. If you're a large brand, you may want to use a market research firm to help you understand the ongoing buzz about your brand in the physical world.

Connect influencers at meet-ups

I've talked about marrying events with social influence marketing so that your potential customers expose their influencers to your brand too. You may want to run specific programs just for the influencers who play a significant role in impacting brand and purchasing decisions in your category. Whether they be expert, referent, or positional influencers, you may want to consider organizing programs that address them directly. Some of these can be real world events too. Insurance companies put a lot of effort into developing relationships with parents of new drivers because they know they heavily impact the first car purchase. And because parents are always concerned about the well-being of their children, they're more likely to push for better auto insurance. Two services that you can use to create those events are MeetUp (www.meetup.com) and HouseParty (www.houseparty.com), which enable companies to connect with local communities around their products or categories.

Treat your stores as cybercafés

Bookstores like Barnes & Noble and Borders have blurred the lines between their physical stores and their online storefront. You can buy books online and return them in the store. You can get notifications about in-store events in your neighborhood through e-mail and encourage customers to look up books online while in the stores. They also organize readings and book clubs and encourage customers to bring their friends to them and promote the events online too. Online or offline, these bookstores don't care: They encourage deeper interaction and encourage customers to bring their social influencers with them at every stage.

Put Twitter on the big screen

Twitter is all the rage these days, and with good reason. The follow-follower dynamic and the 140-character limit lend themselves to frequent, short bursts of communication. But have you considered promoting your Twitter account in your physical stores? Or better still, have you considered having a live Twitter stream in each of your stores to show customers how you're answering the queries of others, responding to problems, promoting specific products, and deepening relationships with your community? Call it the Twitter influence, but the way in which you're interacting with your other customers on the social platforms can strongly influence a customer to purchase from you as well. Don't miss that opportunity.

Part III
Old Marketing Is New Again with SIM

The 5th Wave   By Rich Tennant

"Here's an idea. Why don't you start a social network for doofuses who think they know how to set a broken leg, but don't."

In this part . . .

In Part III, you learn how to transform your own Web site to allow for social influence marketing. I also explain what it means to be an authentic and engaged advertiser — in other words, how to take your existing advertising efforts social and get more mileage out of them.

In Chapter 9, I give you recommendations on how to retool your corporate Web site to allow for social influence marketing. In Chapter 10, I show how earned and paid media can help with your social influence marketing efforts and how to leverage your SIM efforts with offline marketing efforts. Chapter 11 discusses how to tap into the mobile phone market to spread your SIM campaign. In Chapter 12, you find out how to get your employees practicing social media marketing in your own company. Chapter 13 goes in depth on how to measure your campaign to find out how successful it was.

Chapter 9

Practicing SIM on Your Web Site

● ●

● ●

*F*or a long time, companies segregated microsites developed to support a digital marketing campaign from their corporate Web sites — for very good reasons. The corporate Web site had multiple audiences, sometimes needed to sell the product directly, and had to create a more timeless, stable impression than the microsite. The corporate site didn't just cater to prospective customers but to existing customers, shareholders, members of the press, business partners, and suppliers, too. It needed to carry information and include functionality that met all their needs. What's more, the corporate Web site needed to reflect the company's brand; the company couldn't change its look and feel based on the whims of a specific campaign.

The microsites were a different story. Companies built these mini Web sites to support display banner campaigns, and the microsites were time bound and oriented toward specific events or audiences. This could be Christmas shopping, Father's Day, or Back-to-School promotions for teenagers. Creative uses for the display banners directly reflected on the microsite, which would typically contain information about the specific offers. After all, with companies spending so much money on the display banners, they needed to drive visitors who clicked the banners to a site that extended the experience of the banner.

This strategy of separating the corporate Web site from the microsite and treating the microsite as an extension of the display banners worked for a long time. But then the social media revolution came, and it all began to change. In this chapter, I discuss why microsites aren't as valuable as they once were. I also give you recommendations on how to retool your corporate Web site to allow for social influence marketing, along with tips for opening your corporate Web site to the social Web in a meaningful fashion.

Moving Away from Microsites

Today's consumers are not as easily impressed as they once were. They want more than a campaign; they want a committed and longer-term relationship with your company to which they give their time and money. And given that you spend so much money in advertising toward your customers, it only makes sense to generate more than an impression or a single sale from your campaign. Yes, consumers will always want those short-term deals and the back-to-school offers, but they do want more.

When consumers click banner links today, they expect to be taken to a Web site that tells them everything about your product or brand that they're interested in. They want to be able to view your offer and make a purchase but also navigate the rest of your Web site. These consumers want to be able to view what else you have for sale, learn more about your company, and share that information with their friends. Having a disjointed microsite experience separate from the corporate Web site makes it more difficult for them to accomplish their goals. Today's consumers visiting your Web site don't want to just depend on your brand or company to tell them what to buy and whether the offer you're pushing at them is special. They want to draw that conclusion themselves with the assistance of their social influencers. So as you think about social influence marketing on your Web site, first and foremost, consider moving away from designing and building microsites to support online advertising campaigns. Your consumers want more.

Making the Campaign and the Web Site Work Together

The best way to make the advertising campaign and your Web site work harmoniously in a social world is to link the two. You should also link with the various social platforms on which you have a presence. In the sections that follow, I tell you how you can create those links.

Treating your Web site as a hub not a destination

The first step in practicing SIM on your Web site is recognizing that it's a hub that fits into a larger digital ecosystem supporting your brand. This digital ecosystem includes your Web site, your display banners across the Internet, your presence on various social platforms, and the conversations about your brand on blogs, the social platforms, in online communities, and discussion forums. Your purpose shouldn't be to bring people to your Web site and entice them to stay on it as long as possible. That might contradict every traditional marketing principle, but it's true.

If someone wants to know everything about your company — good, bad, or ugly — he should feel that your Web site is the best *starting point* for him.

Design your Web site as a hub versus a destination and your Web site will immediately become more valuable to your customers. Even though this may mean that you'll be pointing your consumers to external sites, they'll always treat yours as a starting point in the future.

Recently, the Mars brand Skittles redesigned its Web site (www.skittles.com) so that every navigation item links to a different social platform. No more is there a true Skittles Web site, only a home page (see Figure 9-1). When you click the Products links, you're taken to the Wikipedia page for the corresponding Skittles products. When you click a video link, you're taken to that video's YouTube page, and when you click Pics, you're directed to the Flickr page. Clicking the Friends link takes you to Skittles' Facebook page, and choosing Chatter brings up a Twitter search results page of the Skittles brand. Contact is the only link that takes you to a page on the Skittles site. And while you move between all these social platforms, the Skittles navigation box stays with you so that you can move between all the Skittles social pages very easily.

Figure 9-1:
The Skittles
Web site.

Linking prominently to your presence on social platforms

As long as customers interact with your brand, it matters little where they're interacting with it. For many consumers, the Internet is the social platform on which they share information, connect with their friends, develop business relationships, and get entertained. They're also interacting with brands on these social platforms. That's not a bad thing. Highlight your presence on these social platforms right on your Web site, too. If your customers want to interact with you on social platforms, allow them to do so by showing them how they can. For example, The Perfect Bass, a company that sells bass guitars (not fish), displays links to their other sites on their home page, as shown in Figure 9-2.

Depending on your business model and the strength of your brand, how prominently you link to the social platforms may differ. For example, if you're a luxury handbag brand that likes to entice customers by creating a feeling of mystique and exclusiveness, linking extensively to the social platforms may do more harm than good. However, if you're Coca Cola and are keen to deeply immerse yourself in the pop culture, linking to social platforms where conversations are happening (potentially about events that Coke may sponsor) becomes important.

Figure 9-2:
ThePerfect
Bass.com
displays its
social media
links.

Promoting campaigns on your Web site home page

As I mention earlier in the chapter, your corporate Web site serves many audiences and has many purposes. But that shouldn't stop you from using the featured zone on your home page to promote a campaign. That's the first step in linking the campaigns with the Web site. This may be obvious to you, but many companies don't do this. The Perfect Bass displays its products for sale on its home page, as shown in Figure 9-3.

The benefit of doing this is that once you link the two, you're creating an excuse to direct customers who have come to your Web site through your campaign to areas of your Web site where they can interact with each other. You've suddenly opened the door for social influence to take place.

If you're using featured zones on your home page to promote campaigns, it's important that you update them frequently with new promotions. No one likes to see the same promotions again and again. It implies that the company is neglecting its Web site.

Figure 9-3:
ThePerfect
Bass.com
advertises
its free
t-shirt
campaign.

Encouraging deeper interaction through your Web site

Consumers who respond to your campaign want to learn more about the products or services you're selling them, and you can do more than just provide them with that information. Instead of just bringing them the information, you can connect them with other prospective or current customers by pointing them to a discussion area on your Web site (if you have one) or third-party review sites that discuss your product. You can also introduce a live-chat feature, whereby they can talk to you and other customers in real time. More and more companies are building community functionality into their Web sites, where customers discuss potential products, critique existing ones, and exchange thoughts with one another. These communities go a long way in convincing a prospective customer to buy from you. Electro-Harmonix sponsors a forum for customers to hang out in, as shown in Figure 9-4.

Asking customers to critique the campaign

Customers feel they own a bit of your company when they're loyal to your products. They want to have the inside scoop on your company, products, and advertising campaigns, too. The behind-the-scenes advertising campaign assets fuel their interest in the company. Make sure that your TV, print, and even digital advertisements are available for your fans to view on your Web site. And allow them to critique the campaign assets and provide feedback. It serves to build trust, enthusiasm, and ownership among them.

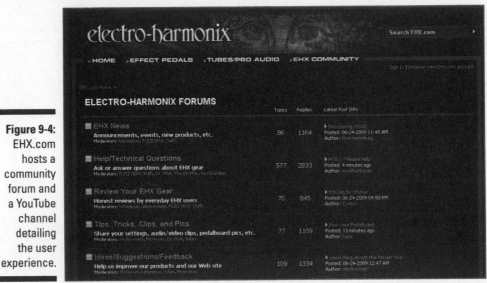

Figure 9-4:
EHX.com
hosts a
community
forum and
a YouTube
channel
detailing
the user
experience.

Rethinking Your Web Site

Practicing SIM philosophies on your Web site isn't only about approaching campaigns differently and tying them into your Web site more strategically. You can also rethink your whole Web site experience to enable more direct social influence to take place. Redesigning your Web site with the social influence elements can increase sales and deepen relationships with your core customers. In the following section, I give you some recommendations on how to do that for four important areas of your Web site.

All these recommendations may not be applicable to your Web site (some require you to sell online, for example), but even those are worth reading nevertheless.

Product pages

The most critical change you can make to product pages on your Web site is to include customer reviews. Nothing sells a product better than actual customer reviews and ratings of the products. The customer reviews provide the shopper with the perspective of other customers. They give your customers the inside scoop on your products — the ins and outs of them and why they're good or bad. Customer reviews are extremely popular. According to a Nielsen Online study published in December 2008, 81 percent of holiday shoppers read online customer reviews. Research by Razorfish shows that when making a purchasing decision, respondents relied on the following sources of information the most: user reviews (60.53 percent), comparison charts (20.48 percent), editorial reviews (15.41 percent), and shared shopping lists (3.58 percent). Amazon is the most well-known example of a company that provides customer reviews, which are shown in Figure 9-5.

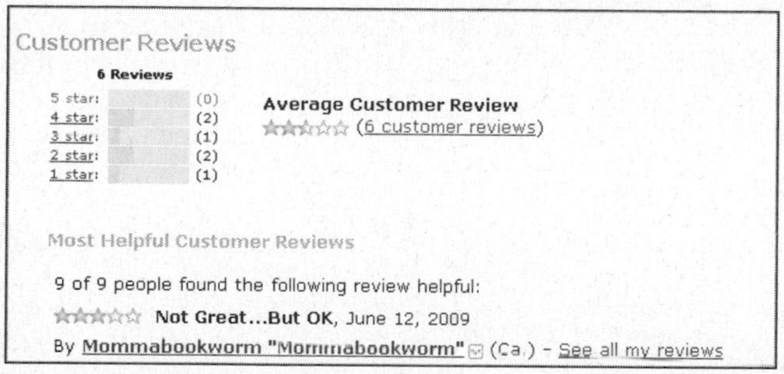

Figure 9-5: Amazon.com's reviews allow plenty of customer feedback.

You'll find that customer reviewers serve a couple of purposes:

🖛 **They help sell products, no matter the review.**

Even though you may be worried that customer reviews may damn your products, they invariably convince customers to purchase, and they lead to more sales. Unflattering customer reviews may drive your customers away from certain products, but they also drive customers to other products.

🖛 **You get feedback about what does and doesn't work.**

The customer reviews also serve as a valuable feedback mechanism, telling you what products are liked and why certain products are purchased more than others. Many a marketer has learned valuable insights about missing features of their products by reading the customer reviews on their Web sites.

According to research by the e-tailing group in June 2008, of merchants who adopted customer reviews, 58 percent said improving customer experience was the most important reason for adding reviews to their sites, followed by building customer loyalty (47 percent), driving sales (42 percent), and maintaining a competitive advantage (37 percent).

In addition to adding customer reviews on your Web site, you can incorporate them in other ways:

🖛 **In your search engine advertisements:** Some retailers have found customer reviews and ratings to be so successful that they now include customer ratings in their search engine advertisements. Including the ratings in those advertisements has also increased the *click-through rate* (the number of clicks in an advertisement that drives users to the Web site) to their Web sites.

> ✔ **On your physical shelves:** Other companies, such as Staples, include customer ratings sourced from their Web site on the display shelves of their physical stores. Even when customers see the ratings in a physical store, they become influenced.

It's in the customer reviews and ratings that your customers truly influence each other. Allow for that social influence and you'll probably see it building trust, increasing sales, and improving customer service.

News and events pages

News and events pages, which are often referred to as the Press Room, provide ample opportunity to allow for social influence with the injection of social features. The first step is to make all content in your press room portable so that journalists and others who use the page can easily pluck the content and publish it elsewhere on the Web, in whatever format may suit them. This means enabling sharing functionality on all your press room pages. You want to make it really easy to share the content here. It's also important to craft your press releases for the blogosophere, in which you'll find the people who can take and amplify your message better than anyone else. But to do so effectively, you need to publish the content in your press release area in a blogger-friendly format.

Making your content blogger friendly means publishing what is referred to as a *social media press release*, which is a press release that's optimized for bloggers, with excerpts and quotes at the top of the press release. From a social media press release, bloggers can also download images and resize them easily. Shift Communications publishes a template for social media press releases (as shown in Figure 9-6). You can find the complete Shift Communications Social Media Press Release template at `www.shiftcomm.com/downloads/smprtemplate.pdf`. It includes the following components:

✔ **Contact Information:** Includes fields for the client contact, spokesperson, and agency contact information. Listed for each are their names, phone numbers, instant messenger addresses, Web sites, Skype usernames, and blog addresses.

✔ **News Release Headline:** This is the headline for the press release. It can also include a subheadline.

✔ **Core News Facts:** Here, in bullet point form, you can list the core news facts for your press release. Be aware that you should use this to list facts only. Hyperbole is not recommended.

✔ **Links & RSS Feeds:** Next comes the link and RSS feed to the Del.icio.us page that you should have setup earlier. That page needs to directly offer hyperlinks to relevant historical, trend, market, product, and competitive sources.

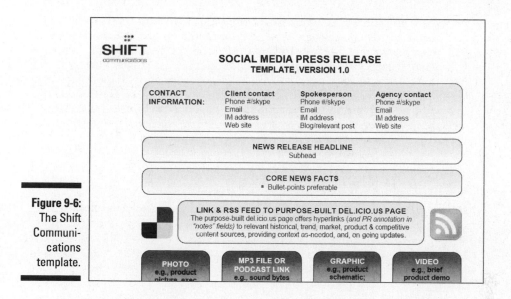

Figure 9-6:
The Shift
Communi-
cations
template.

✔ **Multimedia:** Below that comes the photo, MP3, podcast, graphic, and video links, as required. This can also include links to white papers.

✔ **Pre-Approved Quotes:** Place pre-approved quotes from management, analysts, customers, and partners here.

✔ **Links to Relevant Coverage:** It's important to link to existing coverage of the story, as it's invaluable for any journalist or blogger.

✔ **Boilerplate Statements:** The template includes a place for these, but as you can see, their importance is significantly reduced.

✔ **Tagging & Tracking Links:** You can include Technorati tags, Del.icio.us links, and other RSS feeds here.

Publishing press releases on your Web site (and through the wires) in this format makes them blogger friendly. And as the line between mainstream journalists and bloggers blurs, these press releases become more and more valuable.

About us and contact us pages

The about us pages of a Web site have traditionally included management team profiles, investor information, company history, contact and address information, company values, and fact sheets. Those sections are extremely important, and you can make them all the more so by injecting social features. For example, include links to the blogs and Twitter profiles of the management team along with the traditional profiles. The CEO of the company may want to include a YouTube clip of him sharing his vision for the company, and how the company can serve customers. The company history page can link to external Web sites that explain more about the company's history, and the fact sheet can include quotes and factoids from third-party providers and individual experts. On these pages, you can feature expert influencers who endorse the company. See Chapter 8 for more information on the expert influencers.

The contact us page requires special attention. It mustn't be a page that lists only telephone numbers, e-mail addresses, and locations. In today's world, customers assume *contact us* to mean this: talk to an employee right away about a problem. Include live chat technology on the contact us page (if your company sells a consumer product) and also link to your company's Twitter feed. Figure 9-7 shows the contact us page for EHX, which has links to its forum page, e-mail addresses, and Twitter page (which is further down the page), as well as the traditional contact info, such as phone number and snail-mail address.

The Twitter feed matters because the customer may want to engage in a conversation with someone in your company directly then and there. What better place than Twitter, where you can invariably make a statement that you're authentic and transparent.

Contact Us

Have a question about EHX gear? We'd like to help!

First be sure to visit the corresponding product page -- we've already answered many of the most common questions there.

Next, visit our support & community forums -- you'll find an active and helpful community of EHX staff and everyday users.

Last, if you can't seem to get an answer from the product pages or forums -- we welcome your questions via email.

Email
info@ehx.com

Phone
(718) 937-8300

Mail
Electro-Harmonix
32-33 47th Ave.
LIC, NY 11101

Figure 9-7:
The
EHX.com
contact us
page.

Another potential solution for the contact us page is to enable customers to provide product and business ideas to your company. Call it crowdsourcing, but customers often don't mind giving free advice to companies. The MyStarbucksIdea.com site, as shown in Figure 9-8, solicits feedback from customers, and has been extremely successful. In the last two years, it's received thousands of ideas from thousands of customers about every part of its business. On the site, customers can comment on the ideas submitted and rate them, pushing the best ones to the top. The most successful ideas invariably are implemented by Starbucks in some form or the other. It is a win-win situation already. The customers feel empowered to provide constructive feedback, their voices are heard, and the company benefits from the fabulous ideas. Another good example of crowd-sourcing is the Dell IdeaStorm (www. ideastorm.com), which encourages customers to post ideas about Dell products and services.

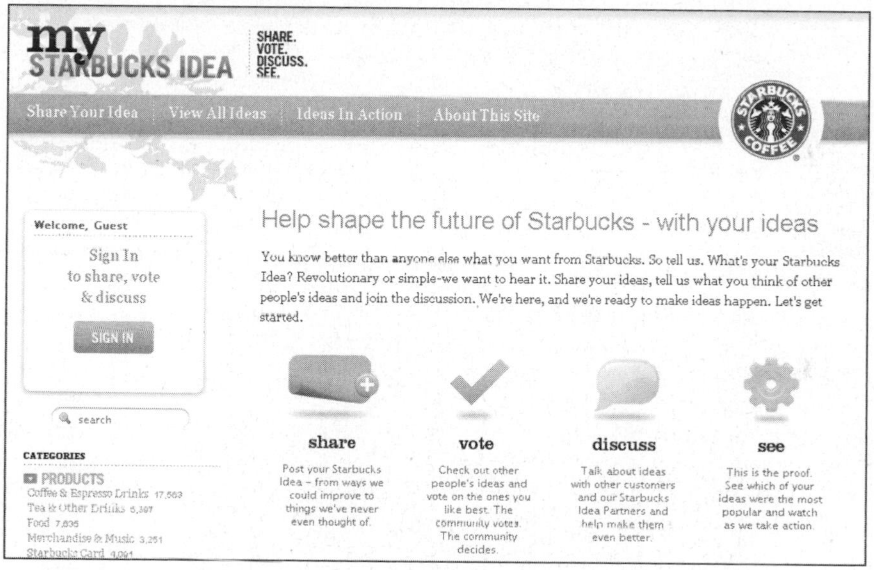

Figure 9-8: My-Starbucks Idea.com

Private online communities

Every day, more companies are building customer communities for the purposes of conducting customer research and soliciting feedback on product concepts. These customer communities (accessible via your Web site) are typically closed communities with only select customers participating by invitation. Customers are recruited either through third-party vendors or mining customer databases for brand advocates who have strong, thoughtful opinions on the products. Marketers use these customers to road-test product concepts and marketing messages and provide feedback on everything from shopping experiences to customer service. These communities typically include live chat, discussion boards, polls, and multimedia sharing. You'll typically give customers special benefits for participating, such as discount coupons, quicker access to new products, and passes to special events and promotions. Rarely do companies directly pay customers for their participation. Communispace (`www.communispace.com`) and Passenger (`www.thinkpassenger.com`) are two leading technology providers of private online communities.

By listening to your customers through these customer research communities, you get important real-time intelligence on shifting patterns of behavior and trends, identify new product ideas and improve existing ones, deepen loyalty by your ability to listen, and invariably develop brand evangelists who can help promote your new products and launches. Think of these private online communities as free focus groups that are with you 365 days of the year, and you'll start to realize how beneficial they can be. Companies — including JC Penney, Mercedes Benz USA, Mattel, Adidas, and Microsoft — use private online communities to test products, learn how to respond to a PR crisis, and launch new initiatives. In fact, Mattel's The Playground, which is a private community of 500 moms, was extremely valuable when the company had a series of product recalls of popular toys in 2007. The company used the group as a sounding board for recommendations on how best to handle the PR crisis. The result was that even though they had a damaging product recall, fourth quarter sales were up 6 percent. This is largely because those 500 moms in the private online community gave Mattel insightful advice on how to respond to the crisis.

In fact, many believe that these private online communities are more valuable than any traditional form of market research. You can use this feedback to support the launch of a new product and create a body of social influencers, who can be provided with the tools with which to promote the launch. In other cases, you can use this community as a way to deepen existing relationships with your customers.

Bringing the Social Graph to Your Web Site

Practicing SIM on your Web site doesn't just mean opening it up to the social Web by making the content more pluckable and including tools that enable consumers to share the content more easily. It also means making your own Web site truly social by bringing your customers' social graphs to your Web site.

With the advent of technologies like Facebook Connect (shown in Figure 9-9), OpenSocial, and Microsoft's own data portability initiatives, it's now possible to bring a consumer's social graph to your Web site. For example, you can include the login information for Facebook Connect on your Web site. Upon login, the user's friends list also appears on your Web site. You can then share their activity for your user. In other words, your Web site becomes a location where a consumer can see and participate with his existing network of friends as he makes brand affinity and purchasing decisions.

Through these technologies, any third-party Web site (including yours!) can take a customer's profile data — including age, gender, region, and interests — from his profile on a social platform and match them to any action, such as purchasing, commenting, or reviewing. If you're a user logging in to a Web site, you can, for example, see user-generated content prioritized to display your friends first, followed by other people in your region, of your age, and with your interests.

Figure 9-9: Facebook Connect.

Probably the most infamous example of portable social graphs is what CNN did on Inauguration Day in 2009, in partnership with Facebook and using the Facebook Connect technology. Users were able to watch a live video feed of President Obama's acceptance speech on their computers via the CNN.com Web site. But more than just that, they could comment on his speech and, in near real time, see comments by other people in their social graph taking place on the CNN.com Web site. Now think about that for a moment. You're watching this live feed, and next to it, there's a window open that is displaying a streaming list of comments from all your friends. The Web site knows that they are your friends because you've connected with them through Facebook. You, in turn, can add comments that are seen just by other friends who are watching the inauguration on the CNN.com Web site, too.

Influencing conversations and getting your brand inserted into conversations has always been difficult and expensive for marketers. But now, with technologies like Facebook Connect, if you can give people reason to talk, you don't have to build a brand new community from scratch, nor do you have to limit your social efforts to Facebook or MySpace. You can design an experience whereby consumers are encouraged to bring their social graphs to your Web site and interact with their friends on your Web site and on your terms. You can use their profile data and the behavior on your Web site to make the experience more personal and meaningful, too. But this truly represents one of the most powerful concepts in social influence marketing: The technology lets you create experiences that let consumers influence each other in a natural fashion with low (or virtually non-existent) barrier to entry.

Without a doubt, Facebook Connect is the most advanced technology to use for enabling social interaction via social graphs on your Web site. Given that Facebook is also the largest social network, it makes sense to use Facebook Connect. Here are some factors to keep in mind when deploying Facebook Connect on your Web site:

- ✔ **Trusted authentication:** Facebook Connect uses Facebook's trusted authentication method. This means that your Web site (when you're using Facebook Connect) can use Facebook's authentication method without having to ask users to register.

- ✔ **Real identity:** Facebook users are represented with their real names and identities when you use Facebook Connect. This can be both good and bad. Some users may not want that.

- ✔ **Friend linking:** Linking established on Facebook is carried through to the external Web sites. You can show a consumer which of his friends already have accounts on your Web site via Facebook Connect.

- ✔ **Dynamic privacy:** The privacy settings that your customers set on Facebook carry through with them to your Web site. This includes changes to photographs, friends, and what information is visible.

- ✔ **Social distribution:** Actions taken by consumers on your Web site can be easily pushed back to Facebook or to their friends via Facebook Feed, requests, and other notifications.

For all the conversations (both here and online) about Facebook Connect, it's important to note that it isn't the only game in town. Google, MySpace, Six Apart, and a few other companies have banded together to provide an alternative to Facebook Connect. You can use Google Friend Connect to accomplish many of the same objectives. While Google Friend Connect doesn't bring your social graph directly from Facebook or another social network, it does let you invite users from them. Because it doesn't require any programming on your end (unlike Facebook Connect, which does require a significant amount of programming effort), it's a popular alternative for smaller companies. It takes care of the authentication, basic social functionality such as commenting and ratings, and also includes polls, events, and member gadgets. These are all very easily installed.

 Just because you don't have to invest huge sums of money in developing and nurturing your own online community, doesn't mean there's no reason for you to develop your own online community. In some cases, that may be a better option — but not always. After all, bringing a social graph to your Web site enables consumers to interact with their friends on your Web site. It doesn't let them interact as easily with other customers about your products.

Tips and Tricks for Web Site SIM

Follow these steps to enhance your Web site's social media potential. Many of these tips and tricks may seem small, but, time and again, I've seen them directly impacting how a potential customer views a brand on a Web site. Keep in mind that some of these tips may require significant organizational change to bring them to life.

Aggregating information for your consumer

Social media has empowered consumers to form stronger opinions and express them more broadly. More people are blogging, commenting, and rating than ever before. Approximately 120,000 blogs are created every day. These contributors provide a rich base of knowledge for other consumers to use while making a purchasing decision. Consumers who tap into these blogs know more about your brand than you probably do. Rather than trying to control the message, serve as the hub and the aggregator of all information regarding the brand. Let your Web site become the amphitheater for the conversation. Even if the conversation is negative, you win over the long term, as Chevy did with its Tahoe campaign. The user-generated advertisement contest resulted in 629,000 visits to the Web site, and Tahoe sales took off.

Articulating product benefits better

Recent research by eMarketer highlights how influential customer reviews are. Approximately 22 percent of U.S. online buyers always read customer reviews before making a purchase; 43 percent of U.S. online buyers read customer reviews at least most of the time before making a purchase. That's social influence at play. So what can you do about it? Recognize that your consumers are informed, and make sure you sell a strong product, articulating its benefits in a more easily understood manner. You'll create happier customers, who'll then do the marketing for you as others will want to identify with them through similar purchasing behavior.

Amplifying the favorite business stories

So you can't control the message anymore. Your consumers would rather listen to each other than to you. But you still have messages that you want to disseminate. You can do that by shaping, influencing, and amplifying business stories that play to your brand's strengths.

Just because your consumers are more interested in talking to each other, it doesn't mean you don't have a voice at all. Edelman research highlights that 28 percent of U.S. online consumers took an action such as calling, speaking, or e-mailing others based on what they read in a blog post. In Belgium, that number is 43 percent. Publish your favorite business stories as widely as possible and also direct consumers to the individuals or groups already predisposed to your products.

Aligning your organization into multiple, authentic voices

Social influence marketing is about providing the space for consumers to influence each other during the purchase process. As a brand, you want them to positively influence each other. Do this by aligning your entire organization into a network of multiple, authentic voices. Don't leave customer interactions to the sales and marketing teams. Empower other internal constituents across the organization to serve as brand ambassadors, maybe via blogs. They'll talk about your brand in their own voices to their own communities. They may not be totally on message, but they'll be authentic — and it'll have a strong, positive influence. Trust them. See Chapter 5 for more information on SIM voices.

Chapter 10

Becoming an Authentic and Engaged Advertiser

In earlier chapters, I briefly touch on social advertising and how it can play an important role in your marketing efforts. I also allude to paid and earned media in the context of the different marketing opportunities on social platforms. I also introduce appvertising.

In this chapter, I go into each of those topics in significantly more detail, as knowing how they can help you achieve your SIM objectives is critical as you become a more authentic and engaged social media advertiser. But that's not all; it's also important to leverage SIM efforts with offline marketing efforts whether it be through television, print, or any other form of media. I discuss that, too, in this chapter.

Social Advertising: A Potential Online Advertising Game Changer

Online display advertising has been in a steady decline recently, with fewer people clicking and interacting with those advertisements everywhere. For the most part, the industry has responded by making the display advertisements more immersive with rollover states, forms, pull-down menus, expandable units, and streaming audio and video clips all built within them.

Those incremental innovations help grab users' attention and provide a decent return on investment (ROI) for the advertisers. But social advertisements, which infuse social content and a user's *social graph* (mapping of the person's friends) directly into the ad unit, promise to make display advertisements far more interactive, engaging, and better performing than other forms of display advertisements that have come before.

The Interactive Advertising Bureau defines a social ad as "an online ad that incorporates user interactions that the consumer has agreed to display and be shared. The resulting ad displays these interactions along with the user's persona (picture and/or name) within the ad content." This definition serves as a good starting point but can be expanded to also include user-generated content.

To explain this in layman's terms, imagine seeing a display advertisement on a Web site like CNN.com or NYTimes.com and uploading a photograph to it. Or you could see *tweets* (Twitter messages) by other people appear within it, and you could respond with comments or tweets of your own. Or imagine you're browsing Facebook and you see a display banner that includes a photograph *of a friend* with a movie recommendation. Those are all social advertisements because they're either infused with social graph data or with user-generated content. In this second example, only people who know your friend will see that advertisement.

Why are these social advertisements such a big deal? Because all of a sudden, display banners that were getting little attention, especially on social networks, now can carry actual, real-time messages from other consumers. Rather than depending on fancy creative images to influence your customers to make a purchasing decision, you can allow customers to influence each other in the display banners. And rather than consumers seeing just static quotes from other consumers (after all customer quotes aren't new in advertising), the consumers can respond to those messages with questions, comments, or endorsements of their own within your advertisement.

From being a medium through which to push a message, the display banner suddenly becomes a location for conversations where consumers can influence each other. The display banner becomes a tool in your social influence marketing toolkit. That's powerful. This matters more than ever because as Forrester analyst Josh Bernoff said, "People don't want to talk about products, they want to talk about their passions or their problems and solutions." Let them use those banner ads to carry on those conversations and influence each other in meaningful ways.

Displaying advertisements on social networks

Every year, Internet pundits predict the demise of online display advertising. They prophesize that consumers will stop looking at banner ads, and as a result, the multi-billion-dollar industry will die a sudden death. And each year, the statistics prove them wrong. In fact, in 2008, $4.8 billion was spent on online display advertising. Marketers continue to invest in display advertising, and with good reason. Year after year, display advertisements produce results, especially for direct-response campaigns, where the dollar investments in display advertisements is traced directly to customer acquisition. Even in down economies like the one we're going through as I write this chapter, companies still use display advertising to reach prospective customers. The amount they spend on display advertising may decrease, but it's still a core component in their media mix simply because those advertisements prove to be worth their investments.

But one type of online display advertising has never really worked well and continues to provide dismal click-through rates: display advertising on social networks. The reason is simple: People click display advertisements less when they're in a social environment engaging with their friends. You've probably seen display ads on social platforms like MySpace and Facebook. They do exist, but they don't perform well.

Appvertisements and How They Can Work for You

Another recent innovation in the online advertising space is appvertisements, which bridge the worlds of advertising and applications. (You get the word *appvertising* when you combine the first part of the word *application* with the last part of the word *advertising*.) These appvertisements are small *applications* (programs) that reside within social networks and tap into people's social graphs. They provide direct entertainment or educational, social interactivity, or utilitarian value to consumers who install them.

When these appvertisements provide value, consumers are typically comfortable with the sponsored branding that comes part and parcel with them. The appvertisements are successful when they have the following attributes: emotional, engaging, social, and simple. I discuss these attributes in the sections that follow.

As you consider building and launching appvertisements on a social platform like Facebook, consider these numbers: The most popular appvertisements average 140,000 installations during their first month, according to Buddy Media Research. Users spend considerably more time interacting with these appvertisements than they do with any traditional display banner ads.

These applications are extremely easy to build and can be personalized based on a user's profile data. For more information on identifying someone to build your appvertisements, see Chapter 7. Here are the attributes that make an appvertisement successful.

Emotional

Appvertisements are typically fun and engaging. They solicit a response from consumers and encourage deeper participation. For example, the Travel Channel Kidnap! appvertisement, created by Context Optional, lets users kidnap friends to exotic locations. The friends escape by correctly answering trivia questions. This appvertisement resides within Facebook, and by the time this chapter was written participation grew to 2.5 million users while also sending 70,000 new visitors to the Travel Channel Web site. Figure 10-1 shows the Kidnap! appervertisement.

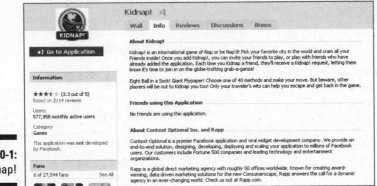

Figure 10-1: Kidnap!

Engaging

For appvertisements to succeed, they must continuously engage users. They should be designed to encourage repeat use and sharing of the appvertisement. The Bud Light Check Your Dudeness application builds on the popular Bud Light television commercial. The application is a photo quiz that calculates each user's "Dudeness." Upon discovering your "Dudeness," you can compare yourself to other friends who have already taken the quiz. It's fun and engaging, and most participants return again to find out how their friends did on the quiz.

Social

The most popular appvertisements are the ones that are deeply social. These are the appvertisements that encourage social interaction with others or enable users to share a side of themselves with their social circles. A good example is the TripAdvisor Cities I've Visited travel map, shown in Figure 10-2. Upon installing the application, users can mark on a map the cities they've visited, the cities they want to visit, and the cities that they're planning to visit. They can also invite friends to recommend cities for them, and users can compare their cities to those of their friends and exchange notes about the comparisons.

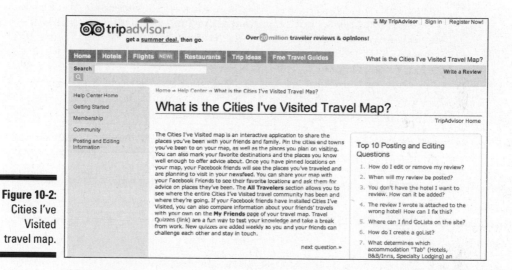

Figure 10-2: Cities I've Visited travel map.

Simple

Probably the most important attribute of successful appvertisements is that they're typically very simple applications. You shouldn't try to build Microsoft Office into your appvertisement. Users are more likely to adopt apps that are simple, straightforward, and focused on doing more with less. If you install the Travel Channel Kidnap!, Bud Light Check Your Dudeness, and the TripAdvisor Cities I've Visited appvertisements, you'll notice that they're all very simply designed, quick to learn, and easy to use.

Getting Your Appvertisement Noticed

Building appvertisements is only half the battle. As with anything else designed and built for the social Web, in order for it to gain traction, you must focus on getting users to adopt the appvertisement and install it on their profile pages on their favorite social platform. That can be very challenging, especially with new appvertisements being launched every single day.

You can get your appvertisements to your consumers in two ways: joining an appvertisement network or *seeding* (building) the appvertisement yourself.

Joining an appvertisement network

Existing appvertisement networks can be very helpful. These appvertisement networks promote new appvertisements on what is called the canvas pages of existing appvertisements. Companies that have built and deployed appvertisements in large quantities charge for the promotion of new appvertisements, typically on a per-installation basis.

Here are some appvertisement networks:

- ✔ Gigya (www.gigya.com), shown in Figure 10-3
- ✔ RockYou (www.rockyou.com)
- ✔ SocialMedia.com (www.socialmedia.com)
- ✔ KickApps (www.kickapps.com)
- ✔ Buddy Media (www.buddymedia.com)

Many of these also build your appvertisements for you.

As each appvertisement network functions differently, both in terms of how you can join the network and how much it will charge you for the promotion of your appvertisement, it's best to shop around when choosing the right one. These should all be factors in determining which platform you go with:

- ✔ Visit their Web sites.
- ✔ Find out how much they charge per installation.
- ✔ Research the *reach* of their networks. (Do they cover all the social platforms?)
- ✔ Understand how robust their analytics systems are.

Keep in mind that some appvertisement networks may be stronger in specific social platforms versus other ones, and you should factor that into your decision based on where most of your prospective customers are spending their time.

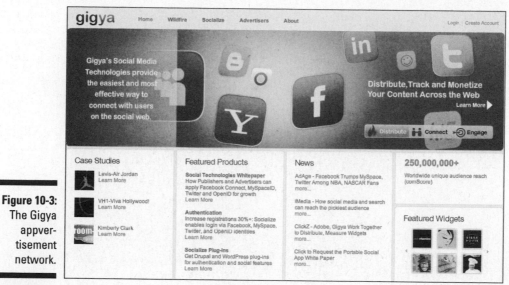

Figure 10-3:
The Gigya
appver-
tisement
network.

Joining a network isn't required, but it does serve as the simplest, quickest way to promote an appvertisement.

Seeding your appvertisement

The other alternative is to manually seed the appvertisement yourself, making sure that it has enough social features to encourage people to share it with others. This typically means manual effort and invariably has a cost of its own.

When you're seeding the appvertisement, you'll want to pay particular attention to the screenshots included, whether it's submitted to all the appvertisement directories, the timing of the release (choose the time in the day when most of your target audience logs in to Facebook, for example), how you invite users to install the appvertisement, and link exchange programs. Also, don't forget to set up a Facebook fan page and a MySpace profile for the application and encourage user feedback through them.

The most important tool in your arsenal of seeding appvertisements is letting users spread the word about your appvertisement for you. You do this by letting them invite their friends and making sure that the appvertisement requires the participation of your users and their friends. You also want to build in a notification system so that you have an excuse to remind your users about the appvertisement. These notifications can, for example, tell your user's friends when your user breaks an existing high score record or notify them when a friend is actually online and playing.

Use the feed functionality built into Facebook to build awareness and repeat use for your appvertisement. How you seed the appvertisement depends on the social platform where you're launching it. Each social platform has its own idiosyncrasies that make the concept of seeding the appvertisement slightly different from the next platform.

Follow these basic steps when you're seeding your appvertisement.

1. **Create the appvertisement and make sure that sharing functionality is built into the appvertisement.**

2. **Launch the appvertisement on your targeted social network by first having it published and approved in the social network appvertisement directory.**

   Each social network has a different policy regarding publishing appvertisements.

3. **Once the appvertisement appears in the appvertisement directory, install the appvertisement on your profile page and encourage your coworkers, friends, and family to install it on theirs, too.**

4. **Install the appvertisement on your company social network profile or fan page and announce the appvertisement via Twitter and other social platforms.**

5. **Alert social influencers with whom you have an existing relationship about the launch of the appvertisement and explain why it may be of value to them and their audiences.**

6. **Start using the appvertisement on a regular basis and use any built-in notification system to remind other users about the appvertisement.**

Making Paid and Earned Media Work Together

Earned media — editorial, radio, or television coverage of an event or product that you don't have to pay for — has its roots in the public relations world. Earned media is usually free publicity through promotional and marketing efforts outside of advertising. Public relations professionals have mastered the art of getting their clients earned media at a cost significantly lower than buying the media attention through paid advertisements or promotions of one form or another.

With the social media revolution, earned media has taken on a new dimension. Your brand no longer has to depend on the mainstream media to earn attention among its consumers. Your brand can also earn that attention directly by interacting and engaging with its consumers and their influencers across the social Web. All of a sudden, earned media means engaging with consumers on social platforms from Twitter and Facebook to MySpace and YouTube. If you can earn your consumer's attention directly, why bother with the mainstream press? And for that matter, why bother with paid media either? In fact, journalists, too, look towards the social Web for story ideas. According to research published by Brodeur and Marketwire and highlighted on Marketing Pilgrim (www.marketingpilgrim.com), more than 75 percent of reporters see blogs as helpful in giving them story ideas, with 70 percent checking a blog list on a regular basis.

Working harder to gain attention

In the early days of the social media phenomenon, brands that engaged in direct conversations with their customers and their influencers automatically gained prominence. After all, what they were doing was revolutionary. The first time a user got a response from a customer service agent via Twitter must have been quite a seismic moment. Similarly, the first time a CEO of a Fortune 1000 company started blogging, it drew a lot of media coverage and won him praise among his customers. Comcast and Zappos have developed a reputation for phenomenal customer service through Twitter; Figure 10-4 shows the Zappos Twitter feed. They were among the first to leverage Twitter strategically for customer service, and anyone who follows them isn't going to get the same kind of attention that they did. Today, Comcast has several employees (on last count, seven employees) who are dedicated to Twitter customer service. All they do every day is address customer service issues via Twitter. (See http://twitter.com/comcastcares.)

The days of participating in the social Web to simply earn attention are over. Your brands must still earn attention as you absolutely need to, but doing so has gotten harder — and it requires more of your time. Every other brand is doing what you're doing online.

So the question is how can your brand earn the trust and attention of consumers online in a meaningful sense? This is where paid and earned media needs to work together. I discuss this in the section that follows.

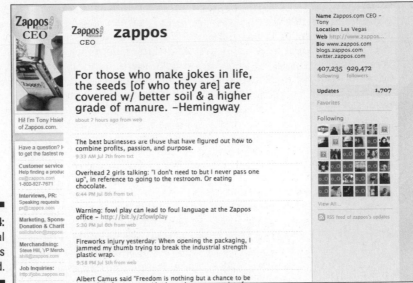

Figure 10-4:
The official
Zappos
Twitter feed.

The most important myth about earned media is this: It isn't, as many people believe, free media. You still have to work for it. In fact, it takes a lot more effort to earn media than buy media. The difference is that earning media requires time and effort and changing your company from within, while paid media is about buying online advertisements. Earned media requires you to devote time to monitoring conversations, building relationships, and engaging with influencers online.

Making paid media jump-start earned media initiatives

So how do earned and paid media work together in this socially-driven digital world? In earlier chapters, including Chapters 6 and 7, I discuss paid media and earned media opportunities on various social platforms. I also discussed when to use what technique. Here, I explore how paid media can support earned media efforts.

At the most basic level, you can use paid media to jump-start your earned media endeavors. Grabbing your customers' attentions and initiating dialogue with them can be hard. All your competitors are trying to do exactly what you're hoping to do, after all. It can be difficult to break through the noise. The sections that follow highlight some specific ways in which paid media can support earned media.

Analysis by Razorfish highlights that it's important to analyze the value of paid media in relation to the value of *incremental reach* (users pass it on) and the value of the endorsement effect (*badging*, or a user promoting a brand via an image on his profile, and so on). The latter two can be jump-started by the first. The point is that when you use paid media to jump-start earned media effort, you must analyze the value of all components to assess the total value of the campaign and how the components support each other.

Build awareness

Paid media is most valuable for building awareness among consumers about a product, service, or promotion. If you're beginning to engage with customers on a social platform or in a hosted online community, an effective way to build awareness for those experiences is to create awareness via paid media across the Internet. Most of your consumers may not know that you're interacting with others on a social platform and providing product sneak peeks, offering discounts, or answering customer service queries. You can build that awareness by using paid media. This paid media can be in the form of advertisements on mainstream Web sites or social advertisements on the social platforms.

Jump-start engagement

Another effective use of paid media is to jump-start appvertisement installations. As I mention earlier in the chapter, your appvertisement is only as successful as the number of installations that it has. Getting people to install your appvertisement virally can be difficult. Promoting the appvertisement through an ad network that guarantees installations is one way to gain traction for it, although some may argue that the quality of the download may be less when you're using an ad network that guarantees the downloads. You can also use paid media to jump-start other forms of social engagement, like activity around a YouTube channel or a Facebook fan page.

Promote interaction

You may have already developed a thriving community and could be looking to increase engagement with a new audience segment. One way to do this is to use paid media to profile community members and highlight the value that the community provides.

For example, Intuit has a very successful QuickBooks Live Community (as shown in Figure 10-5), where customers help each other solve problems. Today, 70 percent of customer service-related issues are resolved with other users answering questions. One accountant has posted more than 5,600 answers. Intuit now has the opportunity to promote the Live Community to prospective customers as a benefit of buying their software. That can be done through paid media.

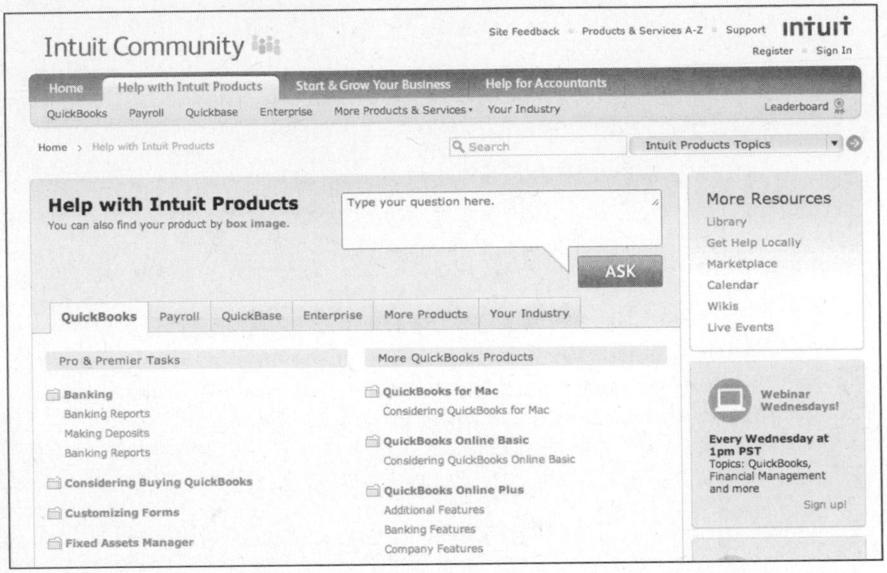

Figure 10-5:
The Intuit
Community.

Win friends and influence

If you want to engage with your customers in a more meaningful way, but don't have the resources, skills, or permission to do so, use paid strategies. For example, American Express hosts a popular business site called Open Forum. The site pays experts like ubermarketer Guy Kawasaki to blog on various topics, which cultivates discussion among the readers. The conversations triggered on the Open Forum percolate to other parts of the Internet, rapidly giving American Express additional exposure. American Express builds its reputation as a company providing valuable advice to its customers, the expert bloggers get a larger audience, the customers get the information, and each post builds brand awareness for the Amex brand.

Tips and tricks for campaigns

When launching and running online campaigns, you can sometimes forget to make sure that your paid and earned media efforts work well together. Your earned media efforts can save you precious dollars and enhance the paid media campaign.

Here are some tips to consider when launching an online media campaign:

✔ **Ask for earned media recommendations.**

When you ask your agency to provide recommendations for a media campaign, ask them to also provide earned media recommendations at the same time. There is no reason why they shouldn't.

✔ **Request a social advertising component.**

Always ask your agency to include a social advertising component to the campaign and push them to explain how you can use the social advertising to jump-start earned media efforts.

✔ **Survey the landscape.**

Look at your presence on various social platforms when you're about to launch a campaign. Is there anything that you can do to amplify the affects of the campaign?

✔ **Design the campaign to be inherently social.**

Ask more of the participants in your campaign and offer more in return. For instance, direct them to your presence on a social platform — where you encourage them to friend, fan, or follow you — instead of directing them to a microsite.

✔ **Promote your brand on social networks.**

Use your social influence on the platforms to highlight the campaign, and use places like Twitter to answer queries, amplify the coverage, and share tidbits about it.

✔ **Establish a fan page.**

Create a permanent home for the campaign, which allows deeper social interaction. It'll strengthen relationships with your customers and help you on the search engine optimization (SEO) front, too. Or use your social network presence as that home.

✔ **Set influence goals and evaluate how well you meet them.**

Make an explicit secondary goal of the campaign to increase your followers on Twitter, your fans on Facebook, and your friends on MySpace and YouTube. With that goal, your creative team will bring more synergistic ideas to the table.

✔ **Don't forget the metrics.**

Measure all digital interactions with your customers and, especially, find out how they reach your microsite or your Web site. Determine how many people were driven from paid versus earned media strategies and how many came from the social platforms. I talk about how to measure a campaign in Chapter 13.

✔ **Identify and reach out to the social influencers.**

And do that as soon as you launch the campaign; maybe they can help promote it for you. Show them the creative. Provide them something in return.

✔ **Offer some sort of reward to influencers who participate.**

Before you launch the campaign, think through whether you can provide consumers who engage with you more deeply on the social platforms with anything. They'll reward your generosity with creating buzz that will nicely complement the paid media campaign.

SIM Working with TV

Research published in July 2009 by interactive agency Razorfish showed that consumers still trust TV advertisements more than they trust advertising on social networks. But consumers do return to branded pages on the social networks at a very high rate if they find them valuable.

This may be a surprising finding on the surface, but it makes sense. There's so much activity on the social networks, with brands trying so many different tactics (and with imposters posing as brands) that consumers aren't ever completely sure what to believe. In contrast, when you see a television advertisement, you know that it comes from the brand because no imposter would spend hundreds of thousands of dollars on television for the attention.

Some traditional advertisers believe that nothing can replace television to build awareness for a brand. These advertisers scoff at the notion of digital advertising displacing television advertising. Asking marketers to choose between the two is a false choice. Each form of advertising has its place, and each one can complement the other effectively to meet the objectives of the marketing campaign. In the following sections, I outline two scenarios of how digital SIM campaigns can effectively complement a television campaign.

Social media has created a perfect storm in the advertising world, which results in new advertising units, like social ads and the rise of earned media working in conjunction with paid media. And the technological innovations in live streaming is changing the nature of television online, leading to a whole new set of marketing implications for traditional TV advertisers.

Awareness through TV, engagement via the Internet

The reach of television is still insurmountable for any other marketing channel. Television advertising provides awareness for a brand, a product, or a new campaign better than other techniques. But television is most effectively used when it serves to build awareness and drive consumers to more deeply engage with a brand on other channels, like the Internet.

Take the Levi's 501 Project Runway Challenge, for example. Levi's 501 sponsored the reality television series Project Runway, in which up-and-coming fashion designers competed against each other in a string of design challenges for a big prize.

Levi's sponsored the TV show to build awareness for its jeans among young women, a target customer that had eluded the brand. Levi's also created a Project Runway design challenge of its own on a specially built Web site.

On this Web site, users were asked to submit their own clothing designs for a competition. Other users voted on the submissions, a panel of celebrity judges weighed in, and a winner was chosen. The online program was promoted extensively through paid media across the Internet and through the television advertisements that aired around the TV version of Project Runway.

Thousands of consumers submitted their designs for this online challenge, with many more visiting the Web site to critique the designs and vote for their favorites. The television advertisements built awareness for the online competition, paid media online promoted it across the Internet, and consumers engaged with the brand more deeply on the Web site by submitting designs, rating others, and discussing them. It was the perfect success story, with television advertisements working in conjunction with a social influence marketing program to meet the brand's objectives. And yes, during the period of the campaign, sales to their target audience jumped.

Awareness, engagement, and conversion with television

Over the last ten years, as digital advertising has gained in prominence, a slew of traditional marketers have bemoaned the attention that the digital space has been getting. Digital marketers have been too proudly explaining how important their form of marketing is because it's more measurable, more quantifiable, and more results driven than other forms of marketing. This tension has created a false divide between television and digital. That's all about to change.

Television is fundamentally going digital itself, in a way that none of us could have imagined a few years ago. The infrastructure that drives television — the content distribution models, the content formats, and the advertising opportunities — are all changing. And what's more, the lines between television and the Internet are blurring. Market research shows that consumers increasingly multitask. They don't just surf the Internet while watching television; they talk to each other online while watching television. And online television sites in the form of Web sites like YouTube, Hulu, and Joost have built-in chat and discussion forum functionality.

The face of television has gone digital, with major cable networks beginning to stream live broadcasts online. This means that as television goes digital, marketers have the opportunity to get the same advertising benefits from television they've always gotten, but with some of the unique attributes of digital such as the measurability, social capability, and interactivity. This is best explained through the example of Netflix Watch Instantly service. This online streaming service allows users to find movies and TV shows via the Netflix Web site and instantly watch them either on their laptops or via a special setup box on their television. (Xbox also can serve as the setup box.) In addition to thousands of movies, for a low monthly fee, users can watch TV shows from ABC, NBC, Fox, and CBS. The technology used to do this streaming is all Internet based, and you can watch a TV show in one computer window while surfing the Internet in another. But what's more is that you can peek into the viewing choices of your friends who are also Netflix members and rate and review shows. Once you've found a highly rated show, you can start watching it right away, and when you've completed it, you can go back to Netflix.com and rate and comment on the show. That's just one example of how television is going digital.

Chapter 11

Building a SIM Mobile Campaign

*P*eople use all kinds of social media to share experiences and create, refresh, develop, and maintain relationships. Consumers use social media, such as full-fledged communities like Facebook, as well as blogs, comment forms, and the like to speak their minds and be heard.

As I outline in Chapter 1, social influence marketing is about employing social media and social influencers to achieve the marketing and business needs of an organization. Using mobile devices like cell phones and other handheld devices in social influence marketing helps you leverage their many capabilities to engage your prospects and customers with your brand, and enable these same people to communicate with each other and share their individual experiences with your brand, products, and services.

In this chapter, you find out how the mobile phone is rapidly becoming the most pervasive communication, entertainment, and social media channel out there, with a future filled with possibilities. You get a feel for what consumers are doing with their phones and the factors that affect their use. I explain how you can use mobile search, branded applications, and mobile-enhanced traditional and new media to engage consumers within a marketing and social media context. Finally, I discuss how you can leverage the convergence of social media and the mobile channel to benefit your business not just tomorrow, but today!

Looking at Consumer Trends in Mobile

The mobile phone has become a key fixture in the lives of nearly everyone in the United States and, increasingly so, around the world. According to the leading research firms, like comScore and Nielsen, nearly 80 percent of the United States population has a mobile phone, which is more than 232 million people. If you consider that Internet use hovers around 260 million people in the United States, or 85 percent, you realize that you can't ignore this marketing channel. Worldwide, the numbers are even more pronounced. Globally, there are 4.1 billion mobile service subscribers, which is 64 percent of the world's population. That's in stark contrast to the estimated 23 percent global penetration for the Internet.

Why the craze? Well, the mobile phone brings value, changes lives, and is changing the way we communicate, socialize, and conduct commerce.

It's more than a telephone; it's a portal to the world and the consumer

For the majority, the mobile phone is quickly becoming more than a simple tool for making and receiving phone calls. Sure, you can still make phone calls with them, but for many of us, the mobile phone has become a portal to the world and a multipath channel for the world to reach you. Today's mobile phones are newspapers, maps, books, magazines, cameras, radios, stores, game consoles, video and music players, calculators, calendars, address books, stereos, TVs, movie theaters, and concert halls. And this is just the beginning. In addition to making and receiving calls on mobile phones, people are doing these things:

- Accessing news and information
- Checking up on the latest celebrity gossip
- Checking the weather
- Looking up addresses and finding directions
- Buying products, images, ringtones — and even pizza
- Receiving the latest coupons and promotional discounts from their favorite stores
- Playing games
- Listening to music and watching movies
- Responding to their favorite brand's mobile messages
- Participating with, and supporting, political candidates
- Donating money to their favorite charities
- Socializing with friends and marketers
- Updating friends and family on their locations and activities

This list is just the tip of the iceberg. Every day, consumers are doing more and more with their mobile phones and you can create new and innovative campaigns that fit in with those uses.

We're shutting off our landlines

In many countries, the mobile phone is the primary means of communication. In the United States, according to a 2009 Center for Disease Control study, nearly 35 percent of Americans don't use a traditional landline phone; this number goes as high as 50 percent or more for some consumer segments. In addition, in the United States, voice is no longer the primary communication channel on the mobile phone. According to Nielsen Mobile, as of October 2008, the average mobile subscriber in the United States sent 357 text messages, compared to 204 voice minutes.

The key to successful consumer engagement, especially in the social media context, is to combine both information delivery and exchange with entertainment; in other words, focus on "infotainment" services.

The release and adoption of smarter phones

No doubt about it, phones are getting smarter. Take the Wayback machine to 1983 (the Wayback is a fictional time-travel machine referenced in the old *The Rocky and Bullwinkle Show* cartoon), and you'd see innovative and/or fashion-conscious road warriors carrying around a mobile phone shaped like a brick and weighing a whopping 30 ounces or more. For all its girth, the grandfather of mobile devices could do only two things: make and receive calls.

Today is a different story. You can find thousands of mobile phones that come in all shapes and sizes. True, many phones are still dedicated for the single purpose of making phone calls, but these devices are smaller, have longer battery lives, and provide clearer calls. However, increasingly, phones are getting *smarter,* meaning that they're capable of doing more. Basically, they're mini (and in many cases not-so-mini) computers. This new class of phone is referred to as a *smartphone.*

Here are the categories of phones:

- **Regular phones:** These are lightweight, dedicated devices for making and receiving phone calls and text messages and sometimes for performing rudimentary data service, such as accessing the Internet via mobile browsers (on what's called the mobile Internet). The Motorola Razr, for example, is a popular featured phone.

- **Smartphones:** These are full-featured, multipurpose, high-bandwidth, networked, multimodal, interactive information, communication, entertainment, and commerce solutions. Some of the more popular smartphones include the Apple iPhone, phones running the Google Android operating system, the Palm Pre, and the BlackBerry from Research in Motion. Juniper Research predicts that 23 percent of all mobile handsets sold by 2013 will be smartphones.

✔ **Wireless-enabled devices:** These devices aren't phones, but each has some form of wireless connectivity — either through Wi-Fi or an embedded wireless access card. The Apple iPod touch, Sony PlayStation 2, Amazon Kindle, and various flavors of netbooks (small laptops) are among the most popular wireless-enabled devices as this book goes to print. With Internet access, these devices naturally support interactive marketing.

The majority of mobile subscribers, roughly 90 percent, carry with them a traditional mobile phone as their primary phone, and the rest have adopted smartphones. But it's expected that more and more people will adopt smartphones and the requisite data plans to send text messages, acquire Internet connectivity, and enjoy related value-added services. That means you can and should start considering making your SIM campaigns smartphone friendly. Also, keep in mind that the 10 percent of the population that uses smartphones today could be a much larger percentage of your target audience.

To learn more about the thousands of mobile devices that are out there (I'm not kidding; there are that many), check out DeviceAtlas at `www.deviceatlas.com`. (See Figure 11-1.)

Figure 11-1:
The myriad of mobile devices: DeviceAtlas.

Even though the iPhone is capturing the lion's share of the press, today it accounts for only 2 percent of all phones and 20 percent of the smartphone class.

Understanding the Many Paths within the Mobile Channel

It's easy to look at a mobile phone and think, "It's just a phone." But it really isn't *just* a phone anymore. Sure, you can make calls with it and engage in social practices, just like the old landline party line phones. However, the telephone capability is just the tip of the iceberg. Today's mobile devices are much more than what most people expect. In fact, for many people, these devices are the primary method of personal communication, social interaction, and even commerce.

Figure 11-2 illustrates the many paths you can use to reach the mobile phone.

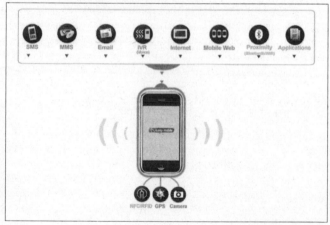

Figure 11-2: The paths through the mobile channel.

Courtesy of iLoop Mobile Inc.

The term used to interact with consumers through all these paths is *mobile channel*. The mobile channel refers to the collection of companies and systems, wireless networks, mobile phones, application providers, marketers, and so on that make it possible for you to interact with an individual audience member directly through a mobile phone or wireless-enabled device. Each of these paths — SMS, MMS, e-mail, voice and IVR, Internet, mobile Web, proximity, and applications — is unique.

Keep in mind what media scholar Marshall McLuhan taught us in 1964: The medium is the message. Each of these paths changes how your message is received and accepted. In the social media context, this is important because if your message isn't accepted, it certainly won't be talked about and shared.

I describe each path as follows:

- ✔ **SMS:** This is short message service, also commonly known as *text messaging*. A text message is comprised of 160 or fewer letters, characters, and numbers delivered through the mobile channel. It is ideal for the sharing and exchange of contextually relevant, timely bits of information — including a brief message to a friend, celebrity gossip, details on the latest sale, impulse impressions, and thoughts on a product or service. In the social media context, SMS is popular with Twitter because people update their accounts (tweet) and/or receive alerts via SMS, even though SMS is just one very small part of the Twitter experience. Keep in mind, though, that SMS is permission based. If you're a marketer trying to reach customers via SMS, they need to have given you permission to market to them.

- ✔ **MMS:** This stands for multimedia messaging service, which is a unique protocol for exchanging digital content, such as videos, pictures, and audio via mobile phones. The term MMS is often generically used for all forms of digital content, including ringtones, images, video, and so on, even if the delivery doesn't follow the proper MMS protocol; more often than not, this content is sent via the Internet rather than through MMS. MMS works well with a SIM campaign where you're inviting customers to share their own pictures and videos with each other.

- ✔ **E-mail:** Traditionally, e-mail has been delivered to a mobile device, such as a BlackBerry or Palm Treo, through a special e-mail service connected to the device. Now, regular e-mail can be delivered through mobile applications (often built in by the wireless carriers or mobile phone manufacturers) or through the mobile Web. Newer phones, such as iPhones and devices such as the iPod touch, deliver and render HTML e-mails, as opposed to the text-only versions of old. For the most part, e-mail is rarely used in marketing specifically to reach mobile devices, due to the difficulty to target a user and know the type of device she's using to read her e-mail.

- ✔ **Voice:** This takes the form of talking with a live person working in a call center, who in turn may trigger mobile data services as a response to the call. Voice can also refer to an interactive voice response (IVR), or automated attendant, system where your audience can interact with your service through various system prompts and menus, such as, "Say or press 1 to tell us what you think of the service." The greatest opportunity here is with social influence marketing campaigns that start online and invite users to have special customized voice messages sent to their friends on their mobile phones. For example, the mobile campaign for the movie *Snakes on a Plane* encouraged participants to create customized voice messages for their friends. When the receivers answered the calls, they heard a message, in the voice of the actor Samuel L. Jackson, about the movie. The message also said that their friends (you could include any name) wanted them to watch the movie together. It appeared as if Samuel L. Jackson was telling them this. This widely successful campaign resulted in more than 4 million calls being placed between friends during the promotional period.

✔ **Internet:** Many mobile devices can connect to the Internet for a wide range of data-enabled services, including the mobile Web, applications, location-based services that tell you about special discounts or recommend restaurants around you, content services like streaming video (for example, Mobile TV or MLB games), as well as mobile-carrier-managed portals, such as Verizon V Cast or T-Mobile T-Zones.

✔ **Mobile Web:** Refers to the experience of browsing the Internet via the mobile phone — for example, going to the Facebook Web site on your phone and posting a status update. You can do this using either the Web browsers built into many of the smartphones to visit mobile versions of Web sites (or in the case of the iPhone, you can actually see the regular Web site) or by using specially created applications that connect you to specific Web sites or Web services. For example, the Facebook iPhone application is extremely popular.

✔ **Proximity spectrum (Bluetooth/Wi-Fi):** Refers to the short-range Bluetooth radio channel and Wi-Fi network capability for connecting to the Internet. Think of *proximity spectrum* as technologies that let you connect your mobile device with others close to you. Typically, Bluetooth is used to connect phones with wireless headsets and related periphery devices, but you can also use it to deliver content to the mobile phone, as you can with Wi-Fi technology. Bluetooth plays a role in social media at live events where you can send content to the phone and encourage users to share it, while Wi-Fi plays a huge role, in that it provides the data network connectivity for mobile Internet, Internet, and application services.

✔ **Applications:** These are software utilities and services downloaded to mobile phones, and they take many forms. Some are unique to the particular platform they're deployed for, such as the Apple iPhone, Google Android, Research in Motion's BlackBerry, the Palm Pre, Nokia Symbian, and Microsoft's line of phones. Applications are incredible ways to interact with social media programs, due to their ease of use and integration into the features of the phone.

Keeping in Mind Mobile Phone Capabilities

Not only are there many paths through the mobile devices to engage and interact with members of your community, as I discuss in the preceding section. Phones today increasingly have a wide range of enabling technologies, including cameras, location detection, and motion and touch sensors to enhance the experience.

It's a snap: Using the camera

Most mobile phones today come with a camera. For this reason, Nokia, the world's leading phone manufacturer, is one of the leading camera manufacturers and distributors as well. A consumer can use the camera in her phone to opt into a mobile marketing campaign by taking a picture of an ad in a magazine, a bar code, a physical product (such as a DVD or soda can), or herself and then use it in the social media context to contribute content to the community.

Consumers are finding that camera phones are easier to use than a standalone camera. And social network applications make it easier to contribute photos directly from a phone's camera than downloading images from a traditional digital camera to a computer and then uploading them to the community site. Most social platforms like Twitter, Facebook, and Flickr allow you to take photographs on your mobile phone and easily e-mail them to the service.

An interesting use of mobile cameras that is emerging is with customers taking photographs of products with the phones, sharing them directly on Facebook, and asking their friends for feedback on whether they should buy the products.

Location, location, location

Location information is a very powerful tool, and it's one of the unique features of the mobile phone. When mobile subscribers are out and about, they *usually* know where they are, but their phones *always* know. Location information can make your programs more contextually relevant to a user's location, and you get those details, depending on the phone, from the user, the service network, global positioning and network triangulation technologies, Wi-Fi networks, and a wide range of other technical alchemy.

All you need to know is that you can use location to make your programs more contextually relevant with the user and the community. For example, you could run a special SIM campaign targeted toward people who are in a 3-mile radius of your flagship store, encouraging them to visit and get an additional discount if they bring a friend into the store with them.

Location-based mobile campaigns can appear as an invasion of privacy. If they're not permission based or aren't explained clearly, they can come across as Big Brother-type efforts. If you're planning a SIM campaign with location-aware elements, I recommend targeting it toward audiences that are already comfortable with location-aware services and advertising.

Near-field communications and RFID

Although RFID and NFC technologies are far from mainstream at this point, some phones are equipped with them. These systems — radio frequency identification (RFID) and near-field communication (NFC) — are similar in concept to Bluetooth in that they're both short-range communication systems, but they have unique identification and commerce capabilities.

In Germany, for example, NFC-enabled phones are used to purchase train tickets. A user simply hovers the phone near an NFC reader, and the reader charges her linked billing account (to a credit card, for instance) for the purchase of the ticket.

RFID chips can be used to identify you and can even personalize signs as you walk by. (Did you see the scene in *Minority Report* in which Tom Cruise walks by a sign and the sign talks to him? That's what I'm talking about.)

Phone interaction

It just takes a tap, a shake, a swipe, or a swing to interact with many of the newer phones coming out on the market. The most recognizable phone on the market leveraging this motion and gesture technology today is the iPhone, but many other phones have it and/or soon will. The motion- and gesture-sensing capabilities of these phones improves the usability and convenience of the device.

For instance, on the iPhone, you can make pinching motions on a picture or mobile Web site to zoom in and out on the screen. With some games, you can tap with one finger, two fingers, three, or more, and the number of fingers you use determines what happens. You can even shake or tilt the device and that has an affect on the experience.

One of my favorite applications that leverages the shake feature is Urbanspoon, which requires you to shake the device, starting a series of jackpot wheels to spin. The application recommends restaurants near you — very cool. See Figure 11-3.

In a social media context, you can have all sorts of fun playing with these input and interaction methods and determining how to use them in your social media program.

The iPhone isn't the first mobile device, however, to use these types of applications. If you ever had a Palm, the early Palm devices were the first ones to come out with gestures as a means of user interface short cuts and data entry.

Figure 11-3:
Urbanspoon
on the
iPhone.

Next-generation mobile services and beyond

If you think mobile networks and devices are going to stop innovating . . . well, don't hold your breath. The horizon holds many exciting developments. Some of the key drivers are increased network bandwidth, longer battery life (including batteries that charge from ambient radio waves), higher-resolution screens, faster processors, and more. Companies are even working on making their processes greener.

Just think of what you could do with faster data speeds on the phone. Today, 3G networks are the norm. 3G is the term commonly used for third-generation mobile networks. The first generation, or 1G, began in the early 1980s; the second generation, or 2G, emerged in the 1990s, and 3G was formed in the late 1990s. With each successive generation, mobile network capabilities and data transfer and network speeds increased. 4G networks, with data-transfer speeds reaching 100 Mbps (megabits per second), are on the horizon. When these hit, you'll be able to do full-motion video conferencing and video exchange on phones and other mobile devices. This will have a big impact on mobile devices' roles in social media.

Fitting Mobile into Your Social Media Practices

As a marketer, it's your job to communicate, deliver, and exchange value with your audience, and the practice of doing those things with and through mobile devices is referred to as *mobile marketing*. Mobile marketing isn't mystical; neither does it fall outside the practice of traditional marketing. The definition of *mobile marketing* is straightforward: marketing on or with a mobile device such as a mobile phone.

Mobile marketing also includes the following:

- **Communicating:** Imparting information and news about your offerings and related activities to your audience members: customers, clients, partners, prospects, leads, employees, advisors, investors, the press, and all the other people and organizations that play a role in your business, as well as society at large. Communicating spreads the word about what your organization does and the value it has to offer.

  You probably use any number of traditional and new-media channels (TV, radio, print, live events, outdoor media, point-of-sale displays in stores, the Internet, e-mail, telemarketing, social media, and so on) to communicate indirectly or directly with members of your audience. *Direct marketing communication* occurs when you initiate contact directly with individual members of your audience, as in the case of sending e-mails or initiating phone calls. Direct marketing communication also occurs when a customer visits your broadband or mobile Internet Web site. *Indirect marketing communication* happens when you advertise or present some other form of promotional message through mass-media channels (such as TV, radio, or print) to expose members of your audience to your communication, but you leave it up to individual audience members to initiate direct contact with you.

- **Delivering:** Providing your products or services and exceptional customer service to members of your audience.

- **Exchanging:** Swapping value (which I define later in this list). Often, you exchange your goods and services for money, but you can determine for yourself what to take in exchange.

- **Offerings:** The products and services produced by your organization.

- **Value:** A sense of worth. People value something when they perceive that the item's worth exceeds what it costs them to obtain, consume, or use.

  ✔ **Mobile-enhanced traditional and new-media channels:** Marketers rely heavily on traditional marketing channels (including television) and new media channels (including Web sites) to build awareness among members of their audience and promote their offerings. Adding *mobile-enhanced* to the mix simply means that you're marketing to people who are accessing the media in those channels from cellphones, smartphones, and other wireless devices.

In addition, a *mobile marketing call to action* is a set of instructions promoted in the media that shows someone how to use his phone or mobile terminal to participate in a mobile marketing program. For example, one mobile call to action might be "Text SONC to 20222 to donate $5 to support Special Olympics Northern California Athletes. You donation will be billed to your mobile phone bill, and 100 percent of the proceeds is received by the charity."

Defining mobile marketing and its place within the social media context

As I mention in the previous section, there are two forms of mobile marketing: direct and indirect.

  ✔ **Direct mobile marketing:** Refers to the practice of reaching out and engaging individual members of your audience via their mobile phones. It also includes individuals reaching out and engaging with you in your marketing campaigns.

  You can proactively engage consumers, — that is, text-message and/or call them — if they've given you explicit permission to do so. If you don't have permission, you can't directly reach out to consumers.

  ✔ **Indirect mobile marketing:** Because mobile marketing requires that individual customers give you permission to interact with them on their mobile phones, you can use indirect mobile marketing to expose people to your offerings and invite them to give you permission to contact them directly. Therefore, indirect mobile marketing is the practice of enhancing your traditional and new-media programs (TV, radio, print, outdoor media, Internet, e-mail, voice, and so on) by inviting individual members of your audience to pull out a phone or mobile device and respond to your mobile call to action. On television, for example, your call to action may ask viewers to text a keyword to a short code to cast a vote. (Think about American Idol or other programs where the audience votes.) Or you may ask participants to fill out a form on the Web or on the mobile Internet, including their mobile phone number, to participate in the program.

Uniting mobile marketing with social media

The mobile aspects of social influence marketing occur within both direct and indirect mobile marketing contexts. As a marketer, you can directly engage your audience either by having them reach out to you or vice versa.

Within the indirect context, you can interlace mobile marketing within your traditional and new media channels — including your Web site, magazine ads, and so on — by adding mobile calls to action. For example, you may

✔ **Offer a text alert service.**

You can send participants updates on your programs in text messages. Create a form on your Web site, where you ask participants to enter their mobile phone numbers and opt in to receiving text messages from you. Or you may invite them to join by asking them to text a specific code to a phone number that you've set up to receive these messages.

If you would like to collect more data on your customers than their mobile phone numbers (their preferences, for example), use the Web form for opt-in, including fields for the additional data you need, and add the customers to your database. However, be aware that it may limit participation in the program because people may not want to fill out the form or provide too much personal information.

✔ **Ask for feedback or content.**

Have participants take pictures with their mobile phones and send them to the community. Or you can ask them to contribute their ideas about the name for your next product, or give a shout-out to a friend.

✔ **Remind participants to share.**

Encourage users to share rewards from a program, such as a coupon offer, with their friends.

Community engagement is all about stimulating interaction between you and members of your audience, as well as among community members. You want them talking to each other. Mobile devices are perfect for this aspect of the social community; you can take advantage of this connectivity and the ability to share experiences whenever and wherever community members want to.

Supporting a cause

Cause marketing is the cooperative use of marketing strategy by a for-profit business and a nonprofit organization for mutual benefit. The business gets to align itself with the value of the nonprofit organization, and the nonprofit organization gets the opportunity to draw attention to its activities and possibly recruit new volunteers and donors.

The mobile channel is ideal for capturing charitable donations. You can mobile-enhance any social media marketing program and put a call to action in this marketing to elicit a response from your audience. In the case of mobile charitable donation programs, the response you're looking for is a financial contribution. For example, the Direct Marketing Education Foundation (DMEF), a foundation dedicated to educating future marketers, raised money by encouraging sponsors to donate via text message. See Figure 11-4 for the call to action featured on the DMEF Web site (www.directworks.org).

The most effective of these channels for charitable donations is SMS because mobile subscribers can participate without registering for a service or using a credit card; the donation can go straight to a subscriber's mobile phone bill, with 100 percent of the donation being passed to the participating charity, less nominal transaction and standard marketing fees.

Group decision making

Group decision making in mobile is just what it sounds like: using the aspects of mobile to stimulate interactions with groups. Mobile allows people to participate in group settings wherever they are, which makes the membership of the group even larger and more diverse than ever before.

Think about something as simple as planning a party. Using a mobile phone, I can invite all of my friends in my address book with a few button presses using a text message. Then I can ask my friends what food they would like to bring to the party, and keep a running tally of guests who plan to attend. Additional messages can go to those who haven't replied, and soon, I have a full menu ready to go. Next, I can ask everyone to bring music. And a few button presses later, the evening shapes up nicely.

One use of mobile in group situations is called flash mobs. A *flash mob* is a large group that suddenly appears and disappears in a specific location, with viral marketing as the main driver of the mob. In the past, e-mail was the primary way to let large groups of people know about the event, but SMS is even more effective with this spur-of-the-moment type of activity.

✔ In January of 2008, a flash mob of 200 people congregated in Grand Central Station in New York City and froze in place on cue, for 5 minutes. That type of coordination has mobile written all over it. Although mobile may not have been used at this event, think of the potential ways the mob could have been notified to perhaps change positions or disperse without a word spoken.

✔ In June 2009, to promote *Hammertime* — a TV show starring '80s rap star MC Hammer — a flash mob danced to "U Can't Touch This" at a clothing store on Sunset Boulevard in Los Angeles, and then left as quickly as they came into the store.

Sometimes done for marketing and public relations, and sometimes done as spur-of-the-moment engagement, flash mobs can be very effective at drawing attention. And mobile marketing can play a large role, allowing in-the-moment communications across large groups of people.

You don't always know what will capture people's attention. When it works, it could be very effective. The idea could be great, but it could still fizzle.

Changing the world with your fingertips

Jim Manis, one of the mobile industry's most influential players, founded the Mobile Giving Foundation (MGF) after the sale of his company m-Qube to VeriSign in 2007. Manis and the team at MGF set up a program in which MGF-certified charities, partners, and participating carriers can organize charitable-donation programs using premium short messaging services or PSMS as the means of capturing mobile subscribers' donations. As in any PSMS program, you promote the call to action; people respond to it and donate, and nearly 100 percent of the donation makes its way to the MGF-certified charity.

A 501(c)(3) or related charity can contact the MGF to go through the certification process and use the mobile channel to raise money. A company that wants to make a difference and be socially responsible can use the mobile channel to promote an MGF-certified program. For more information, visit www.mobilegiving.org.

Figure 11-4: DMEF supporting the direct marketing community through SMS.

Building Your Own Mobile-Enabled Communities

Building a mobile-enabled social community isn't as hard as you may think. You can leverage existing social media platforms or build the mobile capability right into your existing interactive marketing channels, like your Web site and mobile Internet site.

Leveraging existing online communities

People are already using Facebook and other social networking sites on their phones today, and they find it easy to accomplish certain tasks, such as uploading photos or posting updates. Some people even prefer to use their mobile phone; it may be much easier to get them to send in a picture from their phone then asking them to go home, find the picture on their computer, and upload it to the community.

As a marketer, you can leverage and use existing social community sites and invite your community to keep in touch with you and follow you. Each community site has varying levels of sophistication and capability for mobile accessibility. Two of the most popular are Facebook and Twitter.

Facebook

Facebook (www.facebook.com) is one of the world's leading social networking communities. Marketers, like you, are increasingly creating Facebook pages for their companies and marketing campaigns so that their community can follow them and keep up to date. Facebook has these existing mobile capabilities that you can leverage:

✔ **Keep your Facebook community updated from your phone.**

You first have to register your phone with your Facebook page. (Go to your Facebook page's mobile settings by selecting Edit Page.) You can then configure your page so that you can update it by sending text messages.

✔ **Keep your community in sync with you via mobile.**

Ask users in all your marketing media to register on your group or fan page to receive text alerts of your status updates, downloading the Facebook application onto their phones, and following you, or visiting you via the Facebook mobile Web site, http://m.facebook.com.

In March 2009, Facebook started trialing a feature to allow community members to subscribe to your fan page via text messaging. They've not rolled it out to every account yet, but when they do, you can encourage your audience to follow you by simply asking them to text the name of your page (www.facebook.com/*yourname*) to Facebook's shortcode, 32665, to become Facebook fans of your company. Keep an eye out for this. Just imagine; you could include this very simple prompt in all of your company's marketing, asking everyone to take their phones out and become fans.

Twitter

Twitter (www.twitter.com) is an increasingly popular social networking service that supports microblogging, which is the journaling of your activities in 140-character or less messages. Twitter is considered the SMS service for the Web and has attracted millions of followers.

Twitter isn't just for consumers. Companies are increasingly using it to share their community information. You can create a Twitter account for free and start *tweeting* (the term used for posting to the service). You can then invite people to follow you so that they can receive updates via e-mail, on the Web, on the mobile Web, and even via SMS. To have people follow you via SMS, invite them to text "follow *username*" to the Twitter short code 40404.

Other social media communities

Countless other social media communities are out there — some general (MySpace), some target niche segments (LinkedIn, Eons, Gather, Glee, Faithbase, Disaboom, Think.MTV, and MyBatanga), and the numerous social media utilities (YouTube, Flickr, Scribd, Eventful, Evite, and others). Some of these already have mobile capabilities and you can extend others to support your mobile programs. You'll need to do some research to find out who is supporting what and determine how you can best leverage mobile-based marketing on what competitors are doing (or not doing).

If you decide to build your own social media program through the mobile Web, use your competitive research to ensure that you're creating something unique, and then make sure that the concept is true to your brand.

Creating your own social offerings: applications and widgets galore

You may also want to offer value to members of your audience by creating your own social media offerings, or something altogether unique. The mobile space is still new, and there's plenty of opportunity to create something that hasn't been done before.

You can deploy these services over and through any of the mobile paths, such as SMS, mobile Internet, and downloadable applications. For example, with SMS, you can recruit opinions and comments, blogs, and more. The key is to consider the content format and the most appropriate path for delivering the content to mobile subscribers. Two popular and emerging social media services are applications and widgets.

Applications and widgets on the mobile front make the mobile experience come alive. Think about what makes sense for your customers, and how you will make sure it is marketed successfully, and then put your imagination to work! There are any number of mobile widget providers, but you may want to check out Snac (www.snac.com) or the thousands of iPhone application developers, including iLoop Mobile (www.iloopmobile.com). *Widgets* and *applications* are phrases used interchangeably, but the best way to think about them is to consider a widget as something that sits in a Web page or within another application, while an application can function independently.

Applications

One visit to iTunes or to one of the many sites that review applications for various phones shows you how many applications already exist. And hundreds, if not thousands, contain social media elements. Chat was one of first to appear, along with mobile versions of most social network sites (Facebook, LinkedIn, MySpace, and so on). Here are examples of taking it to the next step:

- **Confession Booth** (`www.confessionboothapp.com`): Submit your sins, transgressions, or just bad moments (anonymously) and see what the community thinks.

- **iFamous** (`www.nocturnalware.biz/NOCturnalWare/iFamous.html`): Gives everyone their 15 minutes of fame by allowing users to submit their profiles and photos. Every 15 minutes, a new profile is selected and shown to everyone who has the Famous application on their phone.

- **Mig33** (`www.mig33.com`): Works on almost all carrier phones and allows you to share photos, stay connected with friend updates, get free IM and chat, and make cheap international calls. The application has millions of users in 200 countries.

Combining social with mobile technology allows the creativity to flow. The mobile phone provides a unique opportunity to engage with users that you can't achieve through traditional means.

Widgets

A *widget* is a small application that you can easily add to your Web site or to a mobile phone. Widgets can be tools or games, and they can be functional for business or just for fun. A widget typically does only one thing. Single purpose widget examples are:

- Updates from eBay, following auctions

- Stock quote updates

- Weather forecasts dependent on phone location

- Get your latest Tweets from Twitter

- Simple brand loyalty building games, like filling the shopping cart as fast as you can to win loyalty points

You can easily enhance widgets with forms that ask people to enter their mobile phone number to get updates. You can use mobile in this context to get people to come back. For example, if they get knocked off the high score rankings you can send them a text message to get them to come back and play some more to get their ranking back. Companies like ePrize (`www.eprize.com`), FuHu (`www.FuHu.com`), and Clearspring (`www.clearspring.com`) help you build a widget.

Adding Social Media Elements to Mobile

You should consider two additional elements while embarking on a mobile social media campaign: social graphs and search. These are important for any social media marketing program, but they're especially important in mobile ones.

Portable social graphs

*Social graph*s are the relationships that people have with each other, within a social network, an application, a site, or across the social Web. Think of it as a visualization of relationships — how people connect to each other and what interests they share. But then think about the technical application of this concept. What if you knew who your customer's friends are, and then provide user experiences that take advantage of that knowledge?

Facebook Connect allows Facebook data to be integrated into other Web sites and applications. With Facebook Connect, your customer could use a shopping application for the iPhone, and then share mobile offers with their Facebook network. Taking it another step, consider recommendation engines are becoming commonplace (allows users to make recommendations and rate products or services), but imagine if the only recommendation coming was from a Facebook friend.

Research shows that users are more likely to purchase products or services based on recommendations; friends and family are the most effective referrers.

Searching with mobile

Mobile search is just what the name implies. It's how you find things while on a mobile device, such as Web sites, people, and restaurants. It sounds like it should be simple; after all, don't all Web sites "show up" on your phone when you go to them? But what if you don't know the name of the site, or you're trying to find something and the mobile site address isn't what you thought it was.

Here are a few types of mobile searches:

- ✔ **Search engines:** Just like the Web, search engines and portal sites have created mobile versions. Sites like Google and Yahoo! are available on the mobile phone, and are meant for mobile sites. One big difference is the way results are displayed. For example, when you search for restaurants in a particular city, the listings show the address and phone number (allowing you to easily click the phone number and call the restaurant).

✔ **Directories:** Local search and mobile directories are often available through the phone carrier. Some directory services use GPS *(global positioning)* technology to help determine where you are, and provide the right information. Directories assist users to find sites, and are just like the Yellow Pages to the mobile Web.

✔ **Recommendation services:** Not unlike technology on the Internet, mobile recommendation engines help users by providing similar or related content as their next step.

As a consumer, mobile search helps unlock the mystery and helps get the most out of your phone. As a marketer, you need to make sure that consumers can find the sites and campaigns that you work hard on. In order to be "found" by a mobile search engine, you have to look at a couple of things:

✔ **Make sure your mobile site has "good code."**

Search engines don't like messy sites that contain code errors.

Have your mobile site tested and make sure it gets a passing grade by the code police. Two mobile site testers are `http://ready.mobi` and `http://mtld.mobi/emulator.php`.

✔ **Follow search engine optimization (SEO) best practices.**

SEO describes how to get Web sites to appear in search results for specific keywords. Use your most important keywords — the words that your customers use when searching for you — in your pages and your titles. Make sure that the site is accessible by using text links throughout the site. And then submit your mobile site to the mobile search engine: a simple process of going to the mobile search engine submission page and filling out the form.

You must make sure that your social mobile site is search friendly so that people can find you by phone. People may hear about an application or a fun mobile site from their friends and have to rely on a search service to find it. And, your site must be searchable so that people can find each other and the elements of the application. Good user experience goes hand-in-hand with search friendliness.

Harnessing Mobile to Support Social Media

When considering mobile as part of a social influence marketing campaign, plan it like any marketing campaign with a few added considerations.

✔ **Consider how you will support mobile campaigns and call to actions in other channels.**

The mobile campaign won't be successful in a vacuum — you need to market it everywhere.

✔ **Take a look at your customer list and see if you can determine how your customers use mobile.**

Do they have iPhones or other smartphones?

✔ **Consider using a tool that can take advantage of the social graph.**

Such as Facebook Connect or other existing social networks.

✔ **Plan mobile applications or widgets but consider more than the iPhone.**

How can you support Blackberry, Treos, and other smartphones with your widget or application?

✔ **Plan for user experience.**

Use usability testing to ensure that everything you develop is built with the user in mind.

✔ **Do your research first.**

Take a look at mobile usage within supporting applications (Facebook Mobile, Twitter, YouTube Mobile, MySpace Mobile) and integrate where it makes sense.

✔ **Consider using a mobile Web site.**

It allows users to engage with the brand and with each other.

✔ **Plan for success.**

Ensure you know what your objectives are — what do you want to get out of the relationship with people — and ensure that you continually measure and report on your interactions.

✔ **Be relevant.**

With your communications with members of the community.

Chapter 12

Energizing Employees within Your Company for Social Influence

*U*ntil the beginning part of this decade, enterprise software looked and felt very different from the software that was designed for consumers. Enterprise software helped businesses manage customer relationships, handle knowledge management, communicate internally, and handle company operations focused on addressing the needs of IT managers more than the employees who were the users of the software. Emphasis was put on security, compliance, system control, interoperability, and maintenance — and strangely less on what employees wanted or needed. The fact that the software buyers (the IT managers) weren't the users (the employees) was largely to blame for this state of affairs. And then something changed.

When employees went home in the evenings, the software that they were using for their personal lives (Web or otherwise) was progressively a lot better designed and easier to use. And more than that, the software allowed them to contribute content, share, comment, and connect with each other. Savvy technology companies realized that there was an opportunity to make enterprise software more like consumer software and social-oriented Web sites to better meet the needs of companies.

Steadily, these consumer-centric solutions gained traction in the corporate world, as employees started to discover that they could find free (or nearly free) and easy-to-use tools on the Internet. They could install these tools on their machines or access them online to do their jobs better. This consumerization of enterprise software forced IT managers to reevaluate how they chose software and how strict their security policies were. And with that, the Enterprise 2.0 transformation was born.

In this chapter, I discuss how you can practice social influence marketing within your own company by encouraging collaboration, knowledge sharing, and communication. I also discuss the different tools that you can use to help you in this endeavor. After all, if you want your customers to influence each other about your brand and product, you might want to start by figuring out how you can encourage employees to positively influence each other as well.

I included this chapter in the book because if you plan to engage with consumers across the Internet and practice social influence marketing, you had better be practicing those philosophies in your own backyard, too. It's one of the best ways to learn about social influence marketing — to practice those philosophies internally within your organization.

Encouraging Your Employees to Collaborate

Enterprise 2.0 is the use of social software platforms within companies, or between companies and their partners or customers, according to Andrew McAfee, a Harvard Business School professor who coined the term. These software platforms borrow design philosophies, features, and even technology standards from the Web sites and Web software that pervade the Internet.

Every day, more companies install these social software platforms because they want their employees to collaborate, communicate, share, and organize into communities of interest the way they do in their personal lives. There's no reason why your employees shouldn't use software built on these consumer-oriented design philosophies, with the collaboration layer built into the core — software like wikis, blogs, discussion forums, and microblogging solutions.

The best way to understand what Web tools work for your employees is to ask them about the Web sites they visit and the Web tools that they use in their personal lives. How they use consumer Web sites can give you hints at how they want to adopt enterprise tools.

The following sections include some recommendations for how you can get your employees to collaborate and socially influence each other in positive ways. These practices are a direct mirror of how you can engage with social influencers, too.

Employees always compete with each other for promotions, bonuses, and better career opportunities. That will never change, and it will always affect their willingness to collaborate and work with each other. As you encourage employees to socially influence each other, be aware of any insecurities they have.

Energizing employees: It's nothing new

This isn't the first time that energizing employees for social influence and knowledge sharing has been discussed. Debates in the knowledge management community on how best to get employees to collaborate date back to the early 1990s. For a long time, companies saw the Holy Grail of knowledge management being the ability to capture everything that was in an employee's head in a database so that if the employee were to leave the company, it wouldn't suffer.

This thinking evolved to the realization that no firm can truly capture the experiences and knowledge in an employee's brain, and by the time it does so (if that were possible!), the information or knowledge is stale. Since then, the focus has shifted to energizing employees to collaborate, exchange information, and motivate one another to increase innovation and employee productivity.

Rewarding teams

Most companies are organized to reward individual performance and promote the rising stars more quickly than other employees. If you want to foster a collaborative environment where employees learn from each other, share their knowledge generously, and participate in social platforms geared toward harnessing the collective intelligence, think carefully about how you reward performance. You might be well served by putting more emphasis on team versus individual performance.

Treating everyone equally

Employees usually thrive on competition. That's a good thing. But employees who feel left out of the loop or feel that they aren't seen as critical to the organization are less likely to give their time and brain power for the community. Be sure that you treat every employee equally if you truly want to foster collaboration and the free exchange of information among your employees. They'll speak only if you give them ample opportunities and encouragement to do so. You need to let them speak on their own terms, too whether that be through the technologies that they prefer, the locations of, their choice (team meetings, suggestion boxes, or one on one meetings), or with the mentors that they seek out.

Trusting your employees

Just as it's imperative for you to trust consumers and let them share ownership of your brand, so, too, must you trust your employees to converse, communicate, and collaborate with each other respectfully and productively. If you don't trust your employees, they won't trust you, and they definitely won't want to give their time to furthering the objectives of the organization. This matters most when you're trying to energize them for social influence, as it requires a commitment and not just a job description to accomplish.

Creating the right culture

The right office culture is imperative if you want your employees to engage with one another in conversations, be transparent about what they don't know, and be willing to listen and learn from their peers, including the younger or more junior ones. Your culture needs to be one of humility and openness, and one that allows initiative without punishing people too harshly for mistakes. The way you need to behave in the social Web to engage with your customers in a meaningful way applies to the way you must engage with your employees, too. And it all starts with culture.

Placing a premium on groups with a purpose

A key ingredient to energizing employees for social influence is to put the right mix of employees in a room (real or virtual) together to brainstorm, innovate, or accomplish a specific task. Bring an eclectic mix of employees together and ask them to collaborate on a specific task at hand. Their diverse skills and personalities result in unique results and can lay the foundation for a more collaborative work environment.

Collaborating in a work environment is very different from collaborating in one's personal life. You need clearly defined objectives for people to rally around; otherwise, valuable company time may be wasted.

Avoiding excessive snooping

I'm always amazed to learn about companies that peek into their employees' e-mail accounts and watch what Web sites they visit. If you want to create a culture of social interaction where people in different offices or even countries come together and share their insights and learn from one another online, you need to make them feel that they're not being watched, tracked, or evaluated every step of the way. Treat them with the respect that you give your bosses, and they'll deliver amazing work. Whatever you do, don't snoop around. You'll lose their trust, respect, and commitment.

Picking Social Software for Social Influence

A myriad range of social software companies provides solutions for businesses. These vary from free software as a service (SaaS) solutions that you can rent for a few dollars per month to enterprise-grade solutions that cost hundreds of thousands of dollars and have been retooled for the social world. It can be confusing, finding the right solution for your company as you create an environment that energizes employees for social influence, but here are the four classes of software and Web solutions to consider.

Enterprise software

If you belong to a large organization, you probably don't control what software you get to use. In these instances, you should try to influence your IT department to buy emergent social software or enterprise software upgrades that include social functionality that can either be plugged into your enterprise environment or run independently.

- **Microsoft SharePoint** (http://sharepoint.microsoft.com; see Figure 12-1) is probably the most popular collaboration software in companies today and integrates with Microsoft Office and other Microsoft products very easily.

- **SAP** (www.sap.com) is deployed across large enterprises as it handles industrial grade business operations, customer management, financial, and HR needs very well.

- **IBM** (www.ibm.com) with its Web sphere portal is another great option; it's easy to build custom applications on it that can be delivered through a portal environment.

- **Telligent** (http://telligent.com) is known for its rich community functionality (its Community server product) and how it integrates with the rest of a company's IT infrastructure.

Every day, these enterprise-grade collaboration platforms add more social features to their application suites. Most have Web-based interfaces, too.

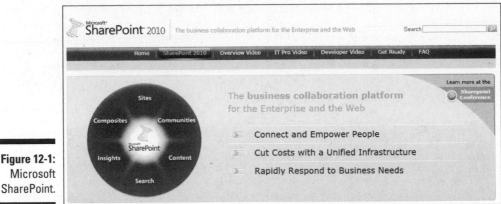

Figure 12-1:
Microsoft
SharePoint.

Emergent enterprise social software

Emergent enterprise social software products are built from the ground up to be collaboration tools, leveraging the design philosophies, needs, and requirements of everyday people. They borrow from the likes of Facebook, Wikipedia, Twitter, and YouTube but add an enterprise flavor that makes them powerful. There are relatively new players:

✓ **Confluence** (www.atlassian.com/software/confluence)

✓ **Socialtext** (www.socialtext.com)

✓ **NewsGator** (www.newsgator.com; see Figure 12-2).

Figure 12-2:
NewsGator's
home page.

These solutions plug into existing corporate software environments and work with the enterprise software effectively. Because the companies who provide enterprise social software understand the needs of big business, they're usually compliant with the security requirements of most IT departments. The software is delivered shrink-wrapped or in some cases as a software as a service model. (With the software as a service model, you don't buy software but lease it on a monthly basis over the Internet.)

Small-scale social software

Smaller, significantly cheaper solutions that work nicely for small business environments are categorized as small-scale social software. Free or nearly-free applications are

✔ **Google's Application Suite** (www.google.com/apps) integrates nicely with Google mail. The Google application suite is mostly free and shares the same user experience of Google search. So if you like the search product, you'll like this.

✔ **Zoho** (www.zoho.com; see Figure 12-3) is similar to the Google Application Suite but far richer in functionality. It is also Web-based and includes several related tools, such as project management and a customer relationship management software.

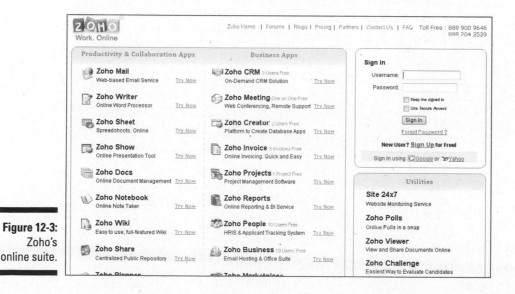

Figure 12-3: Zoho's online suite.

Other strong companies to look at include

- **Traction Software** (www.tractionsoftware.com) is feature rich and combines the best of blogging with a wiki environment. Traction Software isn't free and for some users can appear complex, but it's a great solution for knowledge management.

- **Wetpaint** (www.wetpaint.com) is a simple application that's grounded in all the wiki philosophies. As a result, it's designed to make it very easy for you to build your own site, share it with a select group of people and collaborate around it. It can be used within your organization or for light public facing needs.

- **37signals** (www.37signals.com) takes a different approach in that it has a distinct set of specific Web tools that can help you conduct your business. From a project management application to a tool that tracks leads, it accomplishes a very specific need.

Consumer social software

I'd be remiss if I didn't mention the fact that you can also use consumer-oriented social platforms for your business collaboration needs. Whether it's LinkedIn (www.linkedin.com; see Figure 12-4), Plaxo (www.plaxo.com), Ning (www.ning.com), SlideShare (www.slideshare.net), or even Facebook (www.facebook.com), they're all capable of handling private groups who upload and share files and discussions.

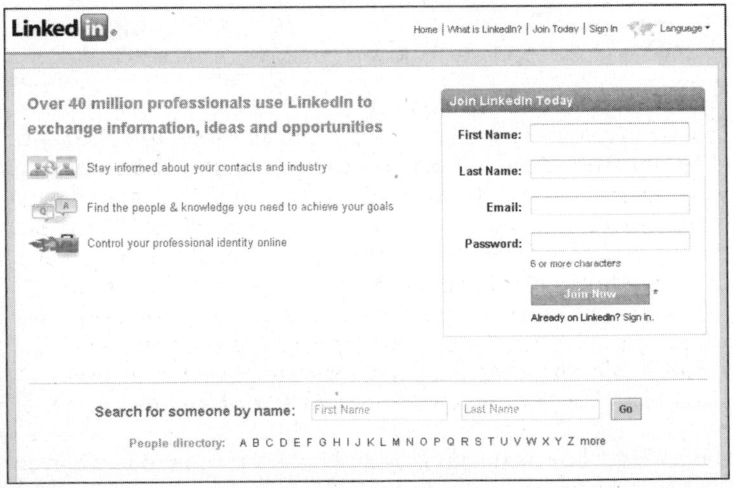

Figure 12-4: LinkedIn's membership page.

Some of these platforms may be more secure than others (especially with third-party tools and plug-ins overlaid on top of them), but they're all options for collaborating among employees, nevertheless. In the case of LinkedIn, its third-party plug-ins let you share presentations, publish news, run polls, and collaborate on documents, all from within LinkedIn and with people in your social graph.

Using Prediction Markets to Pick Winners

I've seen some people define *prediction markets* as speculative markets created for the purposes of making predictions. Sounds simple, doesn't it? Assets are created with financial values and the current market prices can be interpreted as a prediction of the probability of the event or the expected value of the parameter.

Here's what that really means: You can use your employees or your customers — and business partners, too, for that matter — to help you make better decisions. And the way you do it is by setting up a fake stock market-type environment using prediction market software where each participant is given a set amount to invest in different options (whatever you're trying to decide on). How much people invest in an option drives up its price or keeps it low. When you have hundreds and thousands of people participating and placing their bets, you get a clear sense of what the community believes to be the strongest option. Think of it as calculated social influence where the influencers are asked to put their money where their mouth is.

Companies around the world use prediction markets to make decisions. These can be strategic business decisions, such as where to locate a manufacturing plant, or simpler decisions, such as which television advertisement to run. The social influence of the community is automatically factored into the price of each option, providing very tangible guidance on what the community thinks has the greatest chance of success. HP, for example, uses prediction markets to predict workstation computer sales. In six out of the eight times, the results from the prediction market were more accurate than internal corporate forecasts. Probably one of the very first prediction markets was by the University of Iowa Tippie College of Business. Called the Iowa Electronics Market (IEM), it's been accurately predicting political election results since 1988 with only 1.33 percent error rate in voter totals.

As you look at your own company and how you can tap into the collective intelligence of your employees, think about using prediction markets. Not only will you get better advice but you also get a more deeply engaged community of employees participating and feeling that their voices are being heard within the organization. When they're participating in prediction markets internally, they'll probably want to test the same concepts on customers and business partners, too. Your customers will feel more engaged with your company when they become a part of the decision-making process around products and services. It is a win-win situation from whatever perspective that you look.

Prediction markets require participation. This might seem obvious, but you should keep in mind that you need a committed number of participants to make it work and gain collective intelligence. When you establish a prediction market within your organization, make sure the question being posed has resonance and meaning with a large enough community of employees so that you get the maximum participation.

The same goes for external-based prediction markets. Customers aren't spending their time waiting for you to engage with them in prediction markets to help you make better business decisions for them. Be sure to incentivize them to participate and make sure you're asking meaningful questions. Remember that these prediction markets can nicely serve to jump-start your community efforts, whether they're internal communities or external ones!

There are a few prediction market software solutions that you can use for your prediction market needs. These include

✔ Intrade Prediction Markets (www.intrade.com); Figure 12-5 shows the Intrade home page.

✔ Inkling (www.inklingmarkets.com)

✔ NewsFutures (www.newsfutures.com)

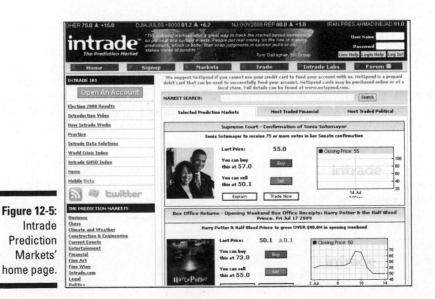

Figure 12-5: Intrade Prediction Markets' home page.

Rethinking Intranet

Historically, an *intranet* was defined as an employee only Web-based network for communication, collaboration, self-service, knowledge management, and business decision making. Most intranets were never designed to allow or encourage social influence, even though they're the ideal platforms for furthering collaboration and knowledge sharing within your company.

Many of the intranets were originally *top-down* (management controlled), rigid, inflexible, and uninviting experiences that served the needs of the Corporate Communications and Human Resources departments but not anyone else. They were used to communicate messages from CEOs and senior management, distribute company announcements, and provide human resources and finance self-service forms to employees.

Intranets slowly evolved to include basic collaboration features and the ability to create and manage department-level pages; they also grew to include key performance indicator dashboards for senior executives. But still for the most part, these intranets were static, top-down, rigid tools that by their very nature discouraged collaboration and social influencing.

For your intranet to go social and truly encourage collaboration and social influence to take place, you must adapt it to enable clear communication, collaboration, navigation, search, accessibility, and more. I give you some tips on optimizing your intranet in the text that follows.

Getting rid of the buzzwords

When you design your intranet, move away from the business and technical jargon that you may have used to describe the intranet or label features on it. Don't use words like *portals, knowledge management, digital dashboards, taxonomies, enterprise collaboration,* and *codification.* Use more inspiring language, words employees can relate to, in all your communications. In other words, humanize the intranet through language but also through the design.

For example, the original intranet at my company was called "Mom 3000," largely because like a mother it had all the answers to questions that employees had. And because it was so advanced the "3000" was added to it. Needless to say, we all loved the intranet and grew attached to it not just because of all its features but because of its personality.

Don't try to control too much

Most intranet managers know now that collaboration functionality is essential for the success of any intranet. But many still launch those collaboration tools with too restrictive controls. Whether it's wiki functionality or group and department pages, make the default setting on all pieces of functionality open to everyone.

Let there be more effort in password protecting something than in opening it to the community. By default let everyone view and edit every page on the intranet unless something has specifically been designated as confidential. And while you're at it, don't dictate how and with what tools your employees should collaborate; let them make those decisions.

Surfacing the connections

Instead of focusing only on publishing information and providing business applications to the employees, look for ways to connect people to one another. Let the intranet reveal strong and weak ties between people and create communities based on the information and collaboration needs of employees.

Make it as easy as possible for the employees by building functionality into the intranet so that people who have shared interests and objectives are linked to each other automatically. This doesn't mean publishing organizational charts but quite the opposite — having the intranet tell people who else within the organization has similar interests or objectives and encouraging them. The Google MOMA intranet approached this by having each employee's goals and objectives visible on the intranet right next to contact information. That way an employee would know whether their proposed conversation or project recommendation would be of high or low interest to the other employee even before contacting him.

Taking search social, too

Intranet managers generally believe — and rightly so — that search is the killer application (in a good way) of their intranet. They also recognize that search is extremely difficult to get right, primarily because employees expect the search to work as well as Google or Bing, even though the intranet search budget is miniscule compared to how much those companies invest in search.

One way to mitigate this is by incorporating social features into the search experience and by combining it with the telephone directory. When you prioritize search results based on what other users find to be useful and link the results with the specific users who find the results valuable, the perception of search increases dramatically because people in an organization are typically interested in the same content that others find useful. And very often, they have deeper questions beyond the content — and are always seeking people who can answer those questions. All the major enterprise search vendors, like Endeca (www.endeca.com) and Lucene (lucene.apache.org), offer some form of social search.

Allowing alternate access

Critical to the success of any intranet today — and even more so if it's one that needs to spur collaboration — is to provide multiple ramps into the intranet. You must build functionality so that employees can install a desktop widget that serves as a mini-window that's easily accessible to the intranet, updating them on who has posted what and making it extremely easy to upload content and share it themselves.

Similarly, it's important to build a mobile version of your intranet so that employees can get updates on their cellphones about new information published and collaboration spaces that they are participating in. Notifications are extremely important tools that further collaboration and social influence. Each time someone submits something to a collaboration space, the other members should be notified (if they so choose).

One company that gives you the mobile technology that you can incorporate into your intranet is Good at www.good.com; see Figure 12-6.

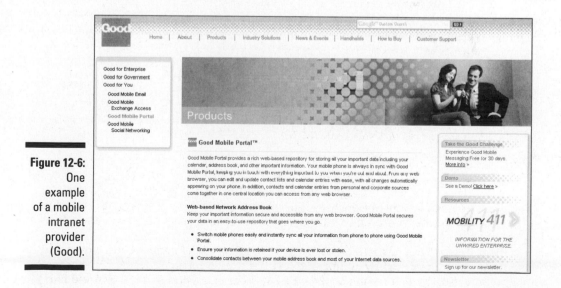

Figure 12-6: One example of a mobile intranet provider (Good).

Promoting the value of historical record

Wikipedia (shown in Figure 12-7) has done an immense amount to teach the value of a historical record. Whether your intranet has wiki functionality (the ability for anyone to format and edit the page), definitely make sure that the pages have *roll-back functionality* (the ability to see previous versions of the page).

With roll-back functionality (or *version control,* as some people call it), employees can always look at previous versions of pages. Or in the case of discussion areas, employees can view earlier collaboration, which often provides great insight as time passes. But more than that, the transparency that comes with having rollback functionality builds trust and openness in a way that no top-down communication can.

Giving your intranet a pulse

Intranet managers can learn a lot from the social Web. Probably the most important lesson is for you to give your intranet a pulse. To fuel those social connections and encourage employees to collaborate with each other on the intranet, you must make sure that the intranet provides the ongoing motivations for people to collaborate.

Figure 12-7:
Wikipedia,
the mother
of all wikis.

The most important way to do this is by showcasing the pulse of the intranet. Think of it as a Twitter-like pulse, which shows all the intranet-related activities of a person's social graph in a streaming list. It encourages the employee to return frequently to the intranet and learn how others are using it. But most importantly, it encourages the employee to respond to the activities of others on the intranet. The streaming pulse should include documents uploaded, comments made, searches conducted, groups joined, discussions initiated, and the like. It should also include the ability for users to publish status updates and comment on the updates of others. Practically all the Enterprise 2.0 software vendors offer this functionality out of the box.

Making the goal to de-structure and de-organize

What is often a company's greatest strength is also its greatest weakness, and that is its organizational structure that enables resources of all kinds to work harmoniously to enable the company to achieve its objectives. But it also means that employees have to be fragmented and divided into teams and departments that in time have difficulty working and communicating with each other.

The social intranet is one where the intranet helps to break down those organizational barriers. It also encourages people to make decisions and collaborate free of positional bias. To encourage collaboration and the natural social influence that usually takes place, encourage de-structuring and build online communities of employees where people are encouraged to be honest, transparent, and willing to declare what influences their points of view. With that in place, you'll be well on the path to having an intranet that truly energizes employees and allows for the social influence to take place most naturally.

Giving employees other choices

Irrespective of how well you design your intranet, there will always be employees who'll want to use some external products or Web sites for their collaboration needs. Some may even want to stick to sharing documents over e-mail and using a file server.

That's fine. Don't force them to migrate to your intranet. Ideally, people should gravitate toward it if it is indeed the best solution. If not, let people use what they want. It's far more important that they collaborate and influence one another than it is for them to use the intranet. Let them make that choice.

Chapter 13

Applying Metrics to the SIM Realm

In This Chapter

▶ Calculating your SIM score

▶ Measuring influencer activity

▶ Analyzing activity on various social media platforms

There's a common myth that social influence marketing isn't really measurable. Many a consultant has said that you can't measure the value of a conversation. Some marketers believe that it's too early to measure social influence marketing because the strategies and tactics are too fresh. They believe that measuring a phenomenon is always difficult, especially when you're still figuring out how to market in it.

The truth is that social influence marketing is as measurable as any other form of marketing. It wasn't the case two years ago — or maybe even a year ago — but that's quickly changing. Today, there are tools, techniques, and mechanisms to measure social influence marketing. These are broader brand metrics, which may not be as measurable as a direct-response marketer may like.

There are also specific campaign or program-oriented metrics that you can capture, analyze, and map to other performance indicators. These may be in the category of a YouTube campaign, an online community effort, a pass-along widget, a blogger outreach program, or a viral video campaign.

It's all well and good to capture metrics about your social influence marketing efforts, whether they're broader brand metrics or specific ones around social influence marketing campaigns. It's extremely important to marry these metrics with your other marketing metrics and see how they correlate. For example, it's no use if you have lots of widget installations if they have no correlation with brand awareness, favorability, or actual sales. As a result, the most important challenge in social influence marketing is not measuring it, but correlating the data to broader business objectives. Therefore, when you put your social influence marketing metrics in place, think about how you can use them to determine whether you met your marketing objectives and also how you want to interpret them in the context of the rest of your marketing and business objectives. Otherwise, you'll just be capturing meaningless data.

A Core Measure of Social Influence Marketing

In this section, I start by suggesting a core brand-oriented metric — the single metric that you must map your social influence marketing objectives against. And not just that. You must map your brand against this metric on an ongoing basis. I call it the social influence marketing score, or the SIM score. It's inspired by the Net Promoter Score, which asks customers, regarding the specific product or service, the question "How likely are you to recommend the product to a colleague or a friend?" It then subtracts the number of detractors from the number of promoters to give a single Net Promoter Score. You'll notice that the while the Net Promoter Score is fundamentally a loyalty metric, the SIM score is a brand-health metric, but based on customer interactions, too.

As you look at the SIM score, keep in mind that the industry is still in the throes of determining the best holistic metric. Expect more from the Interactive Advertising Bureau (www.iab.net) and the Social Media Advertising Consortium (www.smac.org) on this subject in the next six months.

The SIM score is designed to be a pivotal measure that recognizes the participatory nature of branding and, more directly, your brand's health compared to all of your direct competitors in the social Web. Think of the SIM score as the blood pressure for your brand in the social Web. It'll tell you how you're doing but not why or what to do about anything that might be going wrong. Those questions are answered when you dig deeper into understanding the factors that contribute to the SIM score.

You calculate the SIM score based on these two critical attributes:

- The total share of consumer conversations that your brand has online. This is fundamentally about reach — the volume of conversations surrounding your brand.

- The degree to which consumers like, dislike, or have no opinion of your brand when they talk to each other about you. It's centered around impact or consumer sentiment.

These two attributes combined make up the SIM score. This is important because it isn't enough that your brand has a very large share of consumer conversations, especially if most of those conversations are negative in nature. That does more harm than good to your brand. It's important that you adjust the volume of the conversations for the sentiment surrounding your brand.

You should track the SIM score for each brand on an ongoing basis as the brand launches campaigns, brings new products to market, activates influencers, and engages with customers across the social Web. And track your SIM score before your campaigns so that you can always benchmark your score against a baseline.

Here's the formula for calculating the SIM score for your brand, relative to its competitors:

```
SIM score = net sentiment for the brand ÷ net sentiment
            for the industry
```

The components of the formula are as follows:

```
Net sentiment for the brand = (positive + neutral
            conversations - negative conversations) ÷ total
            conversations for the brand
```

```
Net sentiment for the industry = (positive + neutral
            conversations - negative conversations) ÷ total
            conversations for the industry
```

Note four important factors about the SIM score:

✔ **This is a relative score versus your competitors.**

The competitors you choose to include in the calculations directly impact your SIM score. So the SIM score is primarily a relative measurement.

✔ **The SIM score combines positive and neutral sentiment.**

An argument can be made for using only positive sentiment and ignoring neutral sentiment. The SIM score includes neutral sentiment, too, because any mention of your brand helps your brand awareness (as long as it isn't a negative). And therefore, you should factor it into the score.

✔ **The sourcing and quality of the data that you use to compute the SIM score may directly affect the total scores.**

The data that you use to compute your SIM score comes from the conversational monitoring firms that I discuss in earlier chapters. These companies, including Visible Technologies (www.visibletechnologies. com; see Figure 13-1), TNS Cymfony (www.cymfony.com), Nielsen BuzzMetrics (www.nielsen-online.com), Scout Labs (www.scout labs.com), and others count the total number of conversations pertaining to your brand (usually using brand mentions as a way to make the calculation) and then through a technological system add sentiment (positive, neutral, and negative) to each conversational instance.

✔ **Some monitoring vendors let you capture mixed conversations, too.**

These are conversations that include both positive and negative sentiment within them. If you're capturing mixed sentiment for your brand, use those numbers for the denominator (total brand or total industry) calculations, but don't use them for the numerator. Mixed conversations, by definition, can't reliably be ascertained as helping the brand and, therefore, can't be included with positive or neutral conversations in the numerator.

Figure 13-1:
Visible
Technologies.

The data you get from a monitoring firm may not always be good. These technology vendors are getting better and better every day in capturing all the conversations that are happening across the social Web and running those conversations against their sentiment engines. But they don't capture the sum of all the social media conversations. The reason is that a few social platforms, like Facebook, don't allow these vendors to grab the conversation data behind the login, total it, and add sentiment to it. This, of course, may change as Facebook rolls out new versions of Lexicon, which supposedly will let you capture volume and sentiment data.

However, most of the large vendors grab data from all the blogs, forums, microblogging solutions, and community sites online. While they may not include logged-in Facebook pages, they do account for the majority of the conversations happening online and, in that, serve as a good measure.

To give you a perspective on how SIM scoring looks, Table 13-1 shows an example of SIM scores in the auto industry. There were 2,106,523 social media conversations concerning five brands in the auto industry in the last six months of 2008. The brands included were Ford, Honda, Toyota, Nissan, and GM. The table shows their share of voice, net sentiment, and their SIM scores.

Table 13-1	Auto Industry SIM Scores		
Company	*Share of Voice*	*Net Sentiment*	*SIM Score*
Honda	29.6%	81%	30
Ford	31.8%	78%	31
GM	5.8%	73%	5
Nissan	14.5%	80%	15
Toyota	18.1%	80%	18

What's interesting is how share of voice and net sentiment both impact the SIM score. Toyota's share of voice is larger than Nissan's, which contributes to its higher SIM score, for example. Ford, which faced similar challenges to GM in the last half of 2008, has a much higher SIM score. This may be because in the last year they've invested a lot more in managing their brand in social media. While GM was early in experimenting with social media, with a CEO blog and a UGC campaign, its handling of the bailout last year may have hurt its reputation in the social Web.

So what do you do with the SIM score? You track it against all your marketing activities to determine how they're impacting your brand in the social Web. As you track your SIM score over time, you should be able to answer questions like these:

✔ What impact does advertising in all the different mediums have on a SIM score?

✔ How does a SIM score affect overall brand affinity and purchasing decisions for your brand over time?

✔ What does it take to put a program in place to manage one's SIM score effectively? Can you do so in a cost-effective manner?

✔ How does your SIM score differ based on specific topics of conversations?

Along with actual metrics based on customer behavior, you can use heuristic (or expert) evaluations to ascertain how your brand is doing in the social Web in relation to its direct competitors. Wetpaint and The Altimeter Group came together to establish a heuristic framework for ranking the world's most engaging brands. You can see the list and view the methodology (which also allows you to rank your own brand) at Engagementdb (www.engagementdb.com).

Considering Influencer-Specific Metrics

It isn't enough to calculate your SIM score on an ongoing basis. That's a very important measure. It's your brand health in the social Web, but it isn't the only measure. You need to measure how your brand stacks up against the influencers whom you care about, the platforms on which you participate, and for the campaigns that you run.

As I discuss in Chapter 1, there are three types of influencers surrounding your customers: expert, referent, and positional influencers. You need to know how many of the influencers in each of these categories are favorably inclined toward your brand and are, as a result, favorably influencing your customers.

This is no easy task, and the truth is that determining and measuring the favorability of influencers toward your brand is an imperfect science. It simply hasn't been figured out yet. But, here are some tips for measurement surrounding specific types of influencers:

- **Expert influencers:** Once you identify them, track their press mentions, blog posts, Twitter streams, Facebook comments, and discussion forum responses to determine how favorably or unfavorably they talk about your brand. Many of the conversational monitoring vendors provide tools that help you identify these influencers and track their favorability toward you.

- **Referent influencers:** Technology companies like Unbound Technologies (www.unboundtech.com; see Figure 13-2) and Rapleaf (www.rapleaf.com) can help you identify your referent influencers on the specific social platforms by anonymously analyzing the profiles of people for mentions of your industry category or your brand specifically. They then map these to a meta-social graph and can tell you how many people within your demographic and target audience have high networks, influence other people significantly, and talk about your category or brand favorably.

- **Positional influencers:** Other vendors, like Clearspring (www.clearspring.com) and Gigya (www.gigya.com), do the tracking for you by capturing how people download widgets that they see on their friends' blogs and add them to their own pages. This helps identify both positional and referent influencers. For example, Razorfish (my employer) patented an incremental action tag solution that tracks how social media applications (widgets, applications, viral media, and so on) are downloaded and passed along.

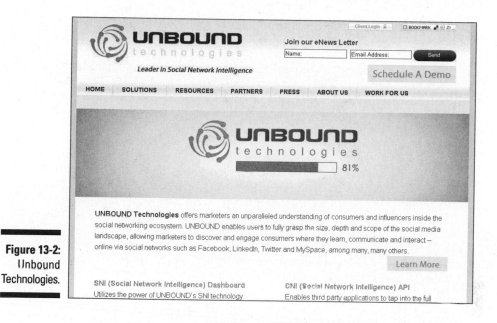

Figure 13-2:
Unbound
Technologies.

After you identify the influencers and you're tracking their favorability toward your brand, the next question is whether they're actually influencing significant conversations across the social Web and pushing people to your Web site or to buy your product. That's not easy to measure, but the industry is moving in that direction. Google, for example, is trying to develop an influencer rank for every person based on how much content people share with their friends and how likely someone is to share that content further along, depending on the source.

Fundamentally, with your social influencers, irrespective of the type, you want to understand who they are, where they're participating, with whom they're participating, what topics they're interested in, and how much they're sharing.

Evaluating Each Platform's Metrics

Different social platforms have different mechanisms for measurement. For each major social platform, you must know what you can measure and what the numbers you get actually mean. In this section, I look at the major social platforms and discuss the forms of measurement on each one of them.

Measurement components fall into four "buckets." Each time you launch a social influence marketing program, try to check off measurement objectives against these four criteria, as defined by Sometrics (www.sometrics.com; see Figure 13-3), one of the leading analytics providers in the social media space:

Figure 13-3:
Sometrics.

✔ **Traffic:** Includes impressions, unique users, and basic engagement, including page views per visit.

✔ **Demographics:** Covers the basics of who is visiting or interacting with your brand. It typically includes age, gender, income, education, and location.

✔ **Sociographics:** Captures your customers' friends and their relative importance, based on their interests and where they lie in your customers' social graphs.

✔ **Social actions:** Includes the actual social activity undertaken by your customers when they interact with you on the social platform — the specifics of what they do.

For every metric that you track for your brand on the different social platforms, try to capture the same metrics for your direct competitors. It's extremely important to know how their Facebook fan pages, YouTube channels, Twitter accounts, and MySpace profiles engage people in contrast to your own presence on the social networks.

Facebook

Your brand probably has a fan page on Facebook. You may even have done some advertising on Facebook. Here's a list of fan-page-related metrics regarding what you can measure, why you should measure those items, and what the measurements actually mean to you and your brand. You can find these metrics by going to your Facebook page, clicking Edit This Page, and choosing All Page Insights. Remember that you need to be designated as a page administrator to see the Edit This Page link.

✔ **Number of fans:** If you have a fan page on Facebook, the most basic measure is the number of fans. These are the Facebook users who have specifically chosen to align themselves with your brand. The number of fans largely represents how popular your brand is on Facebook. This is important because you can blast messages to all your fans. You can also see demographic information about them. Along with number of fans, the average growth of fans is an important metric, too.

For example, one of the most popular fan pages on Facebook is the Victoria's Secret PINK fan page, with more than 1.3 million fans; see Figure 13-4. That, in and of itself, is a huge success. But with an average growth rate of 3,000 fans per day, the PINK page is a continuous success. Keep in mind, though, that Victoria's Secret PINK is one of the top ten Facebook fan pages. Many small businesses have achieved marketing success with even just 1,000 fans.

✔ **Page interactions:** The number of fans is the starting point of Facebook fan page metrics, but page interactions of those fans matter as much. Facebook captures page interactions for you and lets you track the following interactions: total interactions, interactions per post, post quality, discussion posts, and reviews.

Look at each of these metrics in more detail:

- *Total interactions:* The total number of comments, wall posts, and other fan-driven interactions with the page

- *Interactions per post:* The average number of comments, wall posts, and other interactions generated by each post

- *Post quality:* An abstract measurement from Facebook indicating the quality of each post. Increased post quality means deeper engagement with your brand.

- *Stream CTR:* Your stream click-through rate (CTR) and your engagement click-through rate measure how much people engage with your content in a news feed. *Stream* implies clicks to your fan page from a news feed (the first page you see when you log in to

Facebook), and *engagement* implies click-through rates on wall posts that you publish on the Facebook fan page. The social media agency Vitrue (www.vitrue.com) says that click-through rates for content on a brand page (engagement click-through rate) are as high as 6.49 percent. This data is currently based on a sample, and at the time this chapter was written, the engagement rate statistics weren't easily verifiable.

• *Discussion posts:* The number of discussion topics that your fans publish on your fan page.

• *Reviews:* The number of times that fans use the Facebook Reviews application to rate your page.

Figure 13-4:
The Facebook page for Victoria's Secret PINK.

Outside of the fan pages, Facebook applications allow you to capture a lot of important metrics. Building a Facebook application is like building a Web site: You need to define the strategy, brainstorm the concept, and then, with the help of a designer and a developer, actually build it before submitting the application to Facebook for approval so that it can appear in its directory and be made available to all users. If you've built a Facebook application and have it running on your fan page or on the profile pages of Facebook users, you can capture data about the number of users who have

- Added your application tab
- Added your application profile box to their profiles
- Added your application information section
- Bookmarked your application
- Subscribed to your application e-mails

You can also capture a variety of metrics for user activity involving your Facebook applications. These include the number of:

- Active users during the past 7 days
- Active users during the past 30 days
- Canvas page views. (The *canvas page* is the main page for your application.)
- Unique canvas page viewers

And then, If you're more technically minded, here are some more technical metrics:

- Number of API (application programming interface) calls made
- Number of unique users on whose behalf your application made API calls
- Average HTTP request time for canvas pages
- Average FBML (Facebook Markup Language) render time for canvas pages

Outside of the Facebook fan pages and applications, you can also measure the volume of conversation regarding your brand and your competitors on Facebook. This is simply a measure of the number of times that your brand (or its competitors) has been mentioned in conversation on Facebook. The Facebook application Lexicon (www.facebook.com/lexicon) lets you measure the total number of conversations for your brand, as shown in Figure 13-5.

The problem with Lexicon is that your brand needs to be mentioned *a lot* to even appear within the Lexicon tool. The good news is that Facebook is working on a new version of Lexicon, which will tell you the exact number of mentions, sentiment, demographics trends, word association with your brand, pulse, and location on a map. This new Lexicon is in preview mode at the moment, and only select words can be viewed against these metrics. The tool should be made available for the public soon.

Figure 13-5:
Facebook
Lexicon.

As you can see, a lot of activity on Facebook can be measured. What matters most, though, is how those measurements support your business. It's no use measuring a lot of different things on Facebook if it doesn't help your business. Also, metrics aren't useful if you don't know what to do with them. As a result, before you start a social influence marketing program on Facebook, think carefully about what you're trying to accomplish and which metrics are most appropriate for that purpose. And then start the measuring. In fact, this guideline applies to any form of measurement on all the social platforms.

AppData (www.appdata.com) tracks the most popular Facebook applications on a daily basis. You can also view which developers are responsible for the most popular applications. As of August 2009, the most popular applications are Farmville, Causes, LivingSocial, Movies, and We're Related. The developers with the most installations of their applications are Zynga, Playfish, RockYou!, Slide, Inc., and LivingSocial.

YouTube and video clips

With the launch of YouTube Insight (www.youtube.com/my_videos_insight), you have access to more data on the clips you publish and who views them. YouTube Insight gives you the following statistics about your users and clips:

✔ **Views:** First and foremost, you can see the total number of views charted out by week. This is the same data that public users can see. The tool also shows you the number of unique views and the number of views by location (country or state). This can tell you if the people watching your clips are actually in your target market.

✔ **Demographics:** This categorizes the data by age, telling you what percentage of the views came from users in specific age groups, such as 25–34 year olds.

✔ **Community:** This gives you information about the people who have interacted with your YouTube clips. This includes commenting, ratings, and favoriting counts.

You can also export these statistics from YouTube Insights to a spreadsheet to easily keep track of your stats from month to month.

You can also narrow these statistics by video or by geographic region. This is extremely helpful because it can tell you, for example, how much higher your Japanese viewers rated a video clip as compared to ratings from your American viewers.

However, these metrics from YouTube are sometimes not enough to get an accurate picture. In that case, it helps to have more metrics, and fortunately, analytics companies like TubeMogul (www.tubemogul.com; see Figure 13-6) can provide those.

Here are some of the analytics that companies like TubeMogul can provide if you use their services to upload and distribute video clips across the social Web:

✔ **E-mail and embed reports:** Tells you the number of times your video clip has been e-mailed to someone or embedded on a blog or a Web site.

✔ **Link intelligence:** Gives you insight into who is linking to your video clips. The data includes information about links on both blogs and traditional Web sites.

✔ **Aggregation of data:** Lets you view aggregate statistics on several video clips at a time. For example, you can access aggregate data on clips that all belong to a single campaign.

Also, depending on whether you're using a video site with Adobe Flash, you can also track viewed minutes, viewer attention, per-stream quality, syndication tracking, and player tracking.

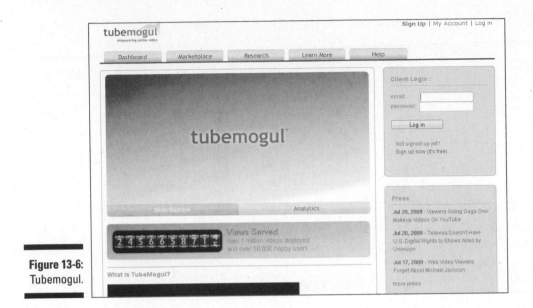

Figure 13-6:
Tubemogul.

Twitter

Because Twitter has an open API (application programming interface), you can measure a lot more on Twitter than elsewhere. This is largely because developers have built dozens and dozens of analytic tools on top of Twitter. All of these can help you understand the reach and frequency of the 140-character tweets.

As with the blogosphere, you can learn a lot about the number of people who get your tweets, how many are retweeted, and which influencers help you the most. But there's something you need to keep in mind: What you can't find out is who those actual people are who are reading the tweets — their demographics, psychographics, and behaviors. In other words, don't expect to get from Twitter the same level of detail around your customers that you do when you run banner campaigns across the Internet. This may change in time, but as I'm writing this book, those numbers aren't as accessible.

Here's what you can find out from Twitter:

✔ **Brand mentions:** The first and most basic metric for Twitter is knowing how your brand is mentioned and with what frequency on Twitter. Twitter Search (`http://search.twitter.com`) lets you scan all published tweets for mentions of your brand. TweetVolume (`www.tweetvolume.com`; see Figure 13-7) can also help with understanding the volume of tweets about your brand.

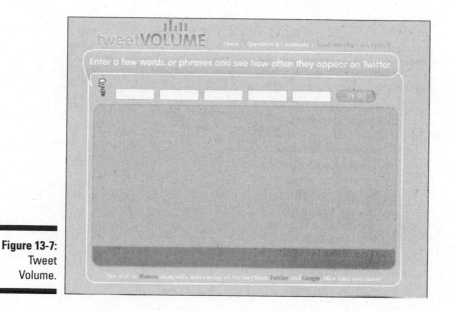

Figure 13-7:
Tweet
Volume.

✔ **Influence:** You can measure influence in Twitter more directly than in any other social platform. With tools like Twinfluence (www.twinfluence.com), you can measure the reach, velocity, and social capital of anyone on Twitter, including your own brand. As you follow people and they follow you, you can use Twinfluence to determine the potential reach of your tweets based on who retweets them. Twitter Grader (www.twittergrader.com) also computes a username's relative ranking compared to other users on Twitter. Twitterank (http://twitterank.com) tells you your rank versus other Twitter uses. That, too, can be considered a measure of influence.

✔ **Pass-along and click-throughs:** Knowing how much your influencers tweet about you is very important to track as well. The best way to do this is by continuously scanning the list of tweets that mention your brand or your username specifically. This helps you understand how much you're being retweeted. Dashboards like TweetDeck (www.tweetdeck.com; see Figure 13-8) can make this tracking much easier because they allow you to list multiple search terms and see all your replies (basically, tweets that reference your username) in one place. To see the most popular conversation topics that are being tweeted and retweeted, consider using a tool like Tweetlists (www.tweetlists.com).

Figure 13-8:
TweetDeck.

In addition to tracking tweets that have been passed along, you may want to understand how many tweets have resulted in clicks to your Web site. This is where services like bit.ly (`bit.ly.com`; see Figure 13-9) and Tweetburner (`www.tweetburner.com`) come into the picture. You can shorten Web site addresses using these services for your Tweets. But the greatest benefit is that when you do so, you can track the exact number of people who clicked the link in your tweet over time. For example, if you're promoting a special discount, you can tweet about that discount and include a link to the page on your Web site using bit.ly. You can see, on an hourly basis, the number of people who actually click the link in your tweet. That way, you can determine the number of clicks and the number of people who took advantage of the discount.

Another loosely related factor to consider with Twitter and your Web site: It's important to track the number of visitors coming to your Web site from Twitter. This is helpful to understand from a lead-generation perspective. Knowing how many people are coming to your Web site from Twitter versus from search engine or display banner campaigns can and should influence how much effort you put into your Twitter marketing efforts.

The Twitter API is very flexible, allowing new developers to quickly build new Twitter applications. So by the time you read this chapter, there may be a new Twitter analytics tool out on the market, which is why I recommend always searching the Web for new Twitter applications or using a Twitter directory like the Twitter Fan Wiki (`http://twitter.pbworks.com/Apps`).

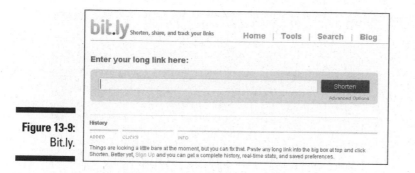

Figure 13-9:
Bit.ly.

The blogosphere

Don't ignore the blogosphere. Outside of Facebook, most online conversations happen within the blogosphere. Measuring the influence and reach of your brand across the blogosophere can be tricky, though. Millions and millions of blogs are published every day with billions of posts published. Does a brand mention on a specific blog matter? How do you know which posts matters over which others?

Here are some metrics that you can and should capture from the blogosphere. These build on the core metrics of unique visitors, page views, and return rates:

- ✔ Number of brand mentions versus your competitors
- ✔ Ratio of comments and *trackbacks* (a method of counting of other bloggers that reference your post) to posts on your own blogs
- ✔ Frequency of posts and comments on your blog and your competitors' blogs
- ✔ Technorati ranking of blogs that mention your brand
- ✔ Technorati ranking of your blog and your competitors'
- ✔ Total number of conversations (unique visitors to all sites talking about your brand)
- ✔ Total number of times that the post has been tweeted or retweeted, saved to Digg, tagged in Delicious, and discussed on FriendFeed

Widgets and social applications

Outside of applications that reside within Facebook, you should measure the impact of your social media widgets and applications elsewhere on the Internet. Here are some of the key metrics to consider, as introduced by the Social Media Working Group of the IAB (Interactive Advertising Bureau):

- ✔ **Installs:** Simply the number of people who have installed your application.

- ✔ **Active users:** The number of total users interacting with your application over a day, week, or month. Some applications lose significant activity in time, so watch this metric carefully.

- ✔ **Audience profile:** Demographics of the people who are interacting with your widget. This may need to be self reported, depending on where you install the widget.

- ✔ **Unique user reach:** The percentage of users who have installed the application among the total audience of social media users.

- ✔ **Growth:** The average number of increase in users within a specific time frame (between two dates).

- ✔ **Influence:** The average number of friends among users who have installed the application. This is a relatively less meaningful metric.

- ✔ **Application/widget installs:** The number of widget installs that a user has on his or her profile. This matters because more installs typically may mean lower interactions with your widget.

- ✔ **Active users/widgets in the wild:** The number of people using the widgets on a regular basis.

- ✔ **Longevity/lifecycle:** Another key metric that tracks how long a widget or application stays installed by a user before he or she uninstalls it.

Needless to say, when examining these metrics, always try to understand how the metrics you capture relate to actual sales. Sometimes the link may be easy, but in other cases, especially if you do not have large numbers, drawing the correlation between the metrics above and the metrics maybe difficult.

Another application to use as you try to understand brand health in the social Web is Status Search (www.statussearch.net). This application lets you search within your Twitter and Facebook friends' statuses. For example, if your brand has 30,000 fans, you'll potentially be able to use Status Search to see if any of your fans are discussing your brand in their own status updates. Keep in mind that this application is still in beta and may be a little buggy at the moment.

Website community metrics

If you're evolving your own Web site for social influence marketing, you may require new metrics to understand how successful you are. Rather than just measure how many people are visiting your Web site and where they're coming from, you're going to need to look at what exactly they're doing on your Web site and how they're interacting with each other. Whether you're using community software from a vendor like Lithium (www.lithium. com) or Pluck (www.pluck.com) or have installed customer reviews from Bazaarvoice (www.bazaarvoice.com) or PowerReviews (www.power reviews.com), the following metrics are important to consider:

- ✔ **Traffic:** The number of people visiting the community pages of your Web site is the first core metric. *Community pages* here means the discussion pages as well as the pages where you have customer reviews and ratings.

- ✔ **Members:** The next most important metric is the number of members of your community pages. These are the number of people that have registered so that they can publish content or share reviews. It's important to track whether the pace of people registering increases or decreases in time. You'll also want to understand who your most prolific contributors are and which have the most influence.

- ✔ **Interactivity:** The number of people who participate in a specific conversation, the number of replies, and the frequency with which they do so is very important. For example, how quickly on average someone replies to a conversation thread and the number of participants engaged in the conversation serve as guides to the health of your community.

- ✔ **Civility:** Another important metric to manage is how civil the conversations in your community are. Whether the community discusses health care or something simpler, such as digital cameras, how much people show that they trust and respect each other through the conversations is important. This can be ascertained by examining the language used, the tone of the conversation, and the way people express disagreement.

- ✔ **Content:** And last but not the least, no community can be measured without establishing metrics around the actual content. To understand your community better, you'll need to understand which pieces of content are the most popular, traffic-generating, and valued over time. You'll also want to understand what type of content is published and shared the most, whether that sharing is done on your Web site or to the social platforms.

Other metrics to consider

As you examine metrics on the major social platforms and analyze your SIM score, be sure to account for activity on the other social platforms. You'll want to track the following information about them:

- ✔ How much your brand and its associated Web sites are bookmarked on sites like Delicious (www.delicious.com) and Flickr (www.flickr.com)

- ✔ Alexa (www.alexa.com), Compete (www.compete.com), and Quantcast (www.quantcast.com) rankings

✔ Brand mentions in discussion forums and on other community Web sites, like Cafe Mom and the microblogging service FriendFeed (`www.friendfeed.com`)

✔ The number of friends and brand mentions on other social network sites that may have a larger presence in certain regions of the United States or in other countries around the world, including

- Bebo (`www.bebo.com`)

- A Small World (`www.asmallworld.net`)

- Flixter (`www.flixter.com`)

- hi5 (`www.hi5.com`)

- LinkedIn (`www.linkedin.com`)

- LiveJournal (`www.livejournal.com`)

- MySpace (`www.myspace.com`)

- Xanga (`www.xanga.com`)

- Orkut (`www.orkut.com`)

Part IV
The Part of Tens

The 5th Wave   By Rich Tennant

"Awww jeez — I was afraid of this. Some poor kid, bored with the usual chat lines, starts looking for bigger kicks. Pretty soon they're surfin' the seedy back alleys of Facebook, and before you know it they're into a profile they can't get out of. I guess that's why they call it the Web. Somebody open a window!"

In this part . . .

Chapter 14 lists ten key SIM best practices that you must absolutely pay attention to. Chapter 15 includes ten common mistakes — mistakes made by the best of us who have been practicing SIM time and again. Finally, Chapter 16 lists ten must-read blogs that will keep you updated with the world of SIM and digital marketing more broadly.

Chapter 14

Ten SIM Best Practices

S ocial influence marketing effort may fail for a lot of reasons. And not surprisingly, hundreds if not thousands of articles are online about why certain SIM efforts failed. Strangely, there's a lot less discussion about what succeeds and why. I certainly don't have all the answers, but what I do know is that by following these ten best practices, your chances of success are much greater.

Open Up Your Brand to Your Consumers, and Let Them Evolve It

This is difficult for many marketers. You've probably spent money and time building your brand only to have someone telling you to let go of it. This may sound absurd. The truth is that the more you let your consumers internalize your brand, talk about it in their own language, and manifest your story in their own way, the more success you will have with your SIM efforts.

Letting your consumers evolve your brand doesn't mean you're losing control of it completely. How you let consumers evolve your brand must be done in a fashion that is in sync with your company values, what your customers expect of you, the industry you operate in, and the appropriateness for your brand. But that doesn't mean you shouldn't let go at all. Brands that hold onto too much mystique run the risk of appearing cold, distant, and alienating. Those risks are accentuated now with the social Web, so be careful, even if you're Chanel or Louis Vuitton.

Develop a SIM Voice without Silencing Other Voices that Support Your Brand

Surprisingly, for every brand that's fearful about opening up to consumers, just as many go the other extreme and inadvertently silence external voices. Your SIM voice is fundamentally about having a mechanism to talk to your consumers in a language and style that they understand. It's a voice to talk to them in a more humane and personal manner.

You shouldn't use your SIM voice to speak the loudest and most exclusively about your brand. Nor should you use it to silence your critics in a heavy-handed manner. To develop a strong SIM voice is to develop strong listening skills, a thick skin, and a nuanced understanding of how to respond to the fuming blogger, for example, without turning him off completely. You want to extend your reach and influence through others. Don't try to do so by being the loudest or by becoming deaf. No one likes a bully.

Respond to Everything, Even If It Means You're Up All Night

For all the hype about social media, one important sobering fact remains: It takes an immense amount of work. Listening in on conversations, even with monitoring tools, is an exhaustive, time-consuming exercise. Responding and participating in those conversations can take the wind out of your sails and ruin many a weekend, if not a marriage. Arguably, many people think that social influence marketing isn't scalable because the larger your company is, the more expensive it gets to participate

But that's the wrong way to think about social influence marketing. Your consumers are talking about you every day across many different channels and platforms. Their attention has become a lot more fragmented, and they're much more impatient, too. The only option is to work harder for their attention and their dollars. If you have to set expectations around the timeliness of your participation, do so, but definitely don't ignore them. For example, a two-day delay in response hurt the Motrin brand immeasurably when customers felt that Johnson & Johnson wasn't hearing their concerns about a Motrin TV advertisement. Now those marketers at J&J thought they were ahead of the game by responding on Sunday evening, but that, too, was to late. To assist in managing responses, you need to build relationships online with influencers before you need them. That way, they can do some of the work for you while you go offline.

Think Beyond the Obvious and Use SIM to Evolve Your Business

To assume that social influence is just about marketing is to take a narrow view of it. The way your consumers communicate, share information, collaborate, entertain, get entertained, work, and do anything has fundamentally changed.

People are influencing each other in new ways all the time and using social technologies to change their lives.

As a marketer in an organization, it's important to recognize that SIM can do more than just help you reach your consumers better. You can learn from your consumers by harnessing their insights about your products and brands; you can change how you conduct customer service or launch new products; and you can change how you interact with your own employees, shareholders, business partners, and external constituents. You can even use it to redefine your core products. Don't miss the opportunity to leverage SIM concepts for every part of your business.

Focus Not Just on Social Media but on Social Influencers

It's easy to lose sight of your social influencers amid the buzz about social media. There's no question that social platforms like Twitter, Facebook, MySpace, and YouTube are hugely popular, and they're changing the way people interact with each other online and approach entertainment. But this isn't just about marketing on those social platforms. After all, consumers don't always respond to brands that dwell on them. They'd rather spend their time talking to one another. That's why it's important to focus on the social influencers, too, as they can reach the consumers for you.

It's important to focus on the social influencers, as they're the ones who increasingly have the largest impact on brand affinity and purchasing decisions. They are the ones who have the most influence on your consumers. They're everywhere, and not just on the social media platforms. By ignoring these social influencers, you're ignoring your largest and most potent sales force. Look beyond the buzz of social media and focus on the social influencers, wherever they may be, interacting with your consumers.

Structure Your Marketing Department for This Social World

Undoubtedly, the Internet and the social media revolution have changed marketing significantly. It's no longer about creating cool, creative ads and pushing messages out to customers via different channels. Nor is it just about print advertisements and in-store displays that may or may not grab the attention of your consumers. It's about a two-way conversation — online and offline — and looking holistically at how all your marketing efforts — digital or not — can work together.

And this begs the question, have you structured your marketing department appropriately for this world? You probably have interactive marketing in one corner of your department organizational chart. But can you still separate interactive marketing from the rest of marketing? Does it make sense? And along similar lines, should you silo market research from product innovation and brand and direct-response marketing when you live in a world with real-time customer feedback? It might be time for you to revisit your marketing department's organizational structure.

Take Your Organization with You, from the CEO to the Field Representative

I discuss in this book how you can apply SIM to different parts of your business and beyond the realm of marketing. I also cover strategies and tactics for making SIM work in conjunction with the other forms of marketing, whether they're digital or offline. But that isn't enough. To succeed in SIM means that you must carry your whole organization with you — everyone from the CEO down to the field representative.

SIM is fundamentally about everyday influence in all its forms and crowd-sourced innovation and product design. To embrace SIM and succeed in it requires your whole organization to orient itself toward it. Your CEO is probably one of the best spokespersons for your organization. He should be one of the people talking to your consumers in a SIM voice that they appreciate, wherever they may be spending their time online. On the other end of the spectrum, your field representatives are out there selling products. Each of them has a network of customers. They, too, are powerful SIM voices. Empower them to speak on behalf of the company to their constituents offline *and* online. Succeeding in SIM means taking everyone in your company in this direction. And a good place to start is by surveying your own employees to understand how much they're using social media today and how they feel it can be harnessed to support your business.

Conduct Many Small Tests Frequently and Build on Each One

Without a doubt, the field of social influence marketing is young. The social advertisement formats are still evolving; companies are just figuring out how to participate in the conversation; customers are discovering how powerful a voice they have online; and the technologies that allow all this to happen and be tracked are in a constant state of flux.

Knowing how to practice SIM and for what specific purposes may not always be easy. The government might have started to regulate blogger outreach programs in your industry, for example (as it recently has with the pharmaceuticals). The only way to succeed in SIM is to conduct many small tests and build on each one. Don't try to boil the ocean all at once, and don't be frozen with paranoia either. Put a strategy in place that means many small, logical steps, each one building on the success of the previous one, deepening your relationships with the influencers and establishing yourself more deeply with your consumers. It takes longer to get where you want to, but it's a safer path to take.

Capture Every Single Piece of Data that You Can

As I discuss in Chapter 13, you can measure a lot of your social influence marketing efforts. SIM is meant to support your overall marketing and business objectives, and you'll know whether it's succeeding in helping you accomplish those only if you're measuring your campaigns, initiatives, and strategies. Everything must be tied to results.

The only way to do that with rigor is to capture every single piece of data that you can about your SIM efforts. From the number of influencers activated to how many views a YouTube clip got that translated into a sale and the brand attitudinal lifts you saw based on a SIM campaign, you must capture all that data. Don't forget about capturing data that supports other parts of your business, such as a reduction in customer service calls or the amount of time it takes to bring products to market, if you've brought customers into your product innovation process. Data is everything.

Make Mistakes, but Make Every Effort to Correct Them as Well

We all learn from our mistakes, and that's a wonderful thing. But when practicing SIM, it isn't enough to learn from your mistakes — you also need to make every effort to correct them. And quickly, too. One of the many attributes that make SIM stand out from other forms of marketing is that you're engaging with your customers in real time as they interact with each other at a scale never seen before.

This means that both the good and bad of your brand (or marketing efforts) can be amplified across the Internet in no time, potentially causing either immense benefit (witness the viral effect of a funny YouTube clip) or immense damage (as Comcast experienced a few years ago). This means that when you make a mistake — and you will, as everyone does — be sure to make every effort to correct it as soon as possible. Otherwise, you'll find yourself in a crisis that spins completely out of your control.

Chapter 15

Avoiding Ten Common Mistakes

. . . .

*Y*ou may follow all the right steps with your social influence marketing efforts and still fail. In fact, however frightening it may seem you may fail completely. The reason is that you may overlook the ten common mistakes of SIM. Steer clear of common mistakes in this chapter, and you have a better chance at enjoying a successful social influence marketing campaign.

Encroaching on Customers' Time

Many companies forget that their customers can have a limited number of conversations at once. They often gravitate to specific social platforms for coincidental reasons, but once they're on them, it's hard to move away. They become accustomed to that social environment, invest in it through their contributions, and bring their friends on board.

Any company thinking of starting a conversation with its customers must begin by asking where its customers currently spend their time, how willing they might be to move their conversations to a new location, and whether they can manage another set of conversations. If you don't think this through before you build something, you may have an empty community.

Your Customers Don't Want to Hear You

The social Web is fundamentally about people talking to each other about subjects that are of interest to them. It isn't designed to be a marketing vehicle. However, some brands naturally have permission, in a manner of speaking, to be a part of those conversations, while others may not. It's important to know whether your brand has that permission. Finding out whether your brand does have permission can be tricky, but the first step is to determine how you want to engage with your customers (what your social voice will be) and how much your customers trust your brand and are favorably inclined toward it. Then ask yourself whether your customers look to you for advice and information beyond the realm of the actual product that you sell. As you answer these questions, you'll discover whether your brand has the permission to participate.

For example, the Barbie brand celebrated its 50th anniversary in early 2009 and ran an extensive social influence marketing campaign. People were excited about the anniversary and welcomed Barbie into their conversations. There was a lot of passion and nostalgia associated with the brand. It was a natural fit for social influence marketing. People wanted to talk about it. But that may not always be the case. Ask yourself whether you have permission to practice SIM with your customers. In contrast to the Barbie example, a brand that has always been aloof, distant, and serious won't have the natural permission to start participating in online conversations in a personal, humorous, and light fashion. It would seem that the brand has been hijacked and customers won't respond favorably to that. That's an example of a brand not having permission.

Choosing the Wrong SIM Voices

It's critical to choose your SIM voices carefully. Don't assign the job to an employee who lacks communication skills or passion for the social Web. And don't choose someone who can't commit the time and effort that it requires to be a SIM voice. This person needs to know the social platforms like the back of his hand. He needs to be willing to invest the time to participate and respond to queries.

Companies that have chosen employees who lack authenticity as their SIM voices are rarely successful. In the case of Whole Foods Market, the CEO was blogging and commenting in discussion forums. The only problem was that he was doing it under a pseudonym and bashing his competitors. The truth surfaced, and he lost all credibility. As a result, be careful whom you choose to be your SIM voices and train them on how to be a SIM voice. This may seem obvious, but you'll be surprised how many obvious mistakes are made around SIM voices.

Not Being Patient

With SIM efforts, it can be difficult to know when it may *break out* (in other words, when your SIM effort may suddenly gain immense traction). Many a marketer has cancelled a SIM effort too quickly, only to see a competitor launch something six months later that turned out to be widely successful. Be patient with your SIM effort; it may not be a runaway success on day one or day one hundred. It could take longer.

With these efforts, recognize that SIM isn't a campaign, rather it's a commitment. Because you're working on the social Web, you're marketing to customers one at a time in a personal, engaging, and conversational manner and that doesn't always happen quickly. Your goal, always, is to get the customers to do the marketing for you. But it may take longer than you'd like. That's something to always recognize. And to do this right, when you start your SIM effort, convince your bosses that it needs to be a 6–12 month commitment at least. If they get cold feet after the second week or the second month, you mustn't let them pull the plug on the effort.

Treating SIM in Isolation

Marketers who don't integrate their SIM activities are always bound to fail. The reason is simple: You can't market to customers in a conversational, personal, and transparent manner on the social platforms but then use a different language, style, and tone elsewhere. Your SIM activities must always complement existing marketing initiatives.

So whether the rest of your marketing efforts constitute display advertising, search engines, TV advertisements, print, outdoor media, advertising on mobile phones, or just a few of the these, make sure that you're thinking about how SIM works with those other marketing efforts. Ideally, each of those marketing initiatives should tie in with the SIM ones, as SIM strategies and tactics can be promoted and extended through these other advertising formats and mediums, too This especially applies to mobile, where increasingly cellphones allow for social influence in new and dynamic ways, with applications that integrate customer reviews and real-time polling for feedback.

Having Only One Approach

Another common mistake of SIM is to treat influencers the way you would treat a member of the press: showering them with attention, inviting them to exclusive launches, and peppering them with press releases. The reality is that influencers in the SIM world are different, and it's important to be aware of those nuances. Otherwise you'll turn them off.

For example, expert influencers who share a lot in common with the mainstream media press would *still* rather not be treated like the press. They want the special attention but expect you to engage with them on their own terms, recognizing the boundaries that they operate in. Many of them now publish guidelines for marketers explaining how they want to be approached. Referent influencers have never been marketed to in the past, and they usually don't know what to expect or how best to manage expectations. And the positional influencers would much rather you not even know that they're a big influence on the customer. So when you market to the influencers, think carefully about the influencer type and how to appropriately market to them.

Thinking of SIM as a Channel

Marketers who treat SIM as a channel have the least success. The reason is that you aren't pushing the message through a channel, as you would in traditional advertising. If you use traditional advertising strategies on the social platforms, you won't get the results that you're looking for. Think of social influence marketing as truly a new form of marketing with new strategies, best practices, and rules of engagement.

Don't Plan for the Worst

If you don't plan for the fact that you'll probably face a PR crisis at some point or other when you practice social influence marketing, you'll be blindsided when it does happen. Now, not every SIM activity results in a PR crisis — most never do at all. But because you're engaging with your customers in a more direct, authentic fashion, there are risks that you may not see with traditional advertising.

The risks take two forms:

- **The actual structure of a SIM campaign:** You may ask users to do something, and they may respond to that negatively. Or a small part of the responses may be so inflammatory in nature that it may undermine the campaign, or your brand.

- **Unintentionally elicit a visceral reaction:** This was the case with the infamous Motrin episode in early 2009, when moms responded extremely negatively to what they considered to be a derogatory TV advertising campaign. The campaign launched on a Saturday, and the marketers didn't notice the firestorm and respond quickly enough. Make sure that you do your scenario planning so that you know how to respond to any different crisis that may arise.

Focusing on One Large Campaign

Social influence marketing is fundamentally about many little efforts that when strung together have as much impact (usually much more) as a single traditional campaign or marketing program. This means that it's always important to plan to launch several small initiatives at once, rather than run one long, mammoth one.

This matters more than ever because your customers are doing a lot of digital snacking. They hop from one platform to another, exchange notes about something in one social network, and then move on to view a video clip, and sometimes go offline for days on end. Putting all your eggs in one basket doesn't serve you well.

Forgetting to Reward Your Participants

You must incentivize, reward, and recognize the contributions of the community. This may seem obvious, but you'll be surprised how many marketers assume that consumers will participate generously without any return. Make sure you match the reward to the level of participation you demand. These rewards don't have to be monetary in nature, but if you're asking something extra of the community that surrounds your product, you better be willing to thank them for their contributions, reward them for their participation, and recognize how they're changing your company for the better. These rewards can be as simple as invitations to special events, discount coupons, featuring customers on your Web site, and sneak peeks of new products and services.

Chapter 16

Ten SIM-Related Must-Read Blogs

• •

A chapter with just ten must-read social influence marketing blogs can't do justice to the wealth of information online that covers social influence marketing. Still, you have to start somewhere, and here are ten of my favorite blogs that help me further my own thinking in SIM. Most of these blogs appear in the Ad Age Power 150 marketing blogs list (which you can find at `http://adage.com/power150`), and if you're looking for other blogs to also follow, look to that list.

Web Strategist

`www.web-strategist.com/blog`

Jeremiah Owyang is one of those Forrester analysts who lives and breathes everything he preaches every day. He's deeply passionate about social media and how you can use it to achieve your business objectives. He provides practical, thoughtful, and actionable advice for you and social media specialists. His blog usually covers topics like the state of social media, how it's changing marketing, and ways in which you can organize your marketing efforts around social media. Because he works for Forrester, many of his posts also contain research nuggets from that company.

Jeremiah publishes daily (how he manages to do that while holding a day job I have no idea) and his posts are usually peppered with links to earlier posts or to external sources. His blog is always a must read and, as someone who knows him, I can attest he's also charming and engaging both in his writing and in person.

The Steve Rubel Lifestream

`www.steverubel.com`

Another must-read blog is Steve Rubel's Lifestream, published by Steve Rubel of Edelman PR. He's also a columnist at Ad Age. While Steve doesn't explicitly cover social influence marketing or social media, at least half of his posts do cover the topic. His posts are typically quite short, visual, and insightful. They generally fit into three categories: news tidbits (which include market statistics and expert interviews), personal reflections on social media and digital marketing, and his own practical experiences. I suggest that you definitely bookmark Lifestream, especially if you're interested in a digital PR angle on SIM. It's worth noting that until June 2009 Steve used to blog at `www.micropersuasion.com` until he moved to the Lifestream format, where all his online publishing efforts are consolidated in one place.

Chris Brogan

`www.chrisbrogan.com`

Here's a man who truly fits the archetype of social media guru. He lives and breathes social media. I like Chris' blog for its unfiltered, passionate, and reflective commentary on how social media forces businesses — large, medium sized, and small ones — to engage with their customers differently. It's an unadulterated look at the social media space from someone who isn't working for a large company but for himself. Filled with passion and raw insight, it's definitely a good read.

Logic + Emotion

`http://darmano.typepad.com`

Now this is a blog that's rather unique, for a very simple reason. It's filled with extremely compelling visualizations that explain social media concepts succinctly and powerfully. David Armano is thoughtful, analytical, and visual with every post, and he's addressed subjects like the evolution of advertising and the relationship between paid and unpaid media extremely well. He's a former agency person who just moved away from the marketing world to help businesses transform themselves with social technologies. As a result, his posts may be a little less marketing oriented now, but the blog is still worth bookmarking and reading.

Conversation Agent

`www.conversationagent.com`

This blog shares similarities with Chris Brogan's but looks at social media more broadly. Valeria Maltoni bills herself as someone who helps businesses understand how customers and communities have changed marketing, public relations, and communications. Her posts cover her own experiences in social media and provide tips and tricks for navigating the social media world. She also analyzes current events from a social media perspective (witness her posts about the Iran election in the summer of 2009), and she interviews thought leaders in the online marketing space.

Influential Marketing Blog

http://rohitbhargava.typepad.com

This blog authored by Rohit Bhargava focuses on the connection points between marketing, advertising, and PR strategy. An Ogilvy Interactive marketer, Rohit discusses what companies can do with social media and explains where they're succeeding and failing. His posts are thoughtful, recommendation-driven, and easily scanable. He focuses on the influence side to social influence marketing more than the others and, therefore, writes more broadly. He also speaks at industry events and discusses social media optimization on his blog like no one else can.

The WOMMA Word

http://womma.org/word

Published by The Word of Mouth Marketing Association (WOMMA), this blog discusses everything that has to do with word-of-mouth marketing, both online and offline. Because the organization is rooted in the offline world, it provides a slightly different perspective on social influence marketing than other blogs. The posts cover word-of-mouth online and offline across all the major channels, from TV and print to digital. The posts on ethics and word of mouth are especially interesting.

Advertising Age's Digital Next

http://adage.com/digitalnext

This group blog covers everything in digital marketing, but because social influence marketing is such a hot topic, more and more of its posts have a SIM orientation. Because its audience is marketers who have to worry about a lot more than just social media, it takes a more conservative, critical, and analytical take on social influence marketing.

Apophenia

www.zephoria.org/thoughts

This is the one academic blog that I'm including in the list. Danah Boyd is a researcher at Microsoft Research New England and an established authority in the field of social network research. She's also a Fellow at the Harvard Berkman Center for Internet and Society. Her research on social media, social networking (especially as it pertains to youth culture), online identities, and online communities has been incredibly important in helping everyone in the industry understand how consumers are actually immersing themselves in the social space. This is definitely another must-read blog, especially if you're trying to understand consumer motivations.

Going Social Now

www.goingsocialnow.com

Going Social Now is my blog, covering all things social influence marketing. I focus on the trends, influencers, and the roles they play, the evolving advertising formats, consumer adoption, and social technologies. I also discuss digital marketing more broadly. The blog serves as a resource for you, the reader, and includes 101 explanations, additional *For Dummies* content that didn't make it into the book, and links to even more wonderful resources beyond the ones I mention here.

Index